D1175969

The Tyndale Old Testament Commentaries

General Editor:
PROFESSOR D. J. WISEMAN, O.B.E., M.A., D.LITT., F.B.A., F.S.A.

LEVITICUS

LEVITICUS

AN INTRODUCTION AND COMMENTARY

by

R. K. HARRISON, PH.D., D.D.

Professor of Old Testament, Wycliffe College, University of Toronto

INTER-VARSITY PRESS

Inter-Varsity Press
38 De Montfort Street, Leicester LE1 7GP, England

First Edition 1980

HARDBACK EDITION 0 85111 633 7
PAPERBACK EDITION 0 85111 834 8
USA ISBN 0 87784 890 4

Text set in 10/10½ pt Linotron 202 Baskerville, printed and
bound in Great Britain at The Pitman Press, Bath

*Inter-Varsity Press is the publishing division of the Universities and Colleges
Christian Fellowship (formerly the Inter-Varsity Fellowship), a student movement
linking Christian Unions in universities and colleges throughout the British Isles,
and a member movement of the International Fellowship of Evangelical Students.
For information about local and national activities in Great Britain write to UCCF,
38 De Montfort Street, Leicester LE1 7GP.*

CONTENTS

GENERAL PREFACE 7

AUTHOR'S PREFACE 9

CHIEF ABBREVIATIONS 11

INTRODUCTION 13
Title of the Book 13
Nature of Leviticus 13
Authorship and Date 15
Unity of Leviticus 25
Purpose of the Book 26
Theology of Leviticus 29
Leviticus and the New Testament 32
The Hebrew Text 34

ANALYSIS 36
The Sacrifices of Leviticus 38

COMMENTARY 39
Probable plan of the tabernacle 46
The high priest's breastpiece 91
The feasts of Leviticus 23 and other Old Testament calendars 214
APPENDIX A: Leviticus 13 241

APPENDIX B: Sex and its theology 249

GENERAL PREFACE

THE aim of this series of *Tyndale Old Testament Commentaries*, as it was in the companion volumes on the New Testament, is to provide the student of the Bible with a handy, up-to-date commentary on each book, with the primary emphasis on exegesis. Major critical questions are discussed in the introductions and additional notes, while undue technicalities have been avoided.

In this series individual authors are, of course, free to make their own distinct contributions and express their own point of view on all debated issues. Within the necessary limits of space they frequently draw attention to interpretations which they themselves do not hold but which represent the stated conclusions of sincere fellow Christians.

In the Old Testament in particular no single English translation is adequate to reflect the original text. The authors of these commentaries freely quote various versions, therefore, or give their own translation, in the endeavour to make the more difficult passages or words meaningful today. Where necessary, words from the Hebrew (and Aramaic) Text underlying their studies are transliterated. This will help the reader who may be unfamiliar with the Semitic languages to identify the word under discussion and thus to follow the argument. It is assumed throughout that the reader will have ready access to one, or more, reliable rendering of the Bible in English.

The book of Leviticus, much prized by our Jewish friends for its emphasis on a distinctive holiness to be displayed by God's people, has too often been neglected by Christians, except for a few selected themes or incidents. Professor Harrison puts emphasis on the purpose and meaning of the various sacrifices and rituals, and on their relation to the New Testament which similarly challenges the reader to lead a holy life. He does much to make the book as a whole clear in its original setting and relevant for us today.

Interest in the meaning and message of the Old Testament continues undiminished and it is hoped that this series will thus further the systematic study of the revelation of God and

His will and ways as seen in these records. It is the prayer of the editor and publisher, as of the authors, that these books will help many to understand, and to respond to, the Word of God today.

D. J. WISEMAN

AUTHOR'S PREFACE

LEVITICUS is a book that is read all too infrequently by the Christian Bible student. Being a rather technical priestly work which deals to a large extent with the rituals and sacrifices of the old covenant, it is commonly imagined to have little relevance for those living in the age of grace.

A closer study of Leviticus, however, provides the reader with remarkable insights into the character and will of God, particularly in the matter of holiness. Amongst the pagan Near Eastern nations, holiness was a state of consecration to the service of a deity, and often involved the practice of immoral rites. For the Hebrews, to be holy as God is holy required a close relationship of obedience and faith, and a manifestation in daily life of the high moral and spiritual qualities characteristic of God's nature as revealed in the Law. This same kind of holiness is demanded also of every believer in Jesus Christ.

Leviticus is thus a work of towering spirituality, which through the various sacrificial rituals points the reader unerringly to the atoning death of Jesus, our great High Priest. An eminent nineteenth-century writer once described Leviticus quite correctly as the seed-bed of New Testament theology, for in this book is to be found the basis of Christian faith and doctrine. The Epistle to the Hebrews expounds Leviticus in this connection, and therefore merits careful study in its own right, since in the view of the present writer it is pre-eminent as a commentary on Leviticus.

I wish to express my sincere gratitude to all who have assisted me in the production of this book, and especially to Professor D. J. Wiseman for his general oversight and unfailing courtesy.

R. K. HARRISON
Wycliffe College
University of Toronto

CHIEF ABBREVIATIONS

AV	The King James (Authorized) Version, 1611.
Heb.	Hebrew.
HIOT	R. K. Harrison, *Introduction to the Old Testament*, 1969.
IDB	Interpreter's Dictionary of the Bible, 4 volumes, 1962.
JB	The Jerusalem Bible, 1966.
LXX	The Septuagint (Greek) Version of the Old Testament.
mg.	margin.
MT	Massoretic Text.
NBD	*The New Bible Dictionary,* 1962.
NEB	The New English Bible.
NIV	The New International Version.
RV	The Revised Version, 1881.
VT	*Vetus Testamentum.*
ZPEB	*The Zondervan Pictorial Encylopedia of the Bible,* 5 volumes, 1975.

INTRODUCTION

TITLE OF THE BOOK

IN the Hebrew Bible the book of Leviticus is the third of the
five books of the Law, or Torah, the authorship of which
was attributed by ancient Hebrew tradition to Moses. The
opening word of the book, *wayyiqrā'*, 'and he called,' was used
as a title by the Jews, who also described Leviticus by such
designations as 'the law of the priests,' 'the book of the priests,'
and 'the law of the offerings.' These latter characterized the
general contents of the book, recognizing it as a work intended
principally for the Hebrew priesthood.

The Septuagint Greek version of the Old Testament entitled
the book *Leuitikon* or *Leueitikon, i.e.,* 'relating to the Levites.'
The Vulgate, which was a revision of the Old Latin version,
rendered the Greek heading by the phrase *Liber Leviticus,* from
which the title in the English Bible was derived. Although the
book is much more concerned with the duties of priests than of
Levites, the English title is not entirely inappropriate, since
the Hebrew priesthood was essentially levitical in character
(*cf.* Heb. 7:11).

NATURE OF LEVITICUS

Since Leviticus is basically a manual of priestly regulations
and procedures, it is only natural that the purely historical
element should be subordinated to ritual and legal considerations. Nevertheless, historical narratives are interwoven with
sections of law and instructions concerning sacrificial procedures in such a way as to make it clear that Leviticus is
closely connected historically with Exodus and Numbers. On
purely stylistic grounds alone Leviticus is linked with Exodus
20 – 40, and the association is demonstrated in the Hebrew
text by means of the opening word of Leviticus, the very first
consonant of which is a 'waw consecutive,' indicating a direct
connection with what has just preceded it, *i.e.,* Exodus 40:38.

Leviticus enlarges upon matters involving the ordering of
worship at the divine sanctuary that are mentioned only

briefly in Exodus. Whereas the latter described the specifications and construction of the tabernacle, Leviticus narrates the way in which the priests are to care for the sanctuary and throne room of the Great King. The work is a fundamentally important legal treatise because it contains the regulations by which the religious and civil life of the Hebrew nation was to be governed once the land of Canaan was occupied.

At Mount Sinai, where the legislation contained in Leviticus was revealed by God to Moses, the tribes of Israel had entered into a special relationship with God which by its very structure had all the marks of a second-millennium BC vassal treaty. Such agreements were made between a great king and a smaller nation with whom the king desired to enter into a political relationship. International treaties of this order were set out according to a traditional pattern, and when the stipulations had been accepted by the vassal, a formal ratification by both parties took place in the presence of their national gods, who acted as 'witnesses'. The Sinai covenant with its associated stipulations is recorded in Exodus 20:1 – 23:33, and was enlarged greatly in content by the addition of related legal and other material to form the book of Deuteronomy, which in effect is a covenant-renewal document. Leviticus differs from both Exodus and Deuteronomy, however, in containing technical regulations which the priests were to apply to the conduct of worship and the regulating of the community's life in Israel.

Leviticus is a well-organized reference manual for the Old Testament priesthood, and consists of two principal divisions or themes which have as their pivot the sixteenth chapter, dealing with regulations governing the annual day of atonement. The first fifteen chapters deal broadly with sacrificial principles and procedures relating to the removal of sin and the restoration of persons to fellowship with God. The last eleven chapters emphasize ethics, morality and holiness. The unifying theme of the book is the insistent emphasis upon God's holiness, coupled with the demand that the Israelites shall exemplify this spiritual attribute in their own lives. The material content is priestly in character, and therefore deals with the covenant obligations of the Israelites at a level which is not found elsewhere in the Pentateuch. The regulations and procedures connected with the observance of the day of atonement are an illustration of this tendency.

At first sight the book of Leviticus might appear to be a haphazard, even repetitious arrangement of enactments involving the future life in Canaan of the Israelite people. Closer examination will reveal, however, that quite apart from the division of the work into two basic themes, many of the chapters have their own literary structure. Examples of this can be seen in material patterned after the fashion of a Mesopotamian tablet, with its title, textual content and colophon, as in Leviticus 1:3 – 7:37–38. Other chapters exhibit a distinct form of construction, which would doubtless prove extremely valuable for purposes of memorizing the contents. Examples of this are to be found in the triadic pattern of the leprosy regulations introduced by the phrase 'The Lord said to Moses' (Lv. 13:1; 14:1, 33), or the concentric arrangement of propositions (palistrophe) in Leviticus 24:16–22. A particularly attractive literary form is the introverted (chiastic) passage occurring in Leviticus 15:2–30, suggesting considerable artistic ability on the part of the writer.

AUTHORSHIP AND DATE

The composition of Leviticus, along with other books of the Pentateuch, was ascribed uniformly by Jewish tradition to Moses, the lawgiver of Israel. Because of the way in which Christ associated Himself with the fulfilment of the law (*cf.* Mt. 5:17), the primitive Christian church also maintained the Mosaic authorship of the Torah or Law, and this became the established position of Christianity. During the mediaeval period there were some writers who attacked orthodox views with regard to the authorship and date of pentateuchal material. Thus in Spain in the tenth century a certain Ibn Hazam of Cordova, who was really an adherent of the Islamic faith, regarded much of the Pentateuch, including Leviticus, as having been compiled by Ezra. Even the celebrated eleventh-century Spanish exegete Ibn Ezra maintained that there were several late insertions in the Pentateuch, although at the same time he managed to regard them as compatible with Mosaic authorship.

INTRODUCTION

A hint of what was to come occurred in the fifteenth century, when Andreas Bodenstein, an opponent of Martin Luther, maintained that Moses could not possibly have composed his own obituary passage in Deuteronomy 34, and argued from that proposition to a rejection of Moses as the author of the entire Pentateuch, since for him the whole corpus of laws was written in the same broad style as the notice of Moses' death. In the following century the deistic philosopher Thomas Hobbes maintained that Moses lived some centuries prior to the appearance of the Torah in its written form, although he accepted the genuine nature of those passages attributed in the text to Moses. The views of Ibn Ezra were followed in the seventeenth century by another philosopher, Benedict Spinoza, who rejected the Mosaic authorship of the Pentateuch, regarding it instead as the outcome of a lengthy process of compilation and editing by various generations of scribes.

While earlier writers had mentioned the possibility of pre-Mosaic sources underlying certain portions of the Pentateuch, these views only began to be developed in the eighteenth century, when the growth of literary criticism presented a serious challenge to the more traditional views. Without using any objective criteria as a guide, various writers began to speculate about the nature and contents of the supposed documents underlying the Pentateuch in its final form. This process was started by a French physician, Jean Astruc, who used *Elohim* and *YHWH* (Jehovah), two of the names by which God was known in the Pentateuch, as a basis for his analysis of the material into its supposed sources.

Although Astruc was aware of the inadequacies of this approach, it nevertheless gained favour with other European scholars of liberal bent, who employed it quite uncritically in their studies. One unfortunate result of this situation was that the Pentateuch became subjected increasingly to dissection into fragments, as successive generations of scholars divided and subdivided the text, attributing the resulting sections on occasions to a wide variety of dates and compilers. By 1805, when J. S. Vater published a commentary on the Pentateuch which identified as many as forty separate underlying sources, many literary-critical writers had already begun to assign the final form of the books of Moses to the exilic period, and to an authorship other than that of Moses, who for many was a legendary figure at best.

In the nineteenth century Graf and Wellhausen took the suggested documents based on the two names of God that had been employed as criteria for source-recognition, along with priestly material, of which the book of Leviticus formed a significant part, and the addition of Deuteronomy, as the supposed 'documentary' sources for the Pentateuch. The 'Jehovistic' source was assigned to a ninth-century BC date, while the alleged document in which the name *Elohim* occurred was attributed to the eighth century BC. Deuteronomy was thought to have been written in the time of king Josiah, who reigned from about 640 to 609 BC, while Leviticus and other priestly materials were dated in the fifth century BC. Wellhausen maintained that Leviticus 17 – 26 was added to the other priestly writings somewhat after the time of Ezekiel, while the remaining priestly passages in the Elohistic 'document' were added by Ezra.[1]

Not merely did the fragmentization of the Pentateuch into alleged underlying 'documents' destroy the basic unity of the narrative material, but it also went far towards denying the historicity of the attributive author. Twentieth-century adherents of the literary-critical theory of pentateuchal origins frequently regarded the beginnings of Israel as at best shrouded in myth and legend, while persons such as Abraham and Moses were held to be completely unhistorical by the more radical critics.

Positive and beneficial for Old Testament study as this approach seemed to be to its adherents, it was in fact marked by serious flaws from the very beginning. Those who initiated the process did so on the basis of a speculative concept that was then developed in the best traditions of Hellenic romanticism. The fact that no attempt was made to test the ideas under consideration at any point against what was known at that time about the compositional techniques underlying ancient Near Eastern literature did not disturb the proponents of the theory. Instead, they set about looking for anything that might serve as evidence for their position, and in the process they

---

[1] For a detailed study of the development of this theory see *HIOT*, pp. 7–32.

denied or manipulated those parts of the Hebrew text that appeared to be inimical to the position that they were advancing.

Unfortunate though this attitude was, it proved to be merely symptomatic of the larger malaise. In essence, the problem was one of method, and the situation was all the more ironic because the nineteenth-century literary critics boasted from time to time about the fundamentally 'scientific' nature of their work. In point of fact, the romanticist ideology which undergirded their speculations was the very antithesis of scientific method, either as it was known in the nineteenth century or at the present time.

Instead of utilizing the *a priori* approach to the problems of the Old Testament, by which deduced consequences were made from assumed principles or propositions, the literary-critical investigators ought to have commenced with the given, objective data and endeavoured to see if they conveyed realistic meaning when interpreted in their own terms. If the data did not make sense at that point, the quest should have been abandoned when further testing confirmed the initial response.

If, however, the data were capable of rational interpretation, they should then have been compared with other relevant evidence, preferably of an objective nature such as archaeological material, and on the basis of the findings some tentative hypothesis could then have been advanced and regarded as subject to modification or rejection in the light of subsequent objective evidence. After still further rigorous testing against the background of other relevant data, which could well have resulted in the severe modification or the abandonment of part or all of the enterprise, any further progress might possibly have advanced in the direction of a working theory.

This *a posteriori* method of examining and explaining data was already in wide use in the nineteenth century, and was successful as an investigative tool because it argued from the data to a possible means of explaining their incidence. In a series of brilliant discoveries the Russian chemist Dmitri Ivanovich Mendeleev (1834–1907) used this approach to classify elements into 'families' characterized by similar properties. By 1871, some six years before Wellhausen published his work on the composition of the Hexateuch,[2] Mendeleev had arranged known elements into tabular form according to their atomic weights and organized them into a preliminary 'family' order. On the basis of this knowledge he was able to predict the existence of elements still undiscovered in his day, and to locate them with complete accuracy in his periodic table of elements.[3] Had contemporary literary critics been truly scientific in their method, they would have endeavoured to discover precisely how ancient Near Eastern documents were compiled and transmitted, instead of asserting that a specific name of God was a criterion for literary analysis, independently of other considerations, and assembling all the verses that utilized that name into a 'document', whether the end-result made sense or not. Whereas Mendeleev's periodic table of the elements is a fundamental and unquestioned part of the modern study of chemistry, the Graf-Wellhausen theory of pentateuchal origins is undergoing fundamental and searching challenges to its credibility and reliability.

With a confidence that was entirely unwarranted even in the light of what was then known about ancient Near Eastern culture, Wellhausen proclaimed that such historic institutions as the tabernacle came from a late period of Hebrew history. Under the influence of Hegelian evolutionary philosophy, Wellhausen rewrote the religious history of the Israelites in such a way as to replace the monotheism of the Genesis narratives with an animistic form of religion, which only after a prolonged period of time emerged as ethical monotheism. In order to effect this reversal of Old Testament tradition it was necessary for Wellhausen to indulge in a wholesale rearrangement of chronological sequences as presented by the Old Testament. By regarding the literary sources which described patriarchal life and religion as completely unhistorical, and by ascribing the origin of monotheistic faith to the work of the prophets rather than to divine revelation during the patriarchal period, he was able to present a reconstruction of events

---

[2] J. Wellhausen, *Die Komposition des Hexateuchs* (1877).
[3] R. K. Harrison in C. H. Pinnock and D. Wells (eds.), *Toward a Theology for the Future* (1971), pp. 18–19.

in which such works as Leviticus appeared at the end rather than at the beginning of Israel's national history.

The fact that this type of study superimposed a highly subjective ideological structure upon the ancient Hebrew narrative, which in general stifled the historical evidence they had to present, appeared to be of no concern to Wellhausen and his followers, who began to apply the literary-critical approach to the rest of the Old Testament with great enthusiasm. In doing this they displayed the most serious weakness of all by regarding as 'scientific' what was in fact an entirely subjective and arbitrary procedure, pursued without any recourse to objective controls.

When archaeological discoveries began to demonstrate the existence of 'monotheistic' worship amongst the pagan Mesopotamians of the fourth millennium BC, and to adduce evidence for the antiquity of such portable shrines as the tabernacle, it became evident the Wellhausen's reconstruction of Hebrew history was in fact riddled with grave deficiencies. While liberal scholars found themselves committed to his theory of pentateuchal origins, they struggled increasingly under the disability of arbitrarily-dated 'documents', the existence of which has never been demonstrated in any way.

To circumvent the difficulty to some extent, certain Scandinavian scholars began to disregard written 'documents' as such, and espoused instead the idea of a reliable oral tradition, transmitted over many centuries and ultimately enshrined in written form. Unfortunately for this view two serious problems arose. The first was that the Scandinavians assumed that Near Eastern oral tradition served in the absence of an earlier written form of that tradition, as was the case in Europe. Like the Wellhausenians before them, they did not take into account the evidence furnished by archaeological discoveries, and this had the unfortunate effect of modifying very seriously the significance of their approach. In this instance it is now known that in antiquity written and oral versions of all important occurrences were promulgated at the same time. The written form normally comprised an official record, whether it was an inscription, a monument, or a portion of the court annals for the particular year in which the event took place. The oral version was for local dissemination, and thereafter could be included in popular or family tradition. This is very different from the European situation, where written and oral forms did not exist side by side.

The second major difficulty to this approach was that, in the end, the units of oral tradition came perilously close to acquiring the fixity of the 'documents' which had been proposed by Wellhausen and his precursors, a situation which could hardly be considered as a forward step in critical thought. The approach to Old Testament study known as form criticism endeavours to isolate specific units of material in terms of their form, rather than concentrating upon documents as such. Once the form has been isolated, the critic then enquires about such things as its use, the cultural context in which it was set, and the purpose of the material.[4] Leviticus is clearly composed of ritual and legislative passages which served a fundamental cultic and regulatory purpose in the life of the ancient Israelites. The first fifteen chapters exhibit a distinctive structure, and seem to have been compiled in a manner that would enable the priests to commit them to memory quite readily. Similarly the material relating to the Passover ceremony is a unique and easily identifiable unit of a liturgical character, intended for obvious cultic usage. The statutes and related social material of the final chapters can be recognized without difficulty by their form, and assessed in terms of their implications for the sedentary occupation of Canaan.

Traditio-historical analysis attempts to investigate the nature of the group that transmitted the particular tradition under study, the location with which it was associated, the life-setting from which the tradition emerged, and the way in which specific themes came to be formulated.[5] This approach relies heavily upon the supposed precedence of oral over written tradition, even though it is now known that the two forms coexisted for all important ancient Near Eastern materials.[6] Tradition analysis would regard Leviticus as having emerged from priestly circles which handed on in oral form the traditions relating to the sacrifices, the care of the sacred

---

[4] Gene M. Tucker, *Form Criticism of the Old Testament* (1971), p. iv *et passim*.
[5] W. E. Rast, *Tradition History and the Old Testament* (1972), p. 19 ff.
[6] *Cf.* K. A. Kitchen, *Ancient Orient and Old Testament* (1966), pp. 135–138.

shrine, and general priestly deportment. Even though the antiquity of Old Testament priestly circles and their traditions has been demonstrated from archaeological and other sources,[7] traditio-historical analysis still regards the literary form of the material as late rather than early, in accordance with the general position of Wellhausen. One disadvantage of this type of approach is that individual creativity is depreciated if not denied completely, despite the fact that a number of Old Testament compositions exhibit distinct indications of individuality in authorship. Another is that the results of such an investigation can be predicted with reasonable accuracy when the process is known to be based upon subjective presuppositions such as the unhistorical nature of much of the early biblical material, or the presumption that the final form of many Old Testament writings was in general late rather than early in date. Since both the methods discussed above are influenced heavily by nineteenth-century European humanistic thought, they will be of limited value to biblical scholarship as a whole until they are integrated into a properly accredited scientific method of study.

While modern liberal scholars still use the old Wellhausenian designation of the supposed 'documents', many of them have come to regard the latter as the fixed form of traditions that had been current for many centuries. Furthermore, the differences of style and content that were once so widely presented as criteria for the recognition of documentary 'sources' have been minimized considerably in the realization that the supposed Elohistic and Jehovistic 'documents' represent the same fundamental Mosaic tradition.

Even the priestly 'document', regarded by Wellhausen as the latest of the pentateuchal sources and therefore less reliable than its precursors, is now acknowledged to be a carefully preserved record of events and procedures. This is particularly the case with Leviticus, which contains a number of very ancient features. Modern discoveries have shown that priestly material from the Near East is always early rather than late in origin, and that priestly traditions are usually preserved in a meticulous manner. Therefore to assign a

---

[7] *Cf.* W. F. Albright, *From the Stone Age to Christianity* (1957 ed.), pp. 252–254.

priestly document such as Leviticus to a late date is to go completely contrary to ancient Near Eastern literary traditions. Furthermore, it is not clear to the present writer how material that is obviously ancient in nature and has been subjected to processes of priestly transmission can be regarded as late in its final form, especially if oral transmission did in fact preserve it accurately. This anomaly deserves some attention on the part of those who maintain the Wellhausenian tradition in one form or other.

In view of these considerations, the most logical conclusion concerning authorship and date would be to recognize the antiquity and authenticity of Leviticus, and to regard it as a genuine second-millennium BC literary product compiled by Moses, with the probable assistance of priestly scribes. It should be noted, of course, that no-one is named directly as the author of specific sections, unlike the book of Exodus (*cf.* Ex. 17:14; 24:4; 34:27). At the same time, Leviticus includes material that formed part of the Sinai revelation (*cf.* Lv. 7:37–38; 26:46; 27:34), which Moses would undoubtedly record subsequently. It is within the realm of possiblity that an editor or a scribe of a later generation could have arranged the Mosaic material of Leviticus in its present order. Even more probable, however, is that the legislation was organized in its extant form in the time of Moses, since the material was needed at that time as a manual for priestly procedures. Distinctive institutions such as the day of atonement and the sacred seasons, which were required to be observed, grew directly out of Israel's historic experiences, and must obviously have been legislated for when they occurred, not many centuries later.

That these enactments would be in written form at an early rather than a late stage in the development of the national life of Israel is thoroughly consistent with what is now known of ancient Near Eastern priestly traditions. There seems little evidence of scribal updating of ancient terminology in Leviticus, and this again is typical of priestly conservatism, especially as exhibited among the Sumerians. A review of Leviticus as a whole against the cultural background of the Late Bronze Age shows that most sections of the book have counterparts in contemporary or earlier Near Eastern writings. This can be illustrated by reference to the cereal and peace offerings, which were somewhat similar to ones found at Ras Shamra (Ugarit), while votive offerings were well known in the Near East. In the view of the present author there is no single element in Leviticus that could not have been known to Moses, or that requires a date later than the end of the Amarna period (fifteenth and fourteenth centuries BC).

According to 2 Kings 17:24–28, organized worship among the Mesopotamians who had been brought to Samaria as colonists commenced in the time of Esarhaddon (681–669 BC). These people intermarried with the Israelite women that remained in the area (cf. Je. 41:5) and the resultant admixture formed the basis of the people that came to be known as the Samaritans. Since this group by uniform tradition employed the Pentateuch alone as the source of their doctrine and worship, the law books from which they were instructed must have been in something close to their final form in the late eighth or early seventh century BC. The Samaritan sectarian recension seems to have been made about 110 BC according to Purvis,[8] but its textual ancestor, which is also regarded as that from which the LXX arose, went back considerably earlier in time, perhaps to the sixth century BC. F. M. Cross has given the designation 'Old Palestinian recension'[9] to the pentateuchal section, and from internal evidence, names and places he concluded that this recension was taken to Egypt in the fifth century BC where after some revision it ultimately became the text from which the LXX was made. Cross has conjectured further that the 'Old Palestinian' type of text emerged from material that had been in the possession of the Babylonian exiles. In view of the highly restricted contents of the Samaritan canon and the emphasis of the sect upon such central rites as the passover, it is difficult to believe that they knew little or nothing in the period following Esarhaddon about the existence or contents of a cultically oriented book such as Leviticus, contrary to the presuppositions of the Graf-Wellhausen theory.

[8] J. D. Purvis, *IDB Supplementary Volume* (1976), pp. 772–775.

[9] F. M. Cross, *The Ancient Library of Qumran and Modern Biblical Studies* (1964), pp. 180–190.

24

Needless to say, the Samaritans have their own theory of literary origins, claiming that their oldest scriptural manuscript reached back to the time of Abishua, the great-grandson of Aaron (1 Ch. 6:3–4). While this is obviously exaggerated, as are certain other Samaritan claims, their tradition clearly supports the existence of Leviticus in written form at a time far earlier than that allowed by liberal scholarship.[10]

UNITY OF LEVITICUS

Although the book is quite clearly a uniform priestly document, scholars of different persuasions have purported to see certain underlying sources in Leviticus. The most prominent of these was the so-called 'holiness code' (chapters 17–26), given this name by Klostermann in 1877. This section deals with the significance of sacrificial blood: various laws and the punishments incurred for their infraction; rules for priestly holiness; and the sacred seasons of the Hebrew religious calendar. The beginning (Lv. 17:1–2) and ending (Lv. 26:46) have been taken as clear indications of the material comprising a separate source, but as noted in the commentary section the contents of this 'code' have been preserved in the style of an ancient Mesopotamian tablet. Since there are other parts of Leviticus that have been written in the same manner (*cf.* Lv. 1:3 – 7:37–38; 27:1–34), the Graf-Wellhausenian view that this 'code' was probably an independent work composed about the time of Ezekiel and added to Leviticus shortly thereafter seems entirely artificial and contrived.

That the kind of situation proposed by Wellhausen simply did not occur is further suggested by the contents of the 'code', in which there is an almost complete lack of interest in the part played by the priests during the sacrifices. This would be most unusual had the material originated in specifically priestly

---

[10] On this sect see also M. Gaster, *The Samaritans, Their History, Doctrines and Literature* (1925); B. J. Roberts, *The Old Testament Text and Versions* (1951); T. H. Gaster, *IDB*, 4, p. 191; J. Macdonald, *The Theology of the Samaritans* (1964); J. D. Purvis, *The Samaritan Pentateuch and the Origin of the Samaritan Sect* (1968); B. K. Waltke in J. B. Payne (ed.), *New Perspectives on the Old Testament* (1970), pp. 212 ff.; *idem* in *Biblical Criticism: Historical, Literary and Textual* (1978), pp. 54–56.

circles independently of the remainder of the book. When, however, it is integrated with the other chapters it harmonizes perfectly well with the ritual and cultic prescriptions affecting the priests as described in Leviticus 1:1 – 9:24. Chapters 11 to 15, dealing with the differentiation between clean and unclean, could also be regarded as a separate section of material, but this again is integrated firmly into the book by means of the references in Leviticus 5:2 and 7:21, which the chapters expound at considerable length. Again, the enactments of chapters 18 to 20 are connected with the laws of chapters 11 to 15 by means of the reference in Leviticus 20:25, which helps to indicate the internal coherence of the book. It is also possible to regard Leviticus 26:46 as applying to the whole of the work, and not just to the 'code' itself, a position adopted by some scholars. While the book may have been assembled in terms of two principal sections, they and other accompanying chapters have been so well integrated as to present the reader with a finished product which exhibits a clear literary and theological unity.[11]

PURPOSE OF THE BOOK

The reason the newly consecrated Israelite priests were given such detailed instructions about the care of God's sanctuary was to ensure His continuing presence with His people. In the covenant relationship God approached Israel and made specific promises to them, contingent upon their obedience to the terms of the Sinai agreement. One of these was the demand that the Israelites should live in a way that would show to contemporary Near Eastern nations the true nature of holiness. This attribute was of an advanced moral and ethical character, and was fundamentally different from the sexual and orgiastic connotations which the term had amongst Israel's neighbours. Only as the chosen people maintained ceremonial and moral holiness could they expect God to honour them with His presence and bring into effect the blessings promised in the covenant.

God's shrine, the tabernacle, had been constructed according to precise instructions, and was the symbol of His presence

[11] *HIOT*, pp. 596–598.

amongst the Israelites. Scrupulous care had to be taken, therefore, to observe the regulations safeguarding the holiness of the tabernacle which God had glorified, lest His presence be removed abruptly through defilement of that sacred place. The regulations of the levitical sacrificial tariff presuppose that man is a sinner, and make provision accordingly for the forgiveness of various kinds of inadvertent or accidental sins. Through the appropriate kind of offering, the transgressor can receive forgiveness from God, mediated by the priesthood which He has appointed to that end.

Not merely are the priests to observe the cultic regulations for ceremonial holiness, but they are required to live lives of moral purity and spiritual dedication, so that they will be examples to Israel of divine holiness. The purpose of this is to establish the chosen people as a holy nation, and thereby to make them distinctive amongst their contemporaries as representatives of the one, true and living God. Holiness of life must therefore characterize both priests and people, and in order that the future sedentary life of the nation might be firmly established on such a basis, a series of social, moral and economic regulations was promulgated. As these and other covenantal prescriptions were obeyed, the nation would be blessed and protected. By contrast, disobedience to the regulations, or rejection of the covenant responsibilities to any degree, would result in severe punishment of the Israelites, since a warning had already been served upon them in the covenant formulation. The function of the Israelite priest was not merely to officiate at the sanctuary but also to instruct the people in God's law. Being a compendium of both ritual and moral enactments, the book of Leviticus would serve as an ideal manual for such a purpose.

Many attempts have been made by scholars and expositors over the centuries to interpret the catalogue of abominable creatures in the book of Leviticus, but with uncertain results. An intriguing investigation of the rationale underlying the differentiation of clean from unclean species has been undertaken by Dr Mary Douglas.[12] As a social anthropologist she

---

[12] Mary Douglas, *Purity and Danger* (1966). Her subsequent writings include *Natural Symbols* (1970) and *Implicit Meanings* (1975).

has discussed the role played by pollution in such areas of existence as the magical rituals of primitive peoples, inter-sex relationships, and dietary regulations. Her basic contention is that rituals of purity and impurity produce unity in experience, a holistic concept closely akin to the ancient Near Eastern tradition of the pairing of opposites to describe totality.

Thus, for her the impurity associated with the avoidance or elimination of faeces is the negative side of a more positive effort to bring our environment closer to some ideal situation. The endeavour to avoid defilement of various kinds would therefore appear to be a creative effort to unify our experience in terms of the environment, and must not be construed as superstitious or irrational. Such laws concerning uncleanness as are found in Leviticus have an obvious symbolic significance in so far as they attempt to introduce an ideal of unity into individual life by showing the ancient Israelites how God required them to live as members of a holy nation.

Dr Douglas argues that since holiness requires individuals to conform to the class to which they belong,[13] the animals that do not exhibit the specified forms of locomotion, namely flying, walking, swimming and running, are unclean. Thus the standard type of insect would appear to be one with only two legs for locomotion, so that any species such as caterpillars, cockroaches and the like would be unclean. This argument encounters difficulties in attempting to explain how sheep, oxen and goats, which have hoofs for walking, reflect the ideal of cleanness, whereas pigs, which also have hoofs, do not. It is hardly sufficient to say, as the author does, that since sheep, oxen and goats were the normal food of pastoral peoples, they would thereby have been regarded as clean. The fact is that in the ancient Near East the flesh of the pig was also more widely consumed than many have been led to imagine hitherto.

Furthermore, on her argument, the legislation of Leviticus was designed to convey God's concept of the ideal to man, not to endorse certain current patterns of social behaviour, which seems to be implied in her understanding of the social background in this instance. Even if one adduces the differ-

[13] *Purity and Danger*, p. 53.

entiating factor of cloven hoofs and the chewing of cud, the rationale of the differentiation is still assumed and not explained.

Before Dr Douglas' stimulating proposals can command general acceptance it will be necessary for more research to be undertaken into human attitudes towards elimination as a bodily function. *Homo sapiens* is a faeces-inspecting animal, as are some of the inferior orders of creation and, if this attitude is as instinctive as it appears to be, it is difficult to see how it can be regarded as other than a normal behavioural mode. Therefore, to describe elimination as a 'negative movement' is to attach a judgment of value to something that is merely a biological function essential to individual wellbeing. Certainly the attitudes of primitive peoples towards this particular activity need to be investigated afresh, since they may well prove to exhibit a surprising diversity. The findings could then be compared profitably with the instructions given by God to members of a 'high culture' regarding the hygienic disposal of faeces (Dt. 23:13).

No research in this field would be adequate without careful enquiry as to possible differences between male and female attitudes towards the avoidance or elimination of dirt. Whatever researches are undertaken with regard to the hygienic practices of primitive peoples must be prepared to interpret those procedures in their own right, otherwise the issue will be confounded by cross-cultural extrapolation. A study of female elimination must also include the foetus as well as the faeces, since the psychological reactions accompanying parturition have been studied only in a very superficial manner to date, with the result that the psychodynamics are poorly understood. Here again, attitudes may well vary from one culture to another, and what may be embarrassing, distasteful and unclean to one may be regarded by others as a normal, and perhaps even pleasurable, activity.

THEOLOGY OF LEVITICUS

In order to understand the spiritual teachings of the book, Leviticus has to be seen, in conjunction with Exodus and Numbers, as literature intimately related to the Sinai covenant. A holy, pure and just God has revealed Himself afresh to the Israelites, and has presented them with a covenant formulation, the terms of which have been accepted. In brief, these contained the assurance that God would provide for all the material and spiritual needs of the people, including the gift of a strategic piece of territory as a national home, if on their part they would acknowledge Him as the one true God, and would undertake not to worship any other deity. As was the custom with certain ancient treaties between a great king and a vassal nation, the responsibilities and obligations of the people to whom the agreement was presented were given in considerable detail, and some of the enactments of the Sinai covenant are enshrined in Leviticus.

Among other things, these provisions furnish a great deal of information about God's character, and His will for those who are in a covenant relationship with Him. In the first instance, Leviticus presents God as a living, all-powerful deity, who has intervened already in Israel's affairs to ransom them from slavery in Egypt and make them a people free to worship Him. This miraculous act of deliverance is a guarantee of His ability to care for the chosen people, and to protect their interests as long as they continue to obey His laws.

Secondly, the book speaks of God's presence with His people Israel, symbolized by the tabernacle in the middle of the encampment, which was the seat of His glory. The people of the Near East were familiar with the concept of a portable shrine as indicative of the presence of a national deity in the midst of his people, and for the Israelites the tabernacle was a reminder of God's supreme power as well as His presence. As has been remarked above, God demanded the exclusive worship of His people as part of the covenant proposals, and Leviticus lays down the terms which alone will result in the acceptance of the worshipper.

The sacrificial system, which is presented in great detail in Leviticus, was one of the means by which community life in Israel was regulated. While the details of sacrificial procedures varied from one kind of sacrifice to another, there is a consistent emphasis in the book upon the fundamental importance of correct ritual behaviour. God can be approached ceremonially only in certain prescribed ways, otherwise disaster could be the result. This situation was not so much a consequence of divine petulance as a means of disciplining the Israelites so that they would obey God's instructions without question. While ancient Hebrew society might be thought to be overgoverned by such legislation, the fact is that the regulations functioned for the protection and guidance of the Israelites. As a result the people were instructed properly in acceptable modes of divine worship, and were also shown by dramatic examples the perils of innovation and disobedience. The legislative sections of Leviticus thus make clear the principle that obedience would be followed by life and blessing, while disobedience would result in death.

Not merely is God a living and omnipotent deity, but He is the essence of holiness. This concept involves ethical and moral, as well as purely spiritual attributes, and must be reflected in the day-to-day existence of the Israelites. Their covenantal relationship to the living God is a matter of supreme importance for mankind, and thus they are to become a kingdom of priests and a holy nation. 'Be holy, as I am holy', an injunction which appears repeatedly in Leviticus, could well be regarded as the motto of Israel's national life. God's holiness involved an abhorrence of anything immoral or sinful, as those concepts were defined by reference to the covenantal legislation, and it also recoiled from anything that was unjust or impure. While God was the One who cared for the enslaved Israelites in Egypt to the point where He had ransomed them and restored their liberty, He demanded that they should observe the requirements of the covenant into which they had entered, and behave as responsible parties to that agreement.

The sacrificial system showed human sinfulness, and the limited means which God had adopted for restoring the sinner to fellowship with Himself. The sinner needs to repent and be forgiven if he is not to die in his sin, and here it must be noted again that the transgressions for which atonement is provided are those of accidental defilement or inadvertent violation of ceremonial regulations. As will be observed in the commentary, there was no forgiveness for the kind of sin which constituted a repudiation of covenant mercies.

Leviticus teaches that atonement for sin must be by substitution. The sinner must bring an offering which he has acquired at some cost as a substitute for his own life. His formal identification with it is followed by the presentation of the offering to God, and a declaration by the priest that atonement has been made.

The book thus makes it evident that no person can be his own saviour or mediator. An individual must come before God in penitence, confess his sin and obtain pardon from a merciful God who repudiates sin but shows covenant love to the sinner. The cardinal importance of blood-shedding in substitutionary atonement is indicated in Leviticus 17:11, for without it there can be no forgiveness of sin. Among other things, obtaining forgiveness involves cost, and the taking of life.

The general legislation of Leviticus shows that all life is lived under the watchful eye of God, and as a result it makes no artificial differentiation between what is holy and what is secular. A holy people will by their lives transform mundane things into beautiful and acceptable offerings to God. Through His indwelling they will be empowered to minister covenantal grace to each other and to those outside the nation of Israel, as opportunity arises. The underlying aim of the teaching is thus to ensure that God's holiness will be able to regulate and direct every area of human activity.

LEVITICUS AND THE NEW TESTAMENT

The importance of levitical law in the mind of Christ can be seen from His remarks (Mt. 22:39) concerning the 'golden rule' (Lv. 19:18). In the synoptic gospels this aphorism is mentioned in Matthew 19:19; Mark 12:31; and Luke 10:27. Paul also referred to it in Romans 13:9 and Galatians 5:14.

The concepts of separation and holiness demanded by the ancient Hebrew priesthood were attractive themes to New Testament writers. Peter was insistent that the fellowship of Christians should be nothing less than a royal priesthood (1 Pet. 2:9), while the author of Hebrews saw in the concept both an individual and a social aspect. What is commonly described as the 'priesthood of all believers' implies that those who have committed their lives to Christ as Saviour and Lord, and thereby have experienced spiritual rebirth, have direct

access to the Father without any recourse to human interme-
diaries. It also means that all true believers must aspire to live
as priests who are consecrated to the Lord's service so that
they will bring continuous honour to God's sacred name.
Therefore they must be moral, upright and holy in their daily
existence. Peter caught the spirit of Leviticus firmly in his
exhortation to Christians to emulate divine holiness in every
activity of life (1 Pet. 1:15).

The author of the Epistle to the Hebrews saw in Leviticus
much that foreshadowed the atoning work of Jesus Christ. In
Hebrews 7, Christ was depicted as the eternal High Priest
whose work far surpassed that of Aaron and his successors in
office. Whereas they ministered locally and died in due course,
Christ's atonement brought about universal redemption, while
His eternity guarantees an unchangeable priesthood. As a
sinless Saviour, Jesus was unique in being able to dispense
with the necessity for making atonement for His own sins
before sacrificing for the iniquities of others. Because grace
and truth came by Jesus Christ, He is the originator of a better
covenant based on divine grace, which enables persons to
approach God freely without the impediments of legalism.
Finally, Christ did what no Hebrew high priest ever accomplished by offering Himself as the supreme sacrifice for human
sin. This atonement was made once for all time, as contrasted
with the annual offerings for national sins of inadvertence
made on the day of atonement. Christ thus transcended the
law in His demonstration of supreme love (Jn. 15:13).[14]

In His death Jesus fulfilled the levitical concept of the sin
offering (*cf.* Rom. 8:1–4; 2 Cor. 5:18–21; Heb. 9:11–28;
10:11–12; 13:10–15), while in other connections Paul described Him as a peace offering (Rom. 5:1–11; Eph. 3:13–18;
Col. 1:18–20). Just as the tabernacle symbolized God's
presence in the midst of Israel, so the incarnation of Jesus
Christ is an assurance that God is present continuously in
human society. The priests and the sacrifices which they
presented were a foreshadowing of the larger work of Christ
for human salvation (*cf.* Heb. 3:1; 4:14–16, *etc.*). The
atonement achieved on Calvary meant that the strict levitical

---

[14] *Cf.* R. A. Ward, *The Pattern of our Salvation* (1978), pp. 52–53.

prescriptions for sacrifice and holiness had been superseded for the Christian by the indwelling of God's Holy Spirit (*cf.* Acts 9:9–16; 15:1–21; Gal. 2:11 – 3:5, *etc.*). Because Jesus Christ lives in the believer by faith, the true living sacrifice to God comprises the daily presentation of the life in the service of Christ and His kingdom (*cf.* Rom. 12:1–2).

THE HEBREW TEXT

Since Leviticus is a priestly work, it is to be expected that the contents will have been preserved carefully. Despite its long history of textual transmission, there are very few areas of difficulty presented by the Hebrew, and such questions as arise are discussed in the appropriate sections of the commentary. The Massoretic Text, which ultimately became the traditional vehicle for the transmission of the Old Testament in Hebrew, has been shown by subsequent manuscript discoveries, including those at Qumran, to have been remarkably free from errors of various kinds. Although it is now known that as many as three different textual types of the Old Testament Hebrew were in circulation in Palestine in the time of Christ, the Massoretic Text contains fewer copying mistakes and is closer to the original manuscripts than the Hebrew texts from which such versions as the Samaritan Pentateuch and the Septuagint were made. These latter are useful for purposes of comparison, however, where difficulties arise in the traditional text, since on occasions they may preserve rather more ancient readings.

Nine Hebrew fragments of Leviticus were found in caves as part of the body of literature known as the Dead Sea scrolls. Only a few of these manuscript scraps from Qumran have been published at the time of writing, and there is some difference of opinion as to their age. Nevertheless they indicate clearly the existence of different types of Hebrew text in the period before Christ. The Leviticus fragment discovered in Cave 11 has been found to diverge in certain areas from the Massoretic Text, the Samaritan Pentateuch and the text underlying the Septuagint version of Leviticus, indicating that it represents an ancient and independent form of the Hebrew textual tradition.

Fragments of Leviticus recovered from Cave 1 have affinity

with the Massoretic Text, whereas those from Caves 2 and 6 are more closely related to the textual types associated with the Samaritan Pentateuch and the Septuagint. The modifications of the Hebrew which result from the slight differences in the various textual traditions seem generally to demonstrate the superiority of the Massoretic Text. Certainly the manuscript discoveries at Qumran have shown that the book of Leviticus has a far longer history of textual transmission than was imagined by nineteenth-century literary critics, and this observation applies to the Pentateuch as a whole.

ANALYSIS

I. REGULATIONS CONCERNING SACRIFICE (1:1 – 7:38)
   a. The burnt offering (1:1–17)
   b. The cereal offering (2:1–16)
   c. The peace offering (3:1–17)
   d. The sin offering (4:1 – 5:13)
   e. The guilt offering (5:14–19)
   f. Conditions requiring atonement (6:1–7)
   g. Burnt offerings (6:8–13)
   h. Cereal offerings (6:14–23)
   i. Sin offerings (6:24–30)
   j. Rules for guilt offerings (7:1–10)
   k. Rules for peace offerings (7:11–21)
   l. Fat and blood forbidden (7:22–27)
   m. Additional peace-offering regulations (7:28–38)

II. CONSECRATION OF PRIESTS (8:1 – 10:20)
   a. Preparation for anointing (8:1–5)
   b. The ceremony itself (8:6–13)
   c. Consecration offering (8:14–36)
   d. Rules for offerings (9:1–7)
   e. Aaron's sacrifices (9:8–24)
   f. Nadab and Abihu (10:1–7)
   g. Drunken priests prohibited (10:8–11)
   h. Rules for eating consecrated food (10:12–20)

III. CLEAN AND UNCLEAN DIFFERENTIATED (11:1 – 15:33)
   a. Clean and unclean species (11:1–47)
   b. Purification following childbirth (12:1–8)
   c. Regulations involving leprosy (13:1 – 14:57)
   d. Purification following bodily secretions (15:1–33)

IV. THE DAY OF ATONEMENT (16:1–34)
   a. Priestly preparation (16:1–4)
   b. The two goats (16:5–10)
   c. The sin offerings (16:11–22)

    d. Rituals for cleansing (16:23–28)
    e. Enactment of the day of atonement (16:29–34)

V. RITUAL LAWS (17:1 – 25:55)
    a. Sacrificial blood (17:1–16)
    b. Various laws and punishments (18:1 – 20:27)
    c. Rules for priestly holiness (21:1 – 22:33)
    d. Consecration of seasons (23:1–44)
    e. Sacred objects: sin of blasphemy (24:1–23)
    f. Sabbatical and jubilee years (25:1–55)

VI. CONCLUDING BLESSINGS AND PUNISHMENTS (26:1–46)
    a. Blessings (26:1–13)
    b. Punishments (26:14–39)
    c. The rewards of contrition (26:40–46)

VII. REGULATIONS CONCERNING VOWS AND OFFERINGS (27:1–34)
    a. Persons (27:1–8)
    b. Animals (27:9–13)
    c. Property (27:14–29)
    d. Redemption of tithes (27:30–34)

The Sacrifices of Leviticus

NAME	REF.	OCCASION	OFFERING	DISPOSITION
Burnt offering (ʿōlâ)	1:1–17	Gaining divine favour	Unblemished male. Individual means governed kind of offering	All burned
Cereal offering (minḥâ)	2:1–16	Thanksgiving and securing divine goodwill	Salted unleavened cakes or cereals	Part burned for God; remainder assigned to priests
Peace offerings (zebaḥ šᵉlāmîm)	3:1–17 22:18–30	Gratitude to God; fellowship with Him; public rejoicing; deliverance from vows	Unblemished male or female animal according to individual means	Fat burned; remainder eaten by priest and worshipper in fellowship meal
Sin offering (ḥaṭṭāʾt)	4:1 – 5:13	Need for purification from sin or defilement	Bull (priest or congregation); male goat (ruler); female goat, lamb, pair of doves or pigeons; meal offering (individual)	Fat burned for God; remainder eaten by priests
Guilt offering (ʾāšām)	5:14–19	Guilt about misappropriation of holy things or some loss to sanctuary	Unblemished ram	Fat burned; remainder eaten by priests

38

COMMENTARY

The first fifteen chapters of Leviticus contain lists of regulations governing the various kinds of sacrifices prescribed for the removal of sin and defilement, the formal initiation of Israel's priesthood into its religious functions, and a statement of fundamental differences between clean and unclean species. The different sacrifices and offerings find their culmination in chapter 16, where the rituals that are to be followed on the day of atonement are prescribed. The remainder of the book deals with a variety of ceremonial laws, and concludes with a statement about the blessings that will come upon Israel if the laws are kept, along with a statement of the punishments which will be the result of neglecting or repudiating covenantal enactments.

I. REGULATIONS CONCERNING SACRIFICE
(1:1 – 7:38)

The laws which govern the sacrificial offerings appear in two contrasting forms in this section. In 1:1 – 6:7, the ritual prescriptions are described from the standpoint of the person making the offering, whereas in 6:8 – 7:36 the narrative considers the various sacrifices as the priests have to deal with them. They come in the same general order, however, except that in 6:8 – 7:36 the peace offering occurs at the end (7:11–21) instead of occupying third place in the list (3:1–17) which comprises 1:1 – 6:17. It is hard to say precisely why the material was organized in this manner. It may have been intended to assist the priests either in memorizing the order of the various rituals,[1] or in giving instructions about the nature and significance of the procedures to be followed. There is literary as well as functional patternism here, and if the purpose of such an arrangement was in any sense didactic, it would imply that the written form of Leviticus served at least in part as a textbook of priestly procedure. As such it would

[1] *Cf.* A. F. Rainey, *Biblica*, 51, 1970, pp. 485–498.

39

compare in function with other ancient Near Eastern cultic manuals designed for priestly use. As distinct from the prescribed festivals of Leviticus 23, which were obligatory for the congregation of Israel, the offerings described in this section were of a more personal and spontaneous nature, intended to meet individual spiritual needs. They thus reflect the liberty of approach to God that the Christian possesses, except that for the latter no mediating priest is necessary because of the atoning work of the great High Priest. In addition, the believer can approach a loving and forgiving God in penitence and faith quite independently of cultic formularies or denominational stipulations, and find grace to help in time of need.

a. The burnt offering (1:1–17)

1. In this introductory verse *called, wayyiorā'*, is the Hebrew name for the book of Leviticus. The conjunction *wa(w)* which begins the word shows that Leviticus is linked with the final chapters of Exodus to form a continuous narrative. It should be noted that the tabernacle had been prepared and the sanctuary set up before the detailed regulations about specific sacrifices were given to Moses. The description of priestly functions was then followed by the ordination of the priests and the account of their first offerings. The literary material which comes after the introductory verse thus belongs properly to the original priestly constitution of Leviticus, and is not a later insertion. The word *called* should probably be rendered 'summoned' (*cf.* Ex. 24:16), since God is instructing Moses in connection with the sacrificial rituals, and is not calling him in the sense in which Christ called His disciples (Mt. 4:19–21; Mk. 1:17–20). On the basis of this instruction Moses is established in his role as teacher of the divine law, and is referred to in this manner by Christ (*cf.* Mt. 19:7–8; Mk. 10:3; 12:19; Lk. 16:29, 31; Jn. 7:19, *etc.*). The introductory statement of 1:1 is paralleled in 6:8 by God's command that Moses should instruct Aaron and his descendants in the ritual procedures, thus establishing an ordered, received tradition. One of the basic functions of liturgical form is to ensure that everything connected with worship is attended to in an orderly and appropriate manner. As long as liturgical procedures are followed rigorously there is little chance of excesses

occurring, or esoteric cultic performances of dubious spiritual or theological value being introduced.

Tent of meeting (Heb. *'ōhel mô'ēd*) was one of the names by which the wilderness tabernacle was known to the Israelites, reminding them that God indeed met there with Moses (*cf.* Ex. 25:22) and revealed to him His will for the nation. Tabernacle terminology presents a rather confusing picture in the various English versions. The RV, RSV and NEB generally use 'tabernacle' for the larger rectangular framework which was covered with curtains, and 'tent' either for the sanctuary (*'ōhel*) containing the altar of incense and the ark of the covenant, or for the entire structure. The AV renders *'ōhel mô'ēd* by 'tabernacle of the congregation', and translates *'ōhel* both as 'tabernacle' and 'tent'. The NIV uses 'Tent of Meeting' for the sanctuary, and 'tabernacle' for the complete cultic enclosure. The sacred meeting place where God revealed Himself to Moses was a small rectangular area framed by acacia boards and covered with curtains and animal skins. Inside, an embroidered curtain divided it into two sections, an outer or holy place, and an inner or most holy place in which the ark of the covenant was kept. Before the tabernacle was constructed, Moses met with God in a temporary 'tent of meeting' pitched outside the Israelite camp (*cf.* Ex. 33:7). This interim structure, which was attended solely by Joshua in the absence of a regularized priesthood, is rendered by NIV as 'Tent of Meeting', which perhaps serves to indicate the link between the precursor and the official tabernacle. It seems best to use the term 'tent of meeting' for the place of divine revelation to Moses and the high priest, and 'tabernacle' for the entire area surrounded by the curtained walls. The word *mô'ēd* has been discovered in an Egyptian source dated about 1100 BC and referring to the assembly of the people of Byblus. In Isaiah 14:13 the term is used with reference to an assembly of the gods in the far northern regions, a familiar theme in pagan Canaanite literature. In the completed tabernacle, God spoke to Moses from above the cherubim (1 Sa. 4:4).[2]

Leviticus 1:1 indicates that the tabernacle was now fully operative, and this fact also serves to link Leviticus with the

---

[2] *Cf.* R. A. Cole, *Exodus* (1973), p. 191.

sequence of events described in the latter part of Exodus.[3] The concept of a leader communing with God in a portable shrine was well understood in Egypt in the Amarna Age (fifteenth and fourteenth centuries BC). The Egyptians normally took such tents with them on their military campaigns, and placed them in the centre of the encampment. The cultic priests would resort to them regularly for worship and also for ascertaining the divine will, looking upon the shrine much as the inhabitants of ancient Troy treated the image of Pallas. The portable shrine brought the presence of the deity into the midst of the encampment, and gave assurance of divine protection for all those in the vicinity. This 'tent' or 'palladium' imagery was employed of Jesus Christ in the fourth gospel, where John spoke of Jesus as the Word who 'became flesh and dwelt (Gk. 'was tabernacled'; 'pitched his tent') among us' (Jn. 1:14). The historic fact of Christ's incarnation is thus a guarantee of God's saving presence and power in human life, because the kingdom has already come among men (Lk. 17:21) in the person of Jesus.

2. The offerings described are voluntary and personal in nature, and the literary form matches the comparative simplicity of the occasion. Group sacrifices do not seem to be entertained here, being described subsequently in terms of the day of atonement (16:1–34) and feasts related to holy seasons (23:1–44). Private sacrifices would be offered in order to express thanksgiving, the desire for renewed fellowship with God and a deepening of the prayer life, or to indicate the need for the forgiveness of sin. Such sacrifices were offered throughout the biblical period. Following the pattern established by some of the prophets (*cf.* Ho. 6:6; Am. 5:21–24), Jesus stressed the motivation underlying the act, and taught that the offering was only truly acceptable to God when the intent of the worshipper was of the highest quality (Mt. 5:23–24; Mk. 12:33). The blood of Christ is infinitely more efficacious than that of any Old Testament offering in purging the human conscience from dead works to serve the living God (Heb. 9:14).

[3] For different interpretations of the tabernacle and selections from the great body of literature, see G. H. Davies, *IDB*, 4, pp. 498–506; C. L. Feinberg, *ZPEB*, 5, pp. 572–583.

The sacrifices touched many aspects of Israelite life, and this fact brought the people into continuous contact with the activities of the tabernacle. Nobody was prevented from bringing an offering to God, for all who so desired could come in penitence and faith to the Lord and be accepted. Jesus still offers a similar invitation (Jn. 6:37). The Hebrews, though laymen, were presumed to know the significance of the sacrificial ritual; hence no explanation is given here. The *offering* (Heb. *qorbān*) was something 'brought near' (*qrb*) to the altar, and was a very general term covering all kinds of sacrificial gifts. The word appears in Mark 7:11 with an explanatory gloss, while in Matthew 27:6 a slightly different Greek word, *korbanas*, described the temple treasury as the place where the offerings were deposited. Those prescribed in Leviticus are to be made specifically to the Lord (Heb. YHWH), the God of Israel, and not to a deity such as El or Baal or any other god (*cf.* *ʾelōhîm* in Ex. 22:20). Offering sacrifices on altars dedicated to the 'unknown god' (*cf.* Acts 17:23) was entirely foreign to the Hebrew tradition. True fellowship with God demands some knowledge and personal experience of His nature (*cf.* Heb. 11:6).

3. Verses 3–9 deal with the burnt offerings of cattle. The inclusiveness of *when any man of you* is now made specific. A donor must bring an unblemished male for his offering of *cattle*. This word is now a general designation of the family *Bovidae*, although in antiquity cattle also included horses, asses, camels and other animals. Such a usage also occurred in Middle English to describe any animal reared for food or for products such as its skin, hair or fleece. For the burnt offering only domesticated animals, indicating a developed stage of agricultural life, were to be presented, since wild species did not cost the donor anything. In addition, wild animals had not received the labour and care that had been expended on *herds* and *flocks*.

Here and in 5:18 alone a male animal is specified for sacrifice. The choice of a male may reflect the dominance of that sex in other than matriarchal societies, but it may well have embraced a more pragmatic purpose also. Where a choice was involved, male animals were more expendable than females in a society in which livestock was equivalent to both capital and income. Fewer males than females were necessary for the survival of the herds and flocks, since the male was utilized only periodically for purposes of breeding. By contrast, the female functioned as a continual provider of milk and its by-products in addition to producing new livestock from time to time. The prescription concerning an unblemished animal sets before the Israelites God's ideal of perfection for the animals (*cf.* Lv. 22:18–25) and also for the priests (*cf.* Lv. 21:17–23) that forms an important part of His service (*cf.* Mal. 1:6–14). Only a ceremonially pure animal would be accounted by God as appropriate to receive the sins of the worshipper by manual transmission.

An important principle underlying Old Testament sacrificial tariffs is enunciated here, namely that any sacrifice must represent a specific cost to the one who offers it to God. However poor a person might be, the sacrificial offering still had to represent some cost on the part of the donor. Thus, in verses 14–17, even the most humble kind of offering, that of doves or young pigeons, still upheld this basic precept. On Calvary Jesus paid the highest price possible in laying down His life for human sin (Jn. 15:13). This great sacrifice is equated with the maximum extent of God's love for fallen man, and also with an individual's care and regard for his fellows.

The *burnt offering* was a gift intended to win divine favour for the worshipper, as indicated by the phrase *that he may be accepted*. By contrast, the sin offering (4:1 – 5:13) was meant to secure divine pardon for the donor. The motive behind the burnt offering is thus made explicit. This is evidently the oldest form of sacrifice, and its name '*ōlâ* indicates 'ascent', suggesting that the essence of the animal gave gratification to God as the sacrificial smoke ascended (*cf.* 1–17). The offering was voluntary (*cf.* 1 Sa. 7:9; 13:9; Ps. 20:3), as the most highly motivated offerings always are, and was presented by the donor at the entrance to the tent of meeting.

4–5. The ritual of sacrifice is described simply but carefully, stressing the consistency of procedure as a safeguard against idolatrous rites. The ceremony thus carries out the intent of the worshipper (*cf.* Jos. 24:14) and precludes the use of strange and erroneous rituals and teachings which would nullify the relationship between God and man. The Christian is also open to such temptations in his worship, and accordingly is urged to follow the pattern of sound doctrine (2 Tim. 1:13) as a basis for true devotion. In this sacrificial procedure the donor is not a passive observer but an active participant. He lays his hand upon the animal's head, indicating that it is his substitute as well as his own property, and that he is giving of himself symbolically in the ritual. Nothing is said about verbal utterances by the worshipper or the priest, but no doubt the sacrificial offering would be accompanied by some statement of purpose as a preliminary. In the time of the temple a psalm might have been said or sung. *Accepted for him*, perhaps indicates a priestly pronouncement to the effect that *atonement* had indeed been made. This atonement (Heb. *kippurîm*) nullifies and removes the effects of sin or uncleanness. (See note on Lv. 4:26). There exisited a special 'atonement' (*kuppuru*) ritual in Mesopotamia, in which the demonic power held responsible for the incidence of illness in a patient was offered a young kid in sacrifice.[4] In New Testament teaching the Christian is urged to present himself as an acceptable sacrifice to God (Rom. 12:1; Phil. 4:18).

5–6. The bull is then slaughtered (Heb. *šāḥaṭ*), a common technical sacrificial term, before the Lord, that is to say, on the north side of the altar located near the entrance of the tent of meeting, and its blood or life-essence (*cf.* 17:11) sprinkled by (NEB 'fling it') the priests around the large altar of burnt offering (*cf.* Ex. 27:1–8). This great altar was made of acacia wood overlaid with bronze. It measured nearly 2.5 m square and about 1.6 m in height, and was located to the east of the tent of meeting. It occupied an almost central position in the entire enclosure. *Aaron's sons* are mentioned to show the specifically priestly side of the ceremony (*cf.* 1:8, 11; 2:2; 3:2). The offering was skinned and cut into pieces by the worshipper, presumably for easier disposition by fire. In Leviticus 7:8 the skin of any burnt offering became the property of the priest, but here there is no mention of the way in which the donor disposed of it. According to 2 Chronicles 35:11, the Levites flayed the

---

[4] See R. C. Thompson, *The Devils and Evil Spirits of Babylonia* (1904), 2, p. 21; *idem, Semitic Magic* (1908), p. 211.

animals offered in the pre-exilic temple, a procedure which appears to be a later development of the Mosaic ritual. The division into pieces is reminiscent of Abraham's covenantal offering (Gn. 15:10), from which this aspect of the Mosaic ceremony was doubtless derived. The worshipper would thus feel doubly rooted in covenant faith and practice. God's self-revelation in Scripture is neither imaginary nor mythical, but instead is of an accredited historical nature which has touched the lives of real men and women as God's purpose for human destiny was unfolding. The faith of the Christian reaches back specifically in time to a Person who came as part of a consciously ordained sequence for man's redemption, and gave Himself as the one perfect sacrifice for human sin (*cf.* Gal. 4:4–5).

Probable Plan of the Tabernacle

North Wall

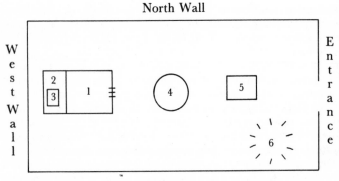

C A M P

1. The holy place in the tent of meeting
2. The most holy place in the tent of meeting
3. The sacred ark
4. The laver
5. The bronze altar of sacrifice
6. Probable site of ash heap

7–13. The kindling of new fire for each sacrifice points to a very early stage of the wilderness wanderings for the origin of this enactment. A more sedentary situation such as that which obtained at Kadesh (*cf.* Nu. 33:37–38; Dt. 1:46; 2:14) is reflected in the regulation of 6:12–13, where the fire was to burn continually on the altar. Only general instructions for the kindling process are given, since the usage was already thoroughly familiar to the priests. The fire had to be sufficiently hot to burn up the offering completely, but the process would certainly be aided by the presence of fatty tissue, placed in order on top of the pieces and the head, feeding the flames as it melted. The entrails and legs were washed so as to cleanse them from excreta, and were also added to the other pieces on the altar. The *head* is mentioned separately because it would have been detached from the body in the process of skinning. The attempt to group 'head and fat' as an appendage to the 'parts', as Noth does,[5] is contrived and artificial. The *pleasing odour* of the burnt offering should not be understood as affording God purely physical satisfaction, but rather as an archaic linguistic survival, here and elsewhere in the Old Testament. The idea of a 'sweet smell' as something that appeased the anger of the gods originated in ancient Sumer (*cf.* Gilgamesh Epic, XI, 160), but the extent to which it was interpreted literally in sophisticated second-millennium BC pagan priestly circles is open to debate. Samuel made it clear that God was gratified most of all by obedience (1 Sa. 15:22), while Hosea 6:6 reiterated God's preference for steadfast love rather than sacrifice (*cf.* Mt. 9:13; 12:7; Mk. 12:33). Psalm 50:13 repudiated the crude anthropomorphic concept of the deity ingesting the sacrificial offering, and instead laid emphasis upon the acceptability to God of such values as thanksgiving, a position which was consistent with the urging of the prophets. In Hebrews 13:15 the Christian is exhorted to offer up to God, through the person of the crucified Christ, a continuous sacrifice of praise that is the product of lips testifying to the saving and keeping power of His name.

14–17. These verses deal with fowls as a burnt offering. There would be persons in Israel who could not afford to slaughter a prime animal, even if they possessed one. For such poor people the law permitted fowl to be presented, and relaxed the specifications for the offering to the extent of not stipulating that the bird must be male and unblemished (*cf.* 5:7; 12:8). The birds most suitable for such offerings were *turtledoves or ... young pigeons*. The dove (Heb. *tōr, Turtur communis; yônâ, Columba livia*) was one of the most commonly mentioned birds in the Bible. Ancient traditions maintained that the dove had no bile,[6] and as a result it was considered to be clean, gentle and inoffensive. Although sometimes attacked by more aggressive birds the dove never retaliates, and for this reason has become a symbol of the Christian virtues. In Matthew 10:16 Christ used the dove as an exemplar of innocence. Its non-aggressive nature has enabled the dove to be employed as an international peace symbol. Isaiah 60:8 indicates that the dove had also been domesticated, although wild doves lived in caves throughout the hilly regions of Palestine, as did pigeons (*Columbae*). Both types of birds continued to be sacrificed in New Testament times, and could be purchased in one of the temple courts (*cf.* Mt. 21:12; Mk. 11:15; Jn. 2:14–16). At the time of Christ's presentation in the temple (Lk. 2:22–24), the sacrificial provisions of Leviticus 12:8 were cited to cover the impoverished conditions of Mary and Joseph. The descent of the Holy Spirit on Christ at His baptism was described in terms of dove imagery also (Mt. 3:16; Mk. 1:10; Lk. 3:22; Jn. 1:32). The *trugōn* of Luke 2:24 ('turtledove') was the LXX equivalent of the Hebrew *tōr*, whereas *peristera*, 'dove', 'pigeon', appeared mostly in the LXX as the rendering of *yônâ*. Attempts to differentiate between the species are not very productive in any language, since both doves and pigeons belong to the same family of *Columbae*.

The priest performed most of the ritual involving the sacrifice of a bird (verses 15–16). The head was wrung off (*cf.* 5:8) and burned, and the blood was drained down the side of the altar. After this the donor removed the bird's feathers and crop, placing them on the ash-heap east of the altar. Perhaps the reason for disposing of the entrails in this manner instead of burning them was that the contents of the stomach, being

---

[6] *Fauna and Flora of the Bible* (1972), p. 23.

acquired indiscriminately, would not be as acceptable to **God** as the food supplied to cattle through human effort. If this **is so** the cost factor is still apparent, even in cases of poverty. **True** blessing for the Christian comes from obeying the gospel **of** Christ and contributing generously to the needs of others (*cf.* **2** Cor. 9:6–12).

The bird was not cut into pieces, as was the case with **a** sacrificial animal, but was held by the wings as its body **was** torn apart (verse 17).[7] Then the offering was placed on the altar to constitute a sacrifice acceptable to God. On Calvary the body of Christ was broken in sacrifice and His blood shed for human sin. This offering can never be repeated (Rom. 6:10; Heb. 7:27; 9:12; 10:10), and now the most desirable sacrifice that anyone, rich or poor, can bring to God is a consecrated life (*cf.* Rom. 12:1; 1 Pet. 1:15–16).

b. The cereal offering (2:1–16)
Like the burnt sacrifice, the meal or cereal offering (AV 'meat offering,' *i.e.* the mediaeval way of rendering 'food offering') was a voluntary gift to God designed to promote or secure His favour. Though this section deals with a vegetable as opposed to an animal sacrifice, the underlying motivation is identical.

1. *When any one* (Heb. *nepeš*, literally 'soul'). The feminine gender of the noun here is purely coincidental, and in no way conflicts with or contradicts subsequent masculine terminology in the verse. *Nepeš* reflects selfhood consistently, and thus should be translated as 'person' or 'self', as in Matthew 16:26; Mark 8:37, where Christ enquires as to what a person proposes to give in exchange for his self-identity. In this way the Semitic character of *nepeš* is maintained, and the contamination of Platonic and similar forms of Greek thought, with their resultant dichotomy between 'body' and 'soul', is avoided. The *cereal offering* (*minḥâ*) was one of native grain, and is considered here as a separate offering, although it often formed a regular part of the burnt offering (*cf.* Nu. 15:1–16). The term *minḥâ* means in general a 'gift', whether as an expression of reverence (Jdg. 6:19; 1 Sa. 10:27), gratitude (Ps. 96:8), homage (Gn. 32:14; 43:11, 15, 25) or allegiance (2 Sa. 8:2, 6; 2 Ch. 17:11). In

7 M. Noth, *Leviticus*, p. 25.

sacrificial terminology it always seems to have had this broad sense of 'gift', as in the earliest Old Testament references, which covered both animal and vegetable offerings (*cf.* Gn. 4:3–5). Perhaps the primitive nature of the *minḥâ* accounts for the special place which it occupies at the beginning of the Levitical sacrificial tariff. By the time of Moses the term had become restricted to cereal or vegetable offerings, *i.e.*, those of a bloodless character.

The material involved was coarsely ground barley or wheat, and according to Talmudic authorities was offered as an independent sacrifice only by a very poor person. But even here motivation was the paramount consideration, and God was believed to view such an offering as though the person had given his very self (*nepeš*). In the same way Christ took account of the motivation underlying the poor widow's gift of two copper coins (Mk. 12:42; Lk. 21:2; AV 'two mites'), which represented her entire living. The total commitment of the individual and his or her resources is the kind of sacrifice that God desires most (Ps. 40:7; Heb. 10:7). Olive *oil* was used commonly by the people of the ancient Near East in cooking, as a shortening agent, and as a means of binding the coarsely ground cereal flour. Like the grain, oil was a product of human labour, so that the cereal offering symbolized the dedication of man's work to God. *Frankincense* (*lᵉbōnâ*), was a balsamic resin obtained from species of shrubs belonging to the genus *Boswellia*. It is not certain if frankincense was produced in Palestine, and if *B. carterii* was the only incense used by the Hebrews it would have been imported from Sheba.[8] Frankincense was symbolic of holiness and devotion (*cf.* Ps. 141:2), and was one of the gifts presented to the infant Jesus by the wise men (Mt. 2:11). Because the sacrificial offering was intended to secure goodwill, the frankincense had to be placed on the ground cereal, in contrast to the procedure required for a sin offering (5:11), where the use of frankincense was forbidden.

---

[8] H. N. and A. L. Moldenke, *Plants of the Bible* (1952), pp. 56–59; W. Walker, *All the Plants of the Bible* (1957), p. 84; R. K. Harrison, *Healing Herbs of the Bible* (1966), p. 43; F. N. Hepper, *Journal of Egyptian Archaeology*, 55, 1969, pp. 66–72.

2. Having mixed the offering, the worshipper presented it to the priest, who took a handful of the meal, making sure that all the frankincense was included. This was the *memorial portion* (*'azkārâ*), a term of uncertain meaning used consistently in connection with that part of the cereal offering which was consumed by fire (*cf.* 5:12; 6:8; Nu. 5:26). There is no evidence for the view that the word was an ancient Semitic designation of 'maleness', to describe the choicest element of the sacrifice. A more probable suggestion links frankincense as one of the four constituent parts of the incense (Ex. 30:34) offered daily by the priest at the time of prayer. In a later age Psalms 38 and 70 were connected in some way with the memorial offering, and it is quite probable that in the days of the Temple one or other of these compositions was recited by the worshipper when a memorial sacrifice was being offered. The reference in Isaiah 66:3 to a memorial offering of frankincense is apparently to Canaanite idolatrous practices. In Acts 10:4 the prayers and alms of the devout Roman centurion Cornelius were described by the visiting divine messenger as having ascended 'as a memorial before God'. It is uncertain whether the original intent of the *'azkārâ* was to remind God of the existence of the impoverished worshipper, to recall to the mind of the offerer the majesty, bounty and provision of God for human needs, or a combination of both. At all events, the intent of the offering was to engender positive feelings ('pleasing odour') on the part of God towards the worshipper.

3. The balance of the cereal became the perquisite of the priests, and being a *most holy part* would be consumed by them in the sanctuary area proper, and not used to support the families of the priests. Here the emphasis upon ceremonial holiness is meant to delineate clearly the property and prerogatives of the priests, so that abuses of privilege will not arise. Such unfortunate happenings did occur, however, at times when the Israelite priesthood was corrupt (*cf.* 1 Sa. 2:12, 22). Because the priest stood in a special spiritual relationship with God, his character and behaviour were matters of the highest importance. The true priest is clothed not so much with ornate cultic garb as with the moral values of righteousness (Ps. 132:9), which become evident in his way of life. The believer in Jesus Christ is even more distinctive in being a member of a 'royal priesthood' (1 Pet. 2:9), and is therefore urged to be 'holy' (1 Pet. 1:16) and to offer spiritual sacrifices acceptable to God through Jesus Christ. Obedience and holiness are the watchwords of the new covenant, as they also were of the old (*cf.* Dt. 7:6, 11 *etc.*).

4–7. The previous section had dealt with an offering of uncooked grain, doubtless the most primitive kind of cereal offering, and thus placed appropriately in this chapter. Subsequent forms comprised dough flattened out by hand and then cooked, either on a hot rock or on the inside of a previously heated stove or *oven*. The resultant bread was an offering of flour baked in the manner familiar in Palestine from the Early Bronze Age, and still in use among Arab peasants.[9] Once more, even the poorest of persons could offer a home-made flat cake or a wafer of bread as a sacrifice to God, and come to know Him more fully in the breaking of bread (*cf.* Lk. 24:35). The *unleavened cakes* would probably be thicker than the wafers, the latter perhaps corresponding to the unleavened bread used by modern Jews at the feast of the passover.

The cereal offering could also be prepared on a *griddle* as well as in an oven or portable stove. The griddle (*mahᵃbat̠*) ould be made ordinarily of ceramic ware, but in the Middle Bronze Age (*c.* 1950–1550 BC) the more affluent Hebrews would be using copper pancake griddles. In the monarchy, at the beginning of the Iron Age in Palestine, some middle-class families would even possess an iron griddle (*cf.* Ezk. 4:3),[10] although they would still be rather expensive. Instructions about breaking it into pieces are given in this form only of the cereal offering. This may have been intended to serve as the counterpart of the procedures mentioned in Leviticus 1:6, where the offering was cut up into small amounts. The breaking of bread ministers in normal life to both physical and social needs within the context of a meal, whether among one's family members or with friends. The sacramental meal which Jesus initiated for his followers as a memorial of His death took place in an upper room (Mk. 14:15), where as part of the pattern to be followed Christ took bread, blessed it and broke

---

[9] Palestinian bread ovens are pictured in *NBD*, p. 166 fig. 43.

[10] J. L. Kelso, *The Ceramic Vocabulary of the Old Testament* (1948), pp. 13, 23.

it (Mt. 26:26; Mk. 14:22; Lk. 22:19). This act symbolized the breaking of His own body on Calvary as the one self-offering by means of which men would be reconciled to God.

A *pan* (Heb. *marḥešet*), whether in ceramic or metal ware, was a stewpot or cooking pot used as a deep fat fryer. In this verse alone, as contrasted with verses 4 and 5, the flour is not spoken of as unleavened, but this is probably intentional to avoid repetition. Authorities suggest that the cereal offering cooked in the *marḥešet* would look rather like a modern deep-fried doughnut.[11]

8–10. The donor brings the offering to the priest, who takes it to the altar and burns the memorial portion, as in verse 2, although incense is not mentioned here. The function of incense seems to have been that of a fumigant and deodorant, cloaking or removing some of the less pleasant smells of the sacrificial ritual, and thereby contributing to the physical effect of making the offering *a pleasing odour to the Lord*. Whatever remained after the memorial portion had been consumed belong to the priests alone. The emphasis upon the holy quality of the offering is significant, since to be truly acceptable the sacrifice consecrated to God by the donor must be matched by an intent to live an equally holy and consecrated life. The term 'holy' does not imply mere dedication to the service of a deity such as was understood among the pagan Canaanites by the use of the word *qudšu* ('prostitute'), but by contrast denotes all the high moral and spiritual qualities inherent in the God of Sinai who demands that His people be holy (*qāḏôš*), as He is holy (Lv. 11:44; 19:2; 20:7, *etc.*; 1 Pet. 1:16. *cf.* 1 Thes. 4:7). The food offerings made to God by fire were regarded as *most holy* (NEB 'most sacred'). As a means of providing for the priesthood, God permitted a *part* of the cereal offering, as well as the sin (5:13) and guilt (7:6) offerings to be eaten by His chosen representatives, and by them alone. The worshippers, by contrast, could participate in votive, freewill and thanksgiving offerings (22:18–30).

11–12. Cereal offerings must not include leaven, this latter substance being prohibited as part of any burnt offering. The

---

[11] J. L. Kelso, *The Ceramic Vocabulary of the Old Testament*, p. 24. For the term see also pp. 12, 13, and figure 16 on page 48.

same was also true for *honey*, the normal sweetener in ancient times. Precisely why these two items were forbidden in burnt sacrifices is unknown. It has been conjectured that honey (Heb *dᵉbaš*, Akkad. *dišpu*) was a favourite food of the gods in some heathen cults, and as a result it was important for the Israelites to exercise great care in connection with any substance that was also sacrificed to pagan deities, lest the incorporating into Hebrew worship of anything dubious might be followed by religious elements alien to the ethics of the Sinai covenant. No doubt much of the honey available for sale in Corinth had first been offered to the Greek gods, and if so the problem with which Paul dealt in 1 Corinthians 8 was of great significance, since it involved the very real possibility of spiritual compromise. The Christian is under obligation to avoid every appearance of evil (1 Thes. 5:22). Leaven (*ḥāmēs*) was basically 'something sour', and in the ancient world consisted of a small piece of dough saved from a previous batch of bread. This portion was allowed to ferment, and when it was mixed with meal (*cf.* Mt. 13:33; Lk. 13:21) the process of fermentation present in the piece of dough was transferred to the whole mixture, lightening the texture of the finished product and improving its flavour and digestibility. Both leaven and honey were agents of fermentation, and in addition it is possible that the term 'honey' was used as an Old Testament euphemism for one form or other of fermented drink. Perhaps the prohibition was intended to prevent interference with the natural constitution of the offerings, which represented the results of honest toil, and would therefore represent the worshipper adequately as being open and unadorned in the presence of the God with whom he had to deal (*cf.* Heb. 4:13).

It should not be assumed that leaven and honey were unclean or symbolic of evil, since both were part of the offering of firstfruits (*cf.* Ex. 23:16–17; 34:22–23; Lv. 23:17–18). Attractive though the suggestion might be that the contrast between honey ('sweet') and leaven ('sour') perhaps parallels that between good and evil, it would not appear to be borne out in practice if only because of the place that leaven occupied in the sacrificial rituals. The firstfruits were in fact the 'beginnings' of the harvest, and the offering of a token first portion to God symbolized the dedication of the entire crop to Him, the giver of all good things. In the messianic reference of Isaiah 7:15, 22, the eating of honey symbolized a time when the Son of the virgin would reject the evil and choose the good, thereby indicating his spiritual maturity. In the New Testament (Mt. 13:33) the kingdom of heaven was likened by Christ to leaven, presumably in an attempt to illustrate the permeating effects of the gosepl as it worked in society to make it Christian. On the other hand, the pervasive nature of leaven was likened by Christ to the character of undesirable teaching (Mt. 16:6, 11–12; 12:1), and by Paul to the insidious spread of evil (1 Cor. 5:6; Gal. 5:9). These references make it clear that the important thing about leaven is its permeating effect. The agent itself is morally neutral, but the results of its activity can be interpreted in terms of positive or negative symbolism, depending upon the circumstances. It is not correct to say, as some authors have done, that leaven is emblematic of a process of corruption,[12] since when leaven is added to meal it enhances and improves the flavour, texture and digestibility of the baked product, rather than causing it to deteriorate. While it might be argued that leaven added to unbaked flour would make the mixture sour if left uncooked, the fact is that the addition of leaven to meal carried with it the intent of cooking, as in the offering of the firstfruits (Lv. 23:17) and in normal domestic use.

13. All cereal offerings were to be accompanied by *salt*. The uniformly preservative and astringent action of this mineral typified permanence and purity, as in the 'salt-covenant' (Nu. 18:19; 2 Ch. 13:5) or the Near Eastern method of establishing a bond of friendship by the eating of salt. Although the believer can be regarded legitimately as the 'salt of the earth' (Mt. 5:13), it is possible for such a person to lose the distinctiveness of faith and witness, thereby modifying the character, permanence and integrity of individual Christian witness to the world. Paul urges the believer to have his speech 'seasoned with salt' (Col 4:6), that is to say, tempered by common sense.[13]

[12] *E.g.* H. F. Beck, *IDB*, 3, p. 105.
[13] F. F. Bruce, *Commentary on the Epistles to the Ephesians and Colossians* (1968 ed.), pp. 299 f.

14–16. The *cereal offering of firstfruits* (NEB *grain-offering of first-ripe grain*) consisted of roasted ears of young corn, a common item of food among the poor. After roasting, the cereal was ground into a coarse meal, and presented as an offering with the addition of oil and frankincense (*cf.* 2:2). Grain and oil were two of the three basic ingredients of ancient Hebrew diet (*cf.* Dt. 12:17): hence this offering, along with a libation of wine which is not mentioned here, would represent the token presentation of man's daily food to the Creator. The prayer of David (1 Ch. 29:14) recognized the propriety of such offerings to God, but in Psalm 40:6–8, commonly attributed to David, it is made clear the God desires wholehearted obedience to His will more than sacrifices and cereal offerings. Christ abolished the latter in His death that He might make obedience an established principle of Christian discipleship (Heb. 10:5–9). The elements of wine and oil in Hebrew diet are sometimes associated symbolically with gladness and joy (*cf.* Ps. 104:15; Is. 61:3; Heb. 1:9).

c. The peace offering (3:1–17)

1. Another in the list of voluntary sacrifices was the *peace offering* (NEB *shared-offering*), better rendered *a sacrifice of well-being*. The word *šālôm* ('peace') has numerous meanings, one of which involves good health. The verb-form means basically 'be intact', 'be complete', and when applied to mankind it refers to the integration of the *nepeš hayyâ* (Gn. 2:7) or human personality. The *sacrifice* (*zebaḥ*) of well-being indicates conscious social communion, in which what is deficient in the offerer will be remedied as he comes in faith and penitence to God, the healer and restorer (*cf.* Ex. 15:26; Ps. 103:3). The ritual follows closely the pattern of the burnt offering.

2. The unblemished offering is presented in the manner described in Leviticus 1, and is killed at the entrance to the tent of meeting. The term *zebaḥ* is from a root denoting sacrificial slaughter, and described an offering intended to promote a sense of communion between the donor and God. In this chapter, however, there is no mention of a meal as part of the ceremony, the narrative concentrating instead upon the disposal of the offering by fire. No details of the way in which the ritual slaughter was carried out are mentioned here, but the animal would obviously have to be secured before the blood was drained from its body. As in all animal sacrificial rites, the *blood* represented the life inherent in the body (see on 17:11). The imposition of the donor's hand indicated, as previously, the dedication of the offering to God and the worshipper's identification with it as his own property (*cf.* 1:4). Like the burnt sacrifice, the peace or well-being offering contains a strong substitutionary element. Christ, the peaceful prince (Is. 9:6), has made peace for us by His atoning death, achieving for us what we could never do for ourselves, and terminating the state of alienation between God and man (Eph. 2:14–16). While the lay worshipper carries out certain duties such as killing the animal, it is the priest's responsibility to dash the blood against the sacrificial altar. After this had been done, the animal was cut into pieces, some of which were offered subsequently on the altar. No mention is made of the skinning process, but this was evidently part of the ritual (*cf.* 1:6), since the regulations in 7:15–36 provided for peace offerings to be eaten by the worshippers, with certain portions being reserved for the priests. In this respect the well-being offering differed from the burnt offering, which was consumed completely on the altar.

3–5. The ritual now diverges from that governing the burnt sacrifice, and only the specially selected portions of the animal carcass offered to God by fire are described. These parts consisted of the *fat covering the entrails*, along with other adipose tissue protecting and nourishing vital internal organs. In the bull or cow this tissue is distributed around the kidneys, which are heavily protected, and is also deposited in layers between the liver and the stomach. The omentum thus formed covers the entire front-quarters of the animal with a thick sheet of fat which has its own blood supply, and which shields and warms the contiguous internal organs. In human anatomical terms this type of adipose structure would correspond to the greater omentum, a fold of peritoneum passing from the greater curvature of the stomach to the large intestine, and this tissue also contains a considerable amount of fat, especially in obese persons. The *fat* (*ḥēleb*), which also included the tissues that it covered, was prohibited to the Hebrews for food, being regarded generally in a metaphorical sense as signifying a

57

particularly choice portion (*cf.* Dt. 32:14), and therefore in the sacrificial rituals the perquisite of God alone. The prohibition of animal fat for human consumption seems also to have been based in part on dietary considerations. Animal fats eaten consistently in significant amounts over a lengthy period of time can raise the cholesterol level already present in the blood and, especially in conjunction with hypertension, can result in such conditions as arteriosclerosis and atherosclerosis, both of which cause circulatory accidents. Had the eating of animal fat and suet been permitted, such an imbalance of cholesterol might well have been precipitated among the Hebrews, since they were already ingesting such saturated fats as butter (*i.e.* curds) and cheese. But by restricting the intake of potentially damaging fats, the circulatory system would be enabled to maintain a reasonable blood-cholesterol level, and allow the factor known as high-density lipoprotein to protect the arteries and the heart against disease. Some modern cancer researchers also maintain that a diet high in saturated fats can lead to mammary gland and colon cancer in those who are constitutionally (*i.e.* genetically) predisposed. The ban on eating the fat of beasts offered for sacrifice was extended in Leviticus 7:23 to all animal meats eaten in a non-sacrificial context. Since tapeworms can sometimes be found in fatty tissues, even those of the 'clean' bovine species, the regulations governing the eating of animal fat would be another important means of protecting the Israelites against this kind of parasitic infestation. The fat protecting *the entrails* was to be removed in a process known to modern Jews as 'porging', and was to be burned with *the two kidneys* and their heavy cover of fat. In Hebrew thought the *kidneys* (*kᵉlāyôt*) of human beings were regarded as the seat of desire and anger, the latter being particularly appropriate in view of the location of the adrenal gland, the medulla of which secretes adrenalin. There is, however, no evidence that any such emotional functions were credited to animals, nor is there any record of the awareness of normal kidney physiology. Also removed for burning was the *appendage of the liver* (AV, RV 'caul, above (upon) the liver'; NEB 'long lobe of the liver') the reference being to the sheet of fatty tissue in the animal's front quarters. The term 'caul' is now of infrequent use, but in medicine it is still employed occasionally to describe the great omentum and certain other structures. From verse 5 it would appear that sacrifices of well-being were usually preceded by regular burnt offerings, perhaps of a daily nature, and that at this time the fat and offal from the animal sacrificed to promote the worshipper's restoration to fellowship with God would be burned on the altar.

6–11. The regulations emphasize again the standard established for sacrificial offerings. Only the choicest animals of the herds and flocks are to be presented to God. In the ritual procedures the fat is once again burned as the Lord's portion, and where a lamb from the principal Palestinian breed of oriental fat-tailed sheep (*Ovis laticaudata*) was being sacrificed, the entire tail was removed and burnt. Such sheep have several extra caudal vertebrae, and the tail serves to store body fat. In mature animals the fatty tail can weigh between 22 and 33 kg, and from very early times it was esteemed as a delicacy.[14] When these separated portions were burned, they were regarded as *food offered by fire to the Lord* (11, Heb. 'bread of the offering to YHWH'). The word 'bread' (*lehem*) here has the ancient nomadic meaning of 'meat' or 'flesh', and this testifies to the great antiquity of the Hebrew sacrificial system.

12–16. The procedures to be followed when a *goat* is offered are the same as those for a lamb, and the formula is repeated accordingly. The fatty portions are to be burned on the altar, though whether in conjunction with the burnt offering or not is unrecorded. The reference to a *pleasing odour* (5, 16) does not compel the reader to think that this ancient phrase was construed in terms of the Hebrews somehow feeding or nourishing God, in the way that their pagan neighbours were imagined by many nineteenth-century writers to have done when presenting votive offerings. The God who is spirit (Jn. 4:24) cannot be worshipped by material agents or means, since He is independent of them. Instead, He desires the love and obedience of His followers, and wishes to have fellowship with them by entering their lives and 'eating' with them (Rev. 3:20). The Lord's supper is correctly designated the 'Holy Communion' in the Christian church, because in proclaiming

---

[14] *Fauna and Flora of the Bible*, p. 75.

the Lord's death (1 Cor. 11:26) the believers are reconciled in fellowship and communion with God through the cross.

17. The prohibition against the eating of fat and blood was intended to be observed as long as the sacrificial system lasted. The phrase *a perpetual statute throughout your generations* occurs seventeen times in Leviticus. The provisions of Deuteronomy 12:15–16, 21–24, which make no mention of a ban on the eating of fat, relate to an entirely different set of ritual circumstances, and in no way affect the prohibitions listed here.

d. The sin offering (4:1 – 5:13)

This section deals with the regulations involving offerings for sins of inadvertence or accident. The position of the wrongdoer in society determined the nature of the animal to be sacrificed. Whereas in Leviticus 3:12 no provision was made for the poor people to sacrifice birds, presumably because they were not considered a sufficiently large offering for a sacrificial meal, in this section a special category of less costly offerings is established for the benefit of persons who could not afford to sacrifice a bull or a goat.

1–2. A new introductory formula ('if any one', *cf.* 5:1)[15] indicates a shift from God's concern with the restoration of well-being to that of means by which accidental trespasses might be expiated. *Sins* (2) is from the Hebrew *ḥāṭā*, a root which means basically 'to miss the mark'. In sinning the offender does indeed miss the real objective of existence, which is to live in obedience to God's commands and be holy as He is holy (Lv. 11:44; 19:2, *etc.*). What is involved in the committing of offences *unwittingly* (NEB 'inadverently'; NIV unintentionally') is doing that which is prohibited in any of the Lord's commands to Israel. The translation 'unwitting' is rather misleading, if only because a degree of conscious disobedience was obviously involved. Thus in the transgressions mentioned in 5:1–4, unwitting sin would include both conscious acts of disobedience and offences committed as the result of human

---

[15] This form occurs frequently in ritual texts from Mesopotamia, as in the *Šurpu* series of incantations, which contained lengthy lists of possible unclean contacts that had resulted in the patient's illness.

weakness and frailty. Subsequent verses deal with the categories of people covered by these provisions.

1. *The high priest (3–12)*

3. As the only anointed individual in the nation when these
laws were instituted, the high priest exercised a position of
great spiritual responsibility. Any offence on his part reflected
on the nation as a whole, thereby *bringing guilt* (3), since he was
the representative of the people before God and would thus
defile the most holy place by reason of his iniquity. Those who
are members of God's royal priesthood in Christ (1 Pet. 2:9)
must be clothed with righteousness (Ps. 132:9), and must not
allow sin to rule in their mortal bodies (Rom. 6:12). The high
priest's *sin offering* (*ḥaṭṭā't*) made atonement for him and
allayed God's wrath. Here, as elsewhere in the Hebrew
sacrificial system, the stress is on something that is done on
behalf of man to remove the barrier set up by sin. The word
ḥaṭṭā't comes from a verbal form meaning 'purify', so that the
noun signifies 'a sacrifice procuring purification'. The function
of this offering is thus to purify the place of worship, making it
holy to the Lord (*cf.* Zc. 14:20), and enabling God to dwell
once again amongst His people.

4–7. The sacrificial procedure follows the general pattern of
earlier offerings in that the sinner brings the animal to the tent
of meeting, identifies himself with it, and kills it *before the Lord*
(4). But there is some difference of detail for the purification of
the high priest, who is required to take some of the sacrificial
blood to the tent of meeting, where the anointed *priest* (6)
sprinkles the blood ritually in the direction of the *veil of the
sanctuary, i.e.,* the curtain separating the holy place from the
most holy place (Ex. 26:33). The use of oil was widespread in
the ancient Near East for toilet, medicinal and other purposes,
as well as for showing respect to guests (*cf.* Lk. 7:46). As a
religious rite, anointing indicated the dedication of persons or
objects to God. A common expression for a theocratic ruler
was 'the Lord's anointed' (*cf.* 1 Sa. 12:3; La. 4:20). The phrase
'the anointed priest' refers to the high priest as the highest
cultic functionary of the chosen people. Aaron was anointed
specifically at his consecration (8:12), while both he and his
sons were sprinkled with anointing oil and sacrificial blood

(8:30) as part of the consecration ritual.[16] The act of blood sprinkling is also performed before the Lord, that is, consciously as in His presence, and not just as a casual part of some elaborate ritual. The awareness of Christ's presence lends a dimension to the various aspects of the believer's life in a manner unknown to unbelievers, making for a greater sense of responsibility towards God and one's neighbour. The Christian now does his work as seeing Him who is invisible (Heb. 11:27). The difference in status between the high priest and all the other members of the congregation is emphasized by the fact that, for him, some of the blood from the sin offering was smeared on the projections of the golden altar upon which *sweet incense* was burned. For the rest of the people, the blood was smeared on the *horns* of the altar of burnt offering.

The incense altar (*cf.* Ex. 30:1–10) was of a design familiar in antiquity, with projections ('horns') rising upwards from the corners.[17] The purpose of these projections, other than being purely decorative, is uncertain, but Jewish interpreters have seen them as directing the thoughts of the worshippers heavenwards as the incense was being burned. Since, however, this small altar was inside the tent of meeting in the holy place, it would not be open to view in the same way as the altar of burnt offering was while the priest was burning the fragrant incense twice daily. In Exodus 30:34–38, the constituents of the incense offered were 'sweet spices, stacte, onycha and galbanum, sweet spices with pure frankincense' in equal proportions. Some doubt exists as to the nature of certain of these ingredients. Thus it is impossible to say precisely what the 'sweet spices' themselves comprised, if in fact they were separate components and not a description of the incense as a finished compound. Stacte, a fragrant resin or gum, has been identified with either the storax tree (*Styrax officinalis* L.) or the opobalsamum (*Commiphora opobalsamum* L.). Onycha was an ingredient most probably obtained by grinding up the claws or

---

[16] Only by assuming uncritically the traditional Wellhausenian position with its reversal of historical sequences can J. R. Porter, *Leviticus* (Cambridge Bible Commentary, 1976), p. 37, maintain that there is no evidence that the priests were anointed originally.

[17] *Cf.* R. A. Cole, *Exodus*, p. 205.

nails of certain molluscs,[18] while galbanum was an aromatic resin from a species of fennel, perhaps *Ferula galbaniflua* Boiss. & Buhse, although this is not absolutely certain. The incense possessed antiseptic and astringent qualities, and in Hebrew tradition it became symbolic of fervent, contrite prayer (*cf.* Ps. 141:2).

8–12. Once the sacrificial blood had been disposed of, all the fatty tissues were collected and burned on the altar of burnt offering, *just as these are taken from the ox of the sacrifice of the peace offerings* (9). All that remained of the bull, *i.e.*, its skin, flesh and entrails, had to be removed outside the camp for disposal *in a clean place* (12). The fact that the animal's skin is mentioned shows that in the sin offering, as in the burnt offering (*cf.* 1:6) the skin was removed before the various parts offered to God were consumed by fire. The clean place was located *where the ashes are poured out* (Heb. *šefek haddešen*), this latter phrase occurring here only in the Old Testament. Presumably the area to the east of the altar of burnt offering, where refuse (*cf.* 1:16), fat-soaked ashes, and similar debris were deposited, is being alluded to here. The animal could not be burnt on the altar, because the ritual was not intended to secure atonement for the high priest so much as to remove the defilement which had been incurred by the high priest behaving unlawfully. Hence the carcass was disposed of by fire at the site of the sacrificial refuse heap outside the camp. This procedure was referred to in Hebrews 11–13, where Jesus was likened to the animals whose blood had been brought into the sanctuary by the high priest as a sacrifice for sin. On Calvary the Saviour suffered outside the gate (*i.e.* outside Jerusalem) in order to sanctify the people through His own blood. The Christian is urged to 'go forth to Him outside the camp'[19] (Heb. 13:13) and to offer up continually through Him 'a sacrifice of praise to God' (Heb. 13:15). To the Israelites the exterior of the camp was unclean territory, but because Jesus was rejected in the holy city and was crucified outside its venerated walls, the old values have been changed completely.

---

[18] W. Walker, *All the Plants of the Bible*, p. 158, identifies onycha with a gum-producing rockrose, *Cistus ladaniferus*.

[19] The Greek *parembolē* ('camp') is cited from LXX of Lv. 16:27.

Any place where Jesus is encountered now becomes sacred for the Christian, who is aware that Christ's converting power changes rules, situations and people alike. The faith once delivered to the saints (Jude 3) is henceforth no longer a tribal or territorial affair, but is cosmic in dimensions, that Christ may be all and in all (Col. 3:11).

2. *The congregation (13–21)*

13–15. This passage is so closely connected with the previous one that the instructions are repeated in an abbreviated fashion for the sake of convenience. *The whole congregation* (13) could have sinned because of improper conduct or advice by the high priest, as happened subsequently in Israel's troubled history and so the ritual for their own sin offering has much in common with that prescribed for the high priest's atonement. In theory the people of Israel were considered 'a kingdom of priests and a holy nation' (Ex. 19:6), and so the blood from the offering of the congregation was dealt with in the same manner as the blood presented for the high priest. Similarly the flesh of the animal sacrificed for both parties was burned outside the camp on the ash-heap. Unwitting sin by the congregation seems to imply that an individual had broken God's commands in some manner, and was unwilling to confess his misdemeanour or atone for it by means of a sin offering. Sooner or later, by unspecified processes, the transgression comes to the notice ('eyes') of the assembly (Heb. *qāhāl*). This group was apparently restricted to community or tribal leaders, and is distinguished carefully from the congregation (*'ēḏâ*), to which they gave guidance.

A choice young bull is brought to the tent of meeting and the transference of community guilt is effected symbolically by the *elders of the congregation* (15). These persons occupied an important place in the community of Israel from the time of the bondage in Egypt, where they apparently held positions of seniority among the tribes (Ex. 3:16; 4:29). This situation was most probably an outgrowth of the patriarchal tradition in which the heads of families had complete power over their households. Such persons would thus be expected to furnish cohesion for the community, but in addition some elders may have been chosen because of their reputation as wise men or counsellors. It was not uncommon in ancient Near Eastern society for leaders of state to gather around them persons of this kind as advisers, to whom they could turn for counsel in times of difficulty or emergency. This can be illustrated from the Old Testament by reference to Pharaoh (Gn. 50:7), the Midianites and Moabites (Nu. 22:7) and the Gibeonites (Jos. 9:11), while at a later period the practice was followed by the Greeks and Romans. The fact that the Hebrew elders in Egypt were the ones instructed about how the passover was to be conducted suggests that they were heads of families originally. They were people who could give leadership in religious matters (Ex. 24:1, 9) as well as in judicial cases, and at one period in the wilderness wanderings seventy of them were appointed to assist Moses with general administrative matters (Nu. 11:16–17). In Leviticus 4:15–21 the elders are seen officiating in a cultic setting. The difference between the elders and the assembly is not made explicit, but the term *qāhāl* seems to mean 'an invited gathering', which would suggest that the assembly could have comprised a small elected group of elders.

16–21. The ritual involving the blood-sprinkling parallels that prescribed for the high priest (verses 7–12), except that the mention of *atonement* (20) is not matched by a similar statement in the passage dealing with the high priest's sin offering. There is no reference to a community meal in connection with this type of sacrifice, the underlying idea evidently being that the one on whose behalf the sin offering is made cannot eat any of it, since the blood has been sprinkled in the holy place (*cf.* 6:30). As a result of this offering the congregation was assured of forgiveness, because God is 'ready to forgive, gracious and merciful, slow to anger and abounding in steadfast love' (Ne. 9:17). It is incorrect to suggest, as Noth does,[20] that in the sin of offering there is an *ex opere operato* effect. While the narrative is in harmony with that of similar passages in emphasizing the importance of ritual propriety, a sense of having committed inadvertent sin and a consequent need for forgiveness is a prerequisite to the offering. Taken in isolation from these conditions, the ritual obviously could not

[20] M. Noth, *Leviticus*, p. 41.

atone by itself. Perhaps Noth did not express himself very clearly about this matter.

3. A ruler (22–26)

22. Precisely who is being described by 'ruler' (Heb. *nāśî'*) is uncertain.[21] The lack of the definite article indicates general rather than specific reference. Clearly such a person was subordinate in status to the anointed priest, but superior to the common people and perhaps even to the elders of verse 15. The Spanish biblical exegete Ibn Ezra (1092–1167) thought of the ruler as a 'prince of a tribe', but Noth seems correct in suggesting that he was one of the ancient tribal spokesmen[22] (*cf.* Ex. 16:22, *etc.*). This again would point to the antiquity of the Hebrew sacrificial system. *Is guilty* is better rendered 'becomes guilty', since this is part of the process of committing sin, whether deliberate or accidental. Christ taught that sin did not consist of isolated incidents of ungodliness, but was essentially a matter of motivation involving the personality (Mt. 5:28; 15:18–19; Mk. 7:21).

23–26. Before the ruler brings his offering he must be told of his sin, whether by the high priest or by some of his fellow-rulers. The process of emotional and spiritual catharsis is frequently aided by public admission of iniquity (*cf.* Jas. 5:16), and has the effect of making the offering for atonement more meaningful. As distinct from the animal presented by the high priest or the entire people, the ruler offers an unblemished male goat (23). The ritual diverged in other respects also, since it required the blood to be smeared on the horns of the altar of burnt offering instead of upon the golden altar of incense. The fat was to be disposed of as in the case of the well-being offerings (26), the reminder to that effect perhaps constituting a procedural direction to the officiating priest. The latter *make(s) atonement for him* to secure forgiveness. The word for atonement comes from a Hebrew root *kpr*, which can have two different meanings. If related etymologically to the

---

[21] D. J. Wiseman, *Bibliotheca Sacra*, 134, 1977, pp. 228 ff., has argued that the term could have described a second-in-command such as a deputy governor or subordinate leader. In 1 Ki. 4:5, 7; 5:7; 22:48, the unrelated term *nissāb* serves the same purpose.

[22] M. Noth, *Leviticus*, p. 42.

Akkadian *kapāru*, 'wipe off,' its sense would be that of 'wiping clean'. In Hebrew sacrificial rituals the thought of making expiation for someone is always prominent, the result being that the individual concerned is thereby exempted from punishment. The atonement which takes place has the effect of ransoming the person, and this seems to be the best sense of *kpr*.

Another meaning, 'to cover' (*cf.* Arabic *kappara*), was familiar to the Hebrews of the Middle Bronze Age, as indicated by the expression for 'appease' (lit., 'I will cover his face') in Genesis 32:21. While some sacrifices are meant to depict the 'wiping clean' of certain polluted objects such as the horns of the altar of incense (4:7) or the mercy-seat (16:14), others are designed to bring cleansing to individuals or to the community as a whole. In the latter case the sin is apparently 'covered', and so blotted out from God's sight. The effect of such a procedure is to reconcile man to God, thereby effecting an 'at-one-ment' and assuring the worshipper of forgiveness.[23] As in other instances, these rites have been performed on behalf of the ruler by *the priest* (26).

4. Ordinary members of the congregation (27–35)

27–35. Offerings for accidental sin by a commoner followed the general pattern prescribed for the ruler. Any of the *common people* (Heb. *'am hā'āres*) could offer a female goat (28) or a ewe lamb (32), neither of which would be beyond the means of the average family. Verses 28–31 and 32–35 are parallel sections which described the rituals to be followed. The blood is smeared on the altar of burnt offering (verses 30, 34), as contrasted with the sprinkling performed by the officiating priest when the inadvertent sin of the whole congregation of Israel was being expiated (4:17). The burning of the fatty tissue, as in the well-being offering (31), has the effect of producing a pleasing odour to the Lord, but this latter is not mentioned in verse 35, which refers instead to the *offerings by fire to the Lord*. Atonement is effected as a result of these rituals, and the penitent sinner is forgiven. Perhaps the flesh of the

---

[23] For this older sense of 'cover' see N. H. Snaith, *Leviticus and Numbers* (1967), p. 30.

sacrifices offered by rulers and commoners was eaten by the priests, although there is no indication here to that effect.

The reader will already have sensed something of the inadequacy of the Old Testament sacrificial system for dealing with sin. The offences described in this chapter are of a rather mechanical nature, for which appropriate expiatory provision was made. But there is no ritual here or elsewhere in the Pentateuch to cover the sins of deliberate and conscious rebellion against God, expressed in such acts as adultery, idolatry, murder or blasphemy. Yet a moment's reflection will enable one to perceive the rationale of such a situation. Had the levitical sacrificial system covered every form of sin and catered for all possible contingencies of transgression, there could have been no room for the work of Christ, since under such conditions it would have been unnecessary. But on Calvary the Saviour dispensed with the need for the blood of bulls and goats, and with His own blood introduced a sophisticated, all-embracing redemption for mankind, thereby making the Hebrew sacrificial system completely obsolete (Heb. 9:11–12). His unblemished self-offering purifies our consciences from dead works to serve the living God.

5. Offences requiring a sin offering (5:1–13)

1. The first few verses of this chapter present the reader with a rather complicated syntactical construction which contrasts with the simplicity and almost mechanical directness of previous sections. These verses deal with three types of transgression, the first of which is a rather special case involving a person who is reluctant to divulge information about a misdemeanour that he has observed, or heard about from another source. Though the verse says nothing about inadvertence, the offence is evidently treated as a sin of ignorance. A person who found himself in such a situation could not assume that the mere offering of a sacrifice would remove the guilt that had been incurred through interfering with the processes of justice. He had first to confess his sin (5) and then make appropriate restitution (6:5). The phrase *he shall bear his iniquity* is in effect an official pronouncement of guilt. The *public adjuration* was frequently known as 'the curse' (Heb. *'ālâ*), presumably because it consisted in part of a solemn denunciation of any witness who continued to be silent about the matter. Scriptural instances of persons who kept their own counsel until placed under some kind of adjuration included Achan (Jos. 7:19), Micah (Jdg. 17:2), a blind man (Jn. 9:24) and Jesus Himself (Mt. 26:63). Being a true and faithful witness was an important consideration under the old covenant (*cf.* Ex. 20:16), since individual integrity and communal justice depended so much upon it.

2–3. The second offence involved contact with either unclean animals or persons. The description of clean and unclean animal species occurs in Leviticus 11, while the next four chapters deal with instances of human uncleanness. More detailed consideration of these regulations will be undertaken at that point, but here it should merely be noted that contact has occurred, and has interfered with the individual's state of cultic or ceremonial purity. The uncleanness is accidental ('it is hidden from him'), hence purificatory rites have not been undertaken. Once the offender knows of his guilt, it is his responsibility to offer expiatory sacrifice, since failure to do so would only worsen his own relationship with God, in addition to affecting the well-being of communal existence. One of the greatest spiritual challenges for the Christian in the complexity of contemporary social life is to keep himself unspotted from the world (Jas. 1:27 av).

4. The third kind of transgression requiring a sin offering was that in which someone pronounced aloud ('with his lips') any kind of *rash oath* (4), without perhaps realizing fully the implications of what was being said. The combination *evil . . good* is an ancient expression denoting totality. Hence the phrase could be translated 'a rash oath to do anything at all'. Such oaths were not infrequently uttered in the ancient world under the influence of alcoholic beverages, and this would doubtless be the case where someone had to be told by someone else ('when he comes to know') of his wrongdoing. The Christian is reminded that the tongue is a powerful instrument (Jas. 3:5–6), and is specifically warned against the swearing of oaths in the sermon on the mount (Mt. 5:34–36) and in Christ's rebukes to the scribes and Pharisees (Mt. 23:16–22). The Lord's servants must be completely credible and reliable as witnesses for Him.

5–10. For these forms of inadvertent sin, the appropriate guilt offering (*'āšām*) was a female lamb or goat, which would be accepted by the priest as a sin offering (*ḥaṭṭā't*). Before atonement could be made, confession was mandatory. The guilt and sin offerings are closely related here (*cf.* 4:13, 22, 27; 5:17; 6:4), but the former receives its proper legislative emphasis in Leviticus 5:14–16, and can be distinguished from the sin offering by the added requirement of restitution. Thus the reference to a guilt offering in verse 6 can be better understood as meaning a 'forfeit'. For those of insufficient means, two doves or two young pigeons could be brought, *one for a sin offering and the other for a burnt offering* (7). The bird killed for the sin offering had its neck broken, but the head was not removed as in the peace offering (1:15).

Some blood was sprinkled on the side of the altar and the remainder at the base, in the fashion of sin offerings (9). This must precede the burnt offering in the ritual procedures, for according to the Hebrew sacrificial system reconciliation had to be effected between God and the sinner before the latter's burnt offering could be accepted. The procedure for this *ordinance* (10) is that described in Leviticus 1:14–17. Some commentators have attempted to answer the question as to why two birds were required by suggesting that, since it was virtually impossible to separate the fat from the flesh in a bird, thereby depriving the priest of the fleshy portion of the sin offering (*cf.* Lv. 6:26), one bird would be burned in its entirety to satisfy the requirements of a sin offering and the other would be given to the priest for his own use. However, a careful reading of the procedural regulations makes it quite clear that the second bird was to be offered for a burnt offering (5:10), so that the carcasses of both birds were utilized in this type of atonement.

11–13. If a person was too poor to bring doves or pigeons, *a tenth of an ephah of fine flour* could be offered instead (11). It is impossible to estimate accurately how much wheat or barley flour this would involve, but it might have been as much as four pints (US dry measure) of flour. The details are reminiscent of Leviticus 2:1–3, but the difference is that in Leviticus 5:11 the meal constitutes a sin offering, and therefore has to be presented without either oil or frankincense. The burning of a

memorial portion (12) gave the offering the status of a blood
sacrifice, since the token was mixed with the other burnt
sacrifices on the altar. There is thus no exception to the
principle that without the shedding of blood there is no
remission of sin (Heb. 9:22). The flour served as a replacement
for a blood sacrifice, thereby emphasizing the concept of
vicarious or substitutionary offering, which is basic to Hebrew
sacrificial thought.[24] Once atonement and forgiveness had
been effected, the remainder of the flour became the priest's
property, as in the cereal offering (*cf.* 2:1-10).

e. The guilt offering (5:14-19)

This short section of legislation begins with a brief annuncia-
tory formula and outlines procedures to be followed for *a breach
of faith* (15), the Hebrew term *ma'al* meaning an act of
infidelity towards God. In this instance the legislation related
to the property of the sanctuary or of the priests being
misappropriated, perhaps because the offerings had been
inferior in character, or had even been withheld due to
forgetfulness or inattention. The guilt or reparation offering
(Heb. *'āšām*) in such a case consisted of an unblemished ram
from the flock, which instead of being sacrificed is assessed in
terms of its monetary worth. This in turn presumes an ability
on the part of the priest to estimate the damages accurately.
The word *be'erkekā* ('your valuation') had aquired the final
syllable (*kā*, 'your') in a possessive sense which made it a
suitable technical term for the holy things of the Lord, as in
Numbers 18:16. Noth renders the word, 'if one compares it',[25]
and this gives a good sense of the relation between the animal
and its monetary value, by which the priests were to be
governed. The silver *shekel of the sanctuary* (*cf.* Ex 30:13) was the
standard for evaluation, and since money was paid out in
weighed amounts of gold or silver in the Bronze Age (*cf.* Gn.
23:16) the shekel is a unit of weight, not a coin at this period. It
is impossible to be certain about the weight of a shekel since
there was no uniformity in antiquity, but the sanctuary shekel
may have weighed about 11 g (or $\frac{2}{5}$ oz.). Its value is equally

[24] O. T. Allis, *The New Bible Commentary Revised* (1970), p. 146.
[25] M. Noth, *Leviticus*, p. 47.

uncertain, since it varied in different periods. The monetary worth needed to be determined in order to assess the amount of the fine, which was one-fifth of the valuation. When the total sum had been given to the priest, he took the ram and made atonement for the offender. This act could not be undertaken until proper restitution had been made.

A more general class of unwitting offence consists of acts forbidden under covenantal legislation. Here provision is made for a person who may have committed an offence, but is not absolutely certain ('though he does not know it') about the matter. To cover all possible contingencies, a compensation offering without the added premium is required, and as in the preceding section this consists of an umblemished ram valued in terms of the monetary standard of verse 15. According to Jewish tradition the ram had to be worth at least two shekels,[26] but this appears to be only a nominal figure, and may have been established at a comparatively late period for those who found it more convenient to make their reparation in money rather then in animals. The significance of this legislation lies in the help it afforded to people of scrupulous behaviour in guarding against the slightest offence. The Hebrew sacrificial system seems pragmatic and rather mechanical to the occidental mind, but here God's wonderful covenant love deals in a special way with people as sensitive personalities, and gives those who respond to this provision an opportunity for easing a tender conscience. To fulfil one's obligations as a member of a holy nation one must aim at being blameless, otherwise reproach will fall upon the people of God. Saint Paul professed to have as his aim a clear conscience towards God and men (Acts 24:16), and to avoid putting any obstacle in anyone's way (2 Cor. 6:3). Thus he urged believers not to give offence to people in such a manner that they would not be saved (1 Cor. 10:32-33), thereby bringing blame upon the Christian ministry. In Philippians 2:14 Paul establishes an ideal of purity for the believer, urging such a person to be blameless and innocent as a child of God in an evil and perverse world. This

[26] K. Elliger, *Leviticus* (1966), p. 77. *Cf.* E. A. Speiser, *Oriental and Bibilical Studies* (1967), pp. 124-128.

can only be achieved when the individual holds fast to the living Word.

f. Conditions requiring atonement (6:1–7)

This section also deals with breaches of faith, but these involve injuries to people in matters of personal property rather than the things of the tabernacle. However, the close relationship between God and His people makes an offence against any of them a sin *against the Lord* (1), since God is the protector of a person's possessions. The three injuries comprise deception regarding deposited property, robbery, and oppression, and all have been done to a *neighbour*. The law taught specifically that a person was not to bear false witness against (Ex. 20:16; Dt. 5:20) or defraud (Lv. 19:13) his neighbour, but was to love him as his very self (Lv. 19:18), a doctrine reinforced by Christ (Mt. 5:43–44; 19:19, *etc.*; *cf.* Rom. 13:9; Gal. 5:14; Jas. 2:8). The neighbour (Heb. *'amît*) was evidently a member of the immediate community to whom the guilty party had lied, either about something deposited with him, or the fact that there was no proof that an article had been left for security or as a pledge. Alternatively the neighbour may have been the victim of robbery or exploitation at the hands of some other community member. Yet another offence involved a person lying about some lost property that had been found (3), and this constituted a form of unlawful appropriation.

In each case the motivating factor was greed, coupled with the expectation that God would not notice the transgression. Such behaviour was inappropriate for the household of faith, because the nature of the covenant community was such that if one member suffered, all the others were affected by the situation (*cf.* 1 Cor. 12:26). Unfortunately many religious persons seem totally unaware that there are such concerns as ethics in social relationships, and therefore need to observe the New Testament's teachings on topics such as honesty, truthfulness, honourable behaviour, purloining, exploitation and the like, as exemplified in Paul's list of spiritual fruits (Gal. 5:22; *cf.* Rom. 12:17; Eph. 4:25, 32; Phil. 4:8; Tit. 2:10, *etc.*).

Before the offender in any of the matters specified could be forgiven, he had first to make appropriate restitution and pay a premium of an extra one-fifth of the value of the property, presumably in weighed amounts of silver. This kind of penalty was obviously intended to bring home to potential transgressors the importance of honesty and truthfulness in social relationships, and to emphasize the cost that might attend a breach of ethical conduct. Only when the recompense had been attended to adequately could the offender bring his unblemished ram, properly valued as a guilt offering (*cf.* 5:15, 18), and receive atonement through confession of sin and sacrifice. The assurance of God's forgiveness for the penitent sinner is a consistent theme of the sacrificial legislation in Leviticus, as it is also in the New Testament (1 Jn. 1:9, *etc.*).

g. Burnt offerings (6:8–13)

Whereas previous sections had dealt with the kinds of sacrifices that God required from His people, the remainder of chapter 6 and the whole of chapter 7, which form a distinct unit in the Hebrew text, comprise a manual of sacrificial procedure addressed to the priesthood. Following normal ancient Near Eastern priestly patterns, this material would be in written form from the very beginning. While the regulations cover the categories of offerings occurring in Leviticus 1:1 – 6:7, they do so with particular emphasis upon the eating of the sacrificial meat, and the extent to which the worshipper could participate with the priest at such meals. *Aaron and his sons* (9), as custodians of the priestly traditions, are instructed in the Law (Heb. *tôrâ*), a term meaning 'direction' or 'instruction' (*cf.* Lat. *doctrina*), which occurs at the head of passages in Leviticus 6:8 – 7:38 dealing with particular laws or groups of laws.

The priests are instructed to keep the altar fire burning continually (9–13), since the *burnt offering* had to be disposed of completely on the altar. The sacrifice now described is the continual burnt offering or *tāmîd* of Exodus 29:38–42, presented morning and evening for the community as a whole. This ceremony reminded the Israelites of their need for continuous worship of the Lord, and assured them of His constant vigilance on their behalf. The believer in Jesus Christ is freed from the necessity of observing prescribed ritual procedures as he walks with the Lord, and can rejoice in God's presence and protection wherever he happens to be. The regulations governing the altar fire merely focus attention upon one aspect of the officiating priest's duties, and are not intended to supplant the instructions already given in Leviticus 1:1–17. The priest was told that he had to keep the sacrificial animal all night *on the hearth* (9), this latter expression being better translated 'on its firewood'. The fat from the sacrifice would drip down on the altar fire and enable it to burn until the following morning, at which time the priest was to follow the ritual prescribed for the removal of the fatty ashes. He wore a linen tunic and breeches for that task (*cf.* Ex. 28:39–42), linen being the material favoured for clothing by ancient Near Eastern priests, and when the ashes had been placed beside the altar he had to change into his *other garments* (11) and take the ashes to a clean refuse-heap outside the camp (*cf.* 4:12). In the meantime it was still his responsibility to keep the altar fire burning, adding more wood if necessary. It appears unlikely that ashes would be left to accumulate beside the altar for any length of time, as some commentators have suggested. Sabbath prohibitions regarding the kindling of fires (Ex. 35:3) did not apply to the tabernacle. Because there were two daily offerings, the altar fire burned *continually* (13). An 'eternal flame' can be amenable to a great deal of symbolism, or none at all. For the ancient Hebrews it typified, among other things, God's presence among His people (*cf.* Ex. 13:21–22), and His own demands that His covenant nation should worship Him alone. Some Christians have seen in this continuous fire the obedience of Jesus Christ our High Priest, who in obedience to the point of death (Phil. 2:8) offered Himself as the perfect sacrifice for human sin.

The emphasis upon the fire ritual will doubtless have impressed the reader with two interesting facts. Firstly, even in so apparently menial a task as the removal of ashes from the altar, it was the officiating priest, and not a deputy, who performed it. Secondly, for this work this same man had to be attired in a different form of dress from that worn in the holy place. There is always a dignity and an importance attached to the performance of the tasks which the Lord assigns to His servants, no matter how trivial the work may appear to be. The way in which one appears physically before God frequently betrays one's attitude of mind (*cf.* Mt. 22:11–14). Indifference and casual behaviour are unacceptable when we are commanded to have our loins girded for service, however lowly that particular service might seem. As far as the priest in this section is concerned, his ministry on one and the same occasion could range from the emptying of altar ashes to the declaration that atonement had been made. Whatever the occasion, he was prepared both in appearance and intent, and by his versatility and readiness serves as a model for the Christian ministry in its widest sense.

h. Cereal offerings (6:14–23)

14–18. In this section the stress is again placed upon the role of the priests and the way in which they are to dispose of the balance of the offering after the memorial portion has been burned. These regulations supplement the material in Leviticus 2:1–16, with which there is considerable verbal correspondence. Once the *memorial portion* (15) has been offered, the remainder of the sacrifice could be eaten by the priests in a consecrated area, in this instance *the court of the tent of meeting* (16). The sacrifice had to be eaten within the tabernacle enclosure or 'court' because it was a most holy offering. This was also true of the sin (*cf.* 5:13) and guilt offerings (*cf.* 7:10), which were also reserved for the use of the Aaronic priesthood. The prohibiting of leaven in connection with the cereal offering (*cf.* 2:4, 11) applied to its use by the priests as well, because *it is a thing most holy* (17). Food designated in this way could only be eaten by the priests in the tabernacle precincts, as contrasted with 'holy things', which could be consumed by the priest and his family under normal conditions of ceremonial cleanliness (*cf.* 2:3). *Every male* (18) Aaronite could eat the cereal offering, even those who exhibited some physical defect and were therefore blemished (*cf.* 21:18–23). The emphasis upon ceremonial holiness describes the status of a gift consecrated to God, as Christ indicated (Mt. 23:19), and implies that ritual holiness could be transmitted by contact, just as ritual uncleanness could. By the post-exilic period the priests in the time of Haggai decided, in response to questioning, that what was ceremonially holy conferred its sanctity upon an immediate object of contact, and nothing more (Hg. 2:12), an opinion which subsequently encountered considerable discussion in Talmudic circles (*cf.* Pesachim 14*a* ff.).

Levitical rituals make it abundantly clear that it is a very responsible matter for persons to stand in the service of the living God. By their initial act of commitment they enter into a relationship of holiness to God, and must fulfil the Lord's will in the manner in which He prescribes it, not as they think it might be done. For the Christian, holiness is the result of the Holy Spirit's work in the individual life, removing that which is alien to the nature of Christ and enabling the believer to grow in grace (*cf.* Eph. 4:15; 2 Pet. 3:18, *etc.*) so that he can begin to match the stature of Christ. Because holiness is a matter of personality, it cannot be conveyed mechanically by contact with 'consecrated' elements, amulets and similar trinkets.

19–23. The high priest was required to present to God a daily cereal offering for himself and the priesthood, comprising *a tenth of an ephah of fine flour* (20). This small quantity was a token offering, divided equally between the morning and evening sacrifices, and prescribed from the time ('on the day') of the high priest's consecration. The offering was mixed with oil and cooked on a griddle (see notes on 2:4–7), after which it was offered in *baked pieces*, Hebrew *tupînîm* (read te̅putennâ), a word of uncertain meaning. This offering was burned completely, since the priests could not eat the most holy portions offered on their behalf. These regulations draw attention to the spiritual integrity of the priestly office. Its holders must not presume upon it, nor must they imagine that, as priests, they are above the law, as happened subsequently in Israel's history (*e.g.* 1 Sa. 2:12, 16–17, 22). Familiarity with sacred activities must not be allowed to breed contempt (*cf.* Mal. 1:6–7). It is a privilege for the Christian to serve the One who had bought him with His own blood, and to be aglow with the Spirit in such a ministry (Rom. 12:11).

i. Sin offerings (6:24–30)

This section deals with the priest's responsibilities in the ritual (4:1 – 5:13), emphasizing the holy nature of the offering. It was subject to the regulations governing other most holy offerings, and conferred ceremonial holiness upon persons or things touching it. Accidental contamination of clothing by the sacrificial blood necessitated the washing of the garment *in a holy place* (27). The Hebrew speaks of the priest's portion being boiled rather than roasted, and prescribes cleansing rituals according to whether the container was made of clay or copper (RSV 'bronze'). A directive to the priests reminds them that certain sacrifices are regarded as too sacred even for them to eat. Christians must not flaunt their spiritual status, but must humble themselves under the Lord's mighty hand (Jas. 4:10; 1 Pet. 5:6), and labour as fellow-workers in the cause of Christ.

j. Rules for guilt offerings (7:1–10)

The guilt or reparation offering (5:14–19) was another *most holy* sacrifice, the consumption of which was restricted to the Aaronic priesthood. When first described, no directions were given about the disposal of the Lord's portion, and the procedure is now outlined. The *'āšām* or offering is killed where the burnt offering is sacrificed, its blood thrown on the sides of the altar (2) and the fatty tissues, corresponding to the list set aside for God in the peace offering (*cf.* 3:9–10), are burned on the altar as a reparation sacrifice. The remainder of the offering then becomes the property of the priests. The closeness of the relationship between the sin and the reparation offering is made explicit here (7). The officiating priest is also given all the cereal offerings that have been cooked, whether in an *oven . . . a pan* or on *a griddle* (9), and the directive is repeated that all of priestly standing are eligible for such offerings (10). These instructions enunciate clearly the principle that those who minister at the altar shall share in the sacrificial offerings (1 Cor. 9:13; 10:18). These constitute their livelihood, and enable them to devote their time and energies to the Lord's service rather than to lesser pursuits (*cf.* Acts 6:2). It is the responsibility of the Lord's people to give proper economic support to those who are full-time ministers of the gospel (*cf.* 1 Tim. 5:17–18), lest they be distracted by purely material considerations from their prime task of proclaiming the crucified and risen Lord.

k. Rules for peace offerings (7:11–21)

11–18. The various portions belonging to the Lord, the priest and the offerer are enunciated to supplement the prescriptions of Leviticus 3:1–17, which dealt predominantly with the mechanics of the ritual. The peace or well-being sacrifice (NEB 'shared-offerings') could be presented as a thanksgiving in connection with a vow made to God (*cf.* Ps. 116:14) or as a freewill offering (16), and it was the only sacrifice in the entire tariff in which the donor was permitted to share. In later Judaism the thanksgiving offering was valued as the highest type of sacrifice, but here it is only one category of offering, meant to promote the well-being of the worshipper. The thanksgiving (Heb. *tôdâ*) gift represented the donor's acknowledgment of God's mercies to him,[27] while the votive (Heb. *neder*) comprised an offering in fulfilment of a vow. The freewill (Heb. *nᵉdābâ*) offering consisted of an act of homage and obedience to the Lord where no vow had been made, and with the other categories of well-being sacrifices lent substance to the conviction in Israel that God valued a tangible response to His blessings more than a mere verbal profession of gratitude, which might or might not be sincere. Similarly, the Christian is commanded to love not just in word or speech, but in deed and truth (1 Jn. 3:18). Along with the thank-offering were to be presented various kinds of unleavened and leavened cakes (13), one of which was the Lord's portion and was given to the officiating priest. The worshipper was not permitted to leave any of the meat from the sacrificial animal for another day but was required to eat it at the time it was offered. For a freewill offering or one made in fulfilment of a vow, however, the donor was allowed an extra day in which to complete the feast (16), at which time he would probably have invited friends to participate (*cf.* Dt. 12:12). Any flesh that remained after that time had to be burned, most probably as a hygienic measure. If this injunction was disobeyed, the well-being offering was null and void. So far from being credited to the donor, it became *an abomination* (18. Heb. *piggûl*), a technical term used to describe sacrificial meat that had become stale through not being eaten in the allotted time (*cf.* Lv. 19:7; Is. 65:4; Ezk. 4:14). As a result the disobedient lay worshipper would *bear his iniquity* (18), which in Leviticus 19:8 meant death at God's hands. In Genesis 17:14 and Exodus 12:15,

---

[27] *Cf.* W. Eichrodt, *Theology of the Old Testament*, 1 (1961), p. 147.

however, the same punishment may only have involved exile, but this is not certain.

The well-being sacrifice followed the general pattern of the burnt offering, except that no birds were allowed to be offered, and the animals had to be female. As well as being the only sacrifice to be eaten by the donor, it was also distinctive in comprising the only animal sacrifice that did not make atonement for sin. The underlying motivation of the peace offerings was that of appreciation or gratitude, which is not always a conspicuous element in Christian living. The believer is instructed to make his requests known to God with thanksgiving (Phil. 4:6), to be watchful in prayer with thanksgiving (Col. 4:2), and to give thanks always and for everything to God (Eph. 5:20).

19–21. These verses deal with the ceremonial conditions of holiness or uncleanness that would affect the outcome of the peace offering. Sacrificial flesh that came into contact with some unclean thing was not to be eaten, while any person who partook of the meat while suffering from some physical impurity ran the risk of death. This fate also lay in store for anyone who ate the sacrificial flesh after having touched anything polluted. The *unclean abomination* (21), Hebrew *šeqeṣ*, was probably some kind of verminous creature, although if the Massoretic Text is read as *šereṣ* it could refer to 'swarming animals'.

It is obvious from the vigorous language of these prohibitions that the layman's participation in sacrifice was taken extremely seriously. It should not be imagined, however, that the main emphasis was upon circumstantial holiness. What is in view consistently is the motivation of the worshipper, for if his condition of ceremonial holiness has been a matter of concern to him, it can be taken as a good indication of his attitude towards the God of Sinai, who was of high moral and ethical character.[28]

l. Fat and blood forbidden (7:22–27)

This section is introduced by a formula, 'Say to the people of Israel', which indicates that the regulations which it contains

[28] D. F. Kinlaw, *Beacon Bible Commentary* (1969), p. 344.

are for general dissemination, and are not restricted to the priesthood. The basic stipulations regarding abstinence from fat had already been given in summary form (3:11), and at this stage a fuller explanation is provided for the populace as a whole. No fat of any kind must be eaten (see notes on 3:3–5), although the fat of animals that had committed suicide, died from natural causes, or had been torn by wild beasts, could be utilized in other ways, which would probably include a method for dealing with the vipers that attacked grazing sheep. These reptiles would emerge from their holes and bite the noses of the sheep as they were eating, causing an injury that the shepherd would have to bathe with oil as the sheep passed under his hands into the sheepfold at the end of the day (Ps. 23:5). In antiquity the shepherds generally counteracted the menace of the vipers by placing the fat of animals, normally hogs, around the edge of the holes where the reptiles lived, and setting fire to the fatty pieces, thereby driving the vipers away. At the present time the fat of pigs is still used for this purpose by Palestinian shepherds. In general Hebrew thought the fat portions of the sacrifice comprised the choice sections, and therefore appropriate to God alone.

Although all things belong to God ultimately, His relationship with the believer demands that the latter assign to God a certain proportion of those material things with which he has been entrusted (1 Ch. 29:14). This requirement removes the spiritual relationship from a purely verbal level, and demands effort from the human participant if his commitment is to be met. This is why God demands His portion of the sacrificial offering, and why that requirement must be satisfied before the ritual proceeds any further, even if it involves burning the entire sacrifice. The principle of returning to God a portion of what He has bestowed was formalized in the system of tithing, or the giving of a tenth part, and this continues to bring blessing to those who apply the words of Malachi 3:10 to their own religious experience.

The emphatic pronouncement in verse 20 about the violator of this provision being cut off from among his people applied with equal stringency to the one who ate blood in any form, whether from animals or birds. These two species are mentioned in order to cover the range of live sacrificial offerings in

Israel. The blood was the seat of life (17:11), and since life was the peculiar property and gift of God, it had to be returned to Him alone and not appropriated by human beings. There are obvious hygienic as well as theological implications in mind, of course, since blood conveys disease as well as health, and if ingested can therefore be the vehicle of a variety of ailments. The traditional insistence of the Jews upon the rightness of their method of slaughtering animals so as to remove all the blood from the tissues is one of the abiding values of their culture which ought to commend itself more consistently to Gentiles. From a hygienic and dietary standpoint, such *kosher* meat is the safest that can be eaten.

m. Additional peace-offering regulations (7:28–38)

As with the preceding section, this passage opens with a formula of annunciation that is intended to give general directions concerning the peace offerings to the congregation of Israel. It deals principally with what might be considered as an appendix to the rules governing these offerings (3:1–17; 7:11–21), and records details about the priests' share which were not mentioned previously. The Israelites are now made fully aware of this situation, and thus know precisely what is involved in the rituals. The unleavened and leavened cakes (12–13), a portion of which was donated to the officiating priests, are not referred to here, since the concern is with the flesh of the sacrifices.

30–34. Following normal procedures, the fat is assigned to God, and when a breast containing fatty tissues is offered it is moved to and fro in the presence of the Lord *as a wave offering* before the fat is consumed on the altar. The breast was then given to the priests as their portion. The act of waving as the offering was presented most probably involved the priest extending the portion in the general direction of the altar and then withdrawing it, as a gesture of dedication. According to the late Chief Rabbi Hertz, something more complex and meaningful was involved than what the present writer conceives of as having been a simple act of presentation to the altar. In discussing the priest's portion of the well-being sacrifices, he described the ancient ritual procedure of 'waving' in terms of the portion prescribed for the use of the priest being first laid upon the hands of the donor. At this point the officiating priest placed his own hands beneath those of the person offering the sacrifice, and moved them first forward and backward, then upward and downward. This act symbolized the consecration of the offering to God, the Ruler of heaven and earth.[29] If the Rabbi is correct in his interpretation, the wave offering has a deeper significance still, because the motions in fact make the sign of the cross. Here, at the heart of the levitical sacrificial system, is a dramatic foreshadowing of Christ's death on Calvary as the event by which atonement and reconciliation (Eph. 2:13–14) are made for all time.

For the officiating priest (32) was reserved *the right thigh* (Heb. *šôq hayyāmîn*), considered then and now as one of the choicest parts of the animal. In 1 Samuel 9:24 it was the portion reserved for the quest of honour. While the thigh would probably be one of the tenderest parts of the carcass, and therefore especially suitable for offering to visitors, it must be remembered that, as far as nourishment is concerned, all sections of meat from a given animal are of equal nutritional value. Older versions rendered the term *offering* (32) by 'heave offering', as in the AV, RV, the American Jewish Version, and others. The NEB furnished a more modern interpretation of 'contribution', which is the general meaning of *tᵉrûmâ*, and implies something 'set aside'. The breast and thigh are prescribed by God as those portions of the peace offerings that belong by right to the Aaronic priesthood, and will remain *a perpetual due* (34) to them from the nation as long as the sacrificial system continues.

Archaeological excavations at Lachish uncovered a well-preserved Canaanite temple which had been destroyed about 1220 BC, apparently by the Hebrews, while in full use. From the ruins were recovered a large number of animal and bird bones, all of which came from the upper section of the right foreleg.[30] This would indicate some ritual consonance between the cultic practices of Israel and those of the Canaanites, especially if the 'thigh' of verses 32–33 is rendered 'shoulder', as in the RV margin. On examination, very few of the bones

[29] J. H. Hertz (ed.), *The Pentateuch and Haftorahs* (1940), p. 434.
[30] G. E. Wright, *Biblical Archaeology* (1960), p. 15.

indicated any contact with fire, suggesting that the meat had been boiled (*cf.* 1 Sa. 2:13–14). This method of preparation would be more suited to shoulder meat than the more tender portions from the thigh, though even the latter can be ruined by indifferent preparation.

35–36. The legislation ensuring the integrity and continuity of priestly food supplies was dated officially from the time that the Aaronic priesthood was constituted and ordained. Consequently the prescribed offerings for the support of the priesthood are to continue into the foreseeable future. It is thus made clear that, even if a person is engaged in such unworldy pursuits as ministering the things of God, he is still a labourer who is therefore worthy of his hire (*cf.* Lk. 10:7). The Lord's servant for his part is instructed not to worry about food, drink or clothing for the morrow (Mt. 6:31), since these are improper preoccupations for those who are seeking Christ's kingdom and His righteousness.

37–38. These verses comprise the concluding statement to the whole body of regulations concerning sacrifices (1:1 – 7:38). This small section is particularly interesting because of its literary form, examples of which are especially prominent in the book of Genesis. It is written in the style of a colophon to a Mesopotamian tablet, and many examples of this device have been recovered during excavations. The use of the word colophon in connection with Mesopotamian literary and other documents should not be identified too closely with its current sense, which merely describes the publisher's imprint at the bottom of the title page of a book.

In ancient Mesopotamia the colophon contained all that one might expect to find on the title page of a printed book, but instead of preceding the material on a tablet, it formed the conclusion to it. Such tablets when intact normally commenced with a title, consisting of the initial words of the material, then continued with the body of whatever was being recorded, and ended with the colophon. This device often included the title or designation of the contents, the date of writing of the tablet and the name of the owner, who could also have been the scribe. Certain types of material, such as the Gilgamesh Epic, were written on more than one tablet, and were linked together by means of a connecting device known as a 'catch-line' so that they would be read in their proper order. When this was the case, the colophon would furnish the number of the tablet when it was part of a series, and would also state whether or not that particular tablet was the concluding one in the series.

As far as the Genesis material is concerned, it is possible to isolate eleven literary units in the form of ancient Mesopotamian tablets from chapters 1:1 – 37:2 by recognizing that the phrase, 'these are the generations of', marks the presence of a colophon in the text. By working backwards from the colophon to the title, the complete literary unit is recovered and shown to conform to typical Mesopotamian patterns. The first of these units (Gn. 1:1 – 2:4) assigns an early date to the material ('when they were created'), which consists of everything prior to Genesis 2:4. The second proposed tablet-form (Gn. 2:5 – 5:2) does not seem to have preserved a title, but perhaps it survived in a damaged form, since many Mesopotamian tablets are broken in various places. The colophon in Genesis 5:2, however, makes it clear that the original material consisted of everything that preceded it.[31]

Turning to Leviticus 7:37-38, it is possible to identify the following elements of an ancient Mesopotamian colophon: the title ('which the Lord commanded Moses'), to be compared with the opening words of Leviticus; the name of the scribe or owner of the material ('Moses'), and a scribal dating of the record ('on the day that he commanded the people of Israel to bring their offerings to the Lord, in the wilderness of Sinai'). Perhaps the enumeration of the principal items (37) dealt with in the sacrificial legislation of the whole section corresponded to the Mesopotamian practice of indicating in a colophon the number of a tablet when it formed part of a series. Moses would be thoroughly familiar with the cuneiform writing and scribal practices of the Babylonians, being himself educated in all the wisdom of the Egyptians (Acts 7:22), since barely a century earlier, in the Amarna Age, Babylonian had been the

---

[31] For a fuller explanation of this procedure as it applies to Genesis, see P. J. Wiseman, *Clues to Creation in Genesis* (1977), pp. 31 ff. This book, edited by Professor D. J. Wiseman, is a combination of P. J. Wiseman's works, *New Discoveries in Babylonia about Genesis* (1936) and *Creation Revealed in Six Days* (1948). See also *HIOT*, pp. 63-64; 545-551.

lingua franca of diplomacy in the Near East. As the person who was most probably responsible for combining the underlying tablet-material of Genesis with the Joseph narratives to produce the book as we know it, Moses would have had first-hand acquaintance with the ancient historiographic sources, preserved perhaps by his time on papyrus or leather.

He may well have decided to present the sacrificial legislation to the Israelites in a literary form similar to that which preserved the earliest written traditions of their ancestors in order to give it the classic type of expression that so fundamentally important a body of regulations required. At all events, the material is arranged in a style that would be recognized readily by the literati of the second millennium BC.

The colophon in Leviticus 7:37–38 marks the termination of an important section of legislative material, authenticates it, and dates it decisively in the second millennium BC. There can be absolutely no question of this colophon being a forgery, or a retrojection by a much later editor to the age of Moses. Like other examples of its kind from Mesopotamia, it testifies to authorship and date, just as the title page of a modern book does. The entire body of legislation gives every indication of antiquity, containing examples of early sacrificial technical terminology, some elements of which had already become obsolete in the time of Moses. The antiquity and continuity of priestly materials is characteristic of the ancient Near Eastern nations, and is thus unexceptional in ancient Israelite circles. Not merely can this section be assigned in its entirety with complete confidence to the Mosaic period, but because of the nature of the material and the degree of veneration accorded to the scribe who compiled it, there must be considerable doubt as to whether any other than the most minor textual modifications were made throughout the entire history of its transmission. This contention is borne out by the purity of the Hebrew text, which contains no difficulties apart from a plural in Leviticus 6:5 ('its fifths'), which the Samaritan Pentateuch and numerous manuscripts read as a singular; the unintelligible term *tup̄înîm* (6:21 – MT 6:14) and the possible substitution of *šereṣ* for *šeqeṣ* in Leviticus 7:21, the latter involving a change of only one consonant, and at that a rather debatable alteration. By any standards these 'difficulties' are of a minor nature, leaving us with an original, unadulterated core of Hebrew sacrificial legislation which, despite the rather stereotyped literary form which is presented on occasions, manages to entertain some variation of style, as is indicated by the rather complex form of Leviticus 6:1–5.

This legal material embodied the means by which an offender against covenant regulations might have sins of omission, inadvertence or accident forgiven, and be reconciled to the living God of Israel. To the modern reader the details of sacrificial procedure may well make for tedious and uninteresting reading, but for the ancient Hebrews it was a fundamentally important element in their spiritual lives, and continued to remain such until the sacrificial system came to an effective end when the Jerusalem temple was destroyed in AD 70. But the meaning of the various prescriptions did not end there, for as the regulations are studied afresh, they remind the reader of certain fundamental aspects of God's self-revelation to man. He is pure and holy by nature, not merely in a ceremonial sense involving ritual propriety, but in an ethical and a moral sense also. Those who would worship Him must do so in spirit and in truth (Jn. 4:23–24), rather than in a formal behavioural manner, if they are to be reconciled to Him and know His blessing in their lives. The ethical and moral aspects of God's nature are the reason for the great degree of seriousness which God attaches to sin. It constitutes an affront to His nature and a defilement of His innate purity, and as a result God is not able to look upon iniquity with equanimity or complacency (*cf.* Hab. 1:13). He hates the sin while loving the sinner, but before the latter can be restored to fellowship, an act of atonement has to take place by which the sin will be removed.

It is important to remember that the only kinds of sin that could be forgiven were those of inadvertence. The law stated explicitly (Nu. 15:30–31) that for sins committed 'with a high hand' against God, *i.e.*, acts done in deliberate defiance of explicit covenantal legislation, there could be no forgiveness. By behaving in such a manner the offender had reviled his God, and would suffer the penalty for such rebellion, which was personal extinction. As observed in the comments on the corresponding verses, this sacrificial legislation points forward to the atoning work of Christ by setting out what might be described as the theoretical basis of atonement. Even sins of accident or omission could not be pardoned without the shedding of blood (*cf.* Heb. 9:22), which embodied the principles of cost and commitment.

Only when an offering had been presented in the appropriate manner, *i.e.*, *recte*, with a genuinely penitent attitude of heart and mind, rather than *rite*, *i.e.*, mechanically, according to the verbal prescriptions of some cultic formulary, could the sinner be assured that atonement had been made. The work of Christ represents a significant advance upon the provisions of the Mosaic legislation in that even deliberate acts of sin against God can be forgiven if the offender is truly penitent and confesses his sins to the Lord. According to the teachings of Christ, the only kind of transgression that can never be forgiven is the sin against the Holy Spirit (Mt. 12:31; Mk. 3:29; Lk. 12:10). This offence consisted of 'blasphemy against the Spirit', namely the attributing to demonic origins of the influence and work of the Holy Spirit in human life. Such a crass perversion of covenant love represents the point beyond which forgiveness cannot proceed because of the total inversion of spiritual values which is involved. No true believer could ever commit so heinous an offence, which has its roots in the powers of darkness. But to guard against falling into temptation and sin, Christians need to stand continually in the shadow of the cross, confessing their offences, pleading earnestly for forgiveness, and experiencing by faith the assurance that the blood of Jesus Christ, God's Son, cleanses the penitent sinner from *all* sin (1 Jn. 1:7).

II. CONSECRATION OF PRIESTS (8:1–10:20)

The first section of Leviticus stood in close relationship to the passages in Exodus dealing with the selection of the Aaronites as the official priestly family (Ex. 28:1), the vestments they are to wear (Ex. 28:2–43), and the manner of their consecration (Ex. 29:1–46). This material followed the initial instructions regarding the design and building of the wilderness tabernacle (Ex. 25–27), and was itself succeeded by covenantal legislation (Ex. 30–34) and by descriptions of the manner in which the tabernacle was ultimately constructed and appointed (Ex. 35–40). Now a major section of Leviticus deals with the consecration of the priests to their important mediatorial office, narrating the way in which the instructions of Exodus 29 were carried out. It might appear at first sight that a better sense of order could have been achieved by describing the consecration of the priests in conjunction with these ritual prescriptions, but the internal organization of the sacrificial system required that the various classes of offerings be enumerated before the priests were actually consecrated and the services of the Tabernacle instituted. The sequence that was adopted proved to be quite proper in view of the fact that sacrifice had first to be offered by Moses on behalf of these priests as part of their consecration rites, and only when the priests possessed the sacrificial manual in its entirety, and the authority to carry out its instructions, could they officiate according to their vocation.[32] At no stage in these narratives is there any deviation from the insistent emphasis upon ritual properiety.

a. Preparation for anointing (8:1–5)

1–2. As with information concerning the various offerings of the sacrificial system, the instructions for the consecration ceremony came from God, thus carrying the highest degree of spiritual and moral authority. The narrative looks back to Exodus 29:4–37, and describes the manner in which that material was implemented. The *garments* consisted of a breastpiece, an ephod, a robe, a coat of chequer work, a turban and a girdle (Ex. 28:4). The robes in question are those to be worn by Aaron, the first High Priest of Israel, and his successors, and their ornate style would have done justice to any temple or royal court in antiquity. It is important to notice, however, that aside from being designated as holy (Ex. 28:2), namely, set apart specifically for service in the tabernacle and later in the temple, no particular cultic or liturgical significance was assigned to the various garments. The passing of time has made it difficult to understand what some of the terms actually described, with the result that some interpretations must be

[32] *Cf.* O. T. Allis, *The New Bible Commentary Revised*, p. 148.

regarded as at best rather conjectural. Because the original record was of contemporary origin, the writer assumed a familiarity on the part of his readers and those who followed them with the objects in question. This would be reinforced over the centuries by visual contact with them, an advantage which we unfortunately do not possess.

Such is the situation with the ephod, which in the case of Aaron was a garment made of richly embroidered material, as compared with the plainer linen ephods worn by other priests (*cf.* 1 Sa. 2:18). It was held in place over the shoulders by means of two straps, but whether the ephod covered the chest, the abdomen, or both is not known. On the shoulder straps were onyx stones, engraved with the names of the Israelite tribes. On top of the ephod was a pouch or 'breastpiece' (Hebrew *ḥōšen*) containing the Urim and Thummim, which were apparently sacred objects employed in casting lots. The term ephod was also used occasionally to describe an 'idol' (*cf.* Jdg. 8:27; 17:5) which was employed in family worship, but precisely why such an image was described by a name used for a well-attested object in Israelite tabernacle worship is unknown. The 'breastpiece' was an elaborately embroidered square of cloth set with four squares of stones. Since it was essentially a small bag, the rendering of *ḥōšen* by 'breastplate' (KJV, RV), 'breastpiece' (RSV, NEB) is entirely conjectural. The article can perhaps be paralleled with the ornate gold breastplate which was found in the tomb of a Middle Bronze Age ruler at Byblos.[33]

The robe of Exodus 28:4, 31–34 was violet in colour, and was apparently to be worn beneath the ephod. It was decorated elaborately with embroidered pomegranates, and had little golden bells around the lower part. The material seems to have been woven in one piece, rather like the robe which Christ was wearing at His crucifixion. If so, the reference in John 19:23 can be interpreted as an allusion to Christ as the great High Priest, about to present Himself as the supreme offering for human sin. The chequerwork robe, normally worn in the Near East by persons of some social standing, was made

[33] For this artifact see P. Montet, *Byblos et l'Egypte* (1928–29), pp. 162–163 and plates. 93, 94.

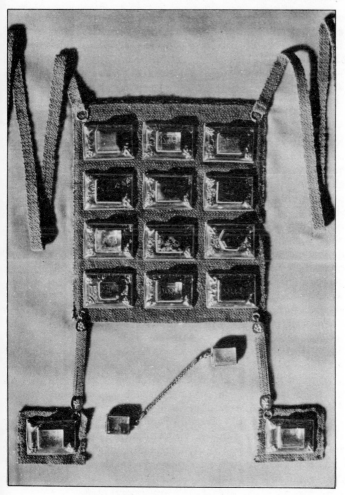

The High Priest's Breastpiece

of striped material or of fabric woven in patterned form. The girdle was more properly a sash which was frequently worn in Egypt by pharaohs and state officials, as well as by members of the priesthood. The turban comprised a length of material wound around the head, as is done at the present day, and had attached on the front a small plate of solid gold engraved with the inscription, 'Holy to the Lord' (Ex. 28:36).

Elaborate though these vestments were, particularly in view of their wilderness milieu origin, their own function was to remind the Israelites that a powerful, holy and just God was indeed present with them in so far as the wearer of the garments was held to be linked to Him. This association of elaborate vestments with a deity was also a traditional aspect of Canaanite cultic worship, as for example at Ugarit, where the robe of the goddess Anat was described as *'epd*. They did not serve to glorify the office of the high priest or other cultic officiants, but instead indicated that there were certain clearly defined standards attached to the worship of the One who had created the universe, and particular avenues by which alone God could be approached.[34] Hurried, casual or disorderly worship had no place in ancient Hebrew religious life, whatever might have been the case in the cultic rites of other Near Eastern nations. The worship of the God of Sinai was a very serious matter, since He was the only true and living God who could deal swiftly and surely with offenders, as even some members of the priestly line were soon to discover. The prescribed forms of the Hebrew rituals and the attire of the priests served the important purpose of maintaining the distinctiveness of worship among the covenant people, and guarded against the possibility of innovations being introduced from pagan sources. Unfortunately even these precautions were circumvented at later periods in Hebrew history.

The *anointing oil* (*cf.* Ex. 30:22–33) for the consecration of Aaron and his descendants was blended by the perfumer (AV

[34] For the symbolic significance of priestly robes see S. H. Kellogg, *The Book of Leviticus* (Expositor's Bible), 1891, pp. 192–201; A. E. Crawley, *Encyclopaedia of Religion and Ethnics,* 5 (1912), pp. 65 f.; J. R. Porter, *Leviticus,* p. 63. For the symbolism of colours in antiquity see Philo, *De Vita Mosis,* 3:6; Josephus, *Ant.* III.7.1.

'apothecary') from a number of costly spices, most of which would come from Arabia or India. This particular mixture was restricted to the anointing of priests, and any other use constituted a capital offence (Ex. 30:32–33) because the substance was holy. The ingredients consisted of liquid myrrh, probably expressed from the shrub *Commiphora myrrha*; sweet cinnamon (*Cinnamomum zeylanicum*); sweet calamus, one of the plant species of the genus *Cymbopogon*, perhaps *C. schoenanthus* L., which has been recovered from tombs in Egypt; cassia, most probably *Cinnamomum cassia*, a tree closely related to the sweet cinnamon; and olive oil as the vehicle. The animals to be offered for sacrifice were *the bull of the sin offering* (*cf.* Ex. 29:10–14) and *the two rams* (*cf.* Ex. 29:15–22), the description of the latter in Exodus indicating that they were a species of fat-tailed sheep. The final element in the preparation for anointing was the *basket of unleavened bread*, described in Exodus 29:2 as unleavened cakes mixed with oil and unleavened wafers spread with oil, all made from finely ground wheat flour.

3–5. Once the preparations had been made, Moses then assembled the people at the entrance to the tabernacle. Since the rite of ordination and consecration of the priesthood to divine service was to affect everyone in Israel, the ceremony was a public one. The duties of Moses the officiant would be carried out within the enclosure of the tabernacle, perhaps in the presence of the elders. The remainder of the Israelites would have to obtain the best view of the proceedings that they could, perhaps by standing on some elevation at the foot of Mount Sinai, where they were encamped at this period.

It is important to notice the position of Moses in relation to God's activities here. Although he functioned as a servant, Moses was still in charge of the household of God (Nu. 12:7; Heb. 3:2), and thus he parallels the obedience and fidelity of Christ, who also became a servant (Phil 2:7) in order to mediate the new covenant. The fellowship of Christian believers is such that it is possible for the chief person to become servant of all (*cf.* Mt. 20:27; 23:11; Mk. 10:44), a concept which makes any type of ranking within the fellowship rather an artificial affair. To Moses was given the revelation on Mount Sinai, and as God's chosen leader he was entrusted with the task of organizing the religious and communal life of the people during the wilderness period. As chief executive officer in Israel he acted as God's visible representative in the impressive consecration ceremony that was to follow.

In this capacity his activities are thoroughly in accord with the ethos of the sacrificial system to which the priests were to be dedicated, since the mediation of divine grace was to be their basic function. The emphasis upon the correctness with which all the procedures and other regulations were to be followed is implied by the statement that Moses carried out all his duties as the Lord commanded him. The people were called to order just prior to the consecration ceremony by a solemn statement from Moses, 'This is the thing which the Lord has commanded to be done.' The proclamation thus makes it clear that the initiative for the entire affair had come from God. Thus no charges of patronage or favouritism could be laid against Moses in the consecration of a close family member as high priest, since the choice was the Lord's. Once that fact had been clearly established, the ceremony could proceed in a thoroughly democratic manner, and, by commending itself to all present as legitimate and authoritative, it could then claim their allegiance and support of the priesthood thus constituted. Despite these precautions, however, there was soon to be a protest against the privileged position of the Aaronites (*cf.* Nu. 16:1–35).

b. The ceremony itself (8:6–13)

6. The great rite of consecration commenced when Moses led Aaron and his sons to the entrance of the tent of meeting, to the east of which stood the copper laver made from the mirrors of the women who served at the sanctuary entrance in some unspecified capacity (Ex. 38:8). Here the Aaronites were washed with water, in order to cleanse them symbolically from sin. It would be comparable to the baptism of adults in the New Testament, one of two sacraments enjoined upon believers by Christ. Some Jewish interpreters have maintained that the washing of Aaron and his sons was by immersion, as was required of the high priest on the day of atonement (Lv. 16:4), but this is not clear from the passage. In a land where good water supplies were few and far between, the washing of one's

94

entire body was a comparatively rare event, and not least in a desert or wilderness environment where water would be scarce except at oases. In practice a perfunctory washing of exposed areas sufficed under normal circumstances for nomads or semi-nomads, aided by the liberal use of scents and ointments, especially where women were concerned. Whereas the Egyptian priests set a standard of cleanliness for their people by washing their entire bodies three times daily, the Hebrew priests usually rinsed off only their hands and feet as they commenced duty in the tabernacle (Ex. 30:19–21).

7. Once the symbolic purification of Aaron and the priests had been accomplished, the ceremony of vesting the high priest took place. The garments mentioned here are listed in the order in which they appear to have been put on, and this might indicate that an eye-witness account had been preserved in some detail. The process formed an important part of the procedure whereby the high priest was inducted into his elevated office, for by this means the emblems of service were bestowed upon him formally in the presence of the entire nation. Dressed in this fashion he would intercede annually in the most holy place of the tabernacle for the inadvertent sins of the Israelite people on the day of atonement. His ceremonial robes thus depicted the functions that, under divine appointment, he was privileged to exercise on behalf of the covenant people. Elaborate and impressive though they were, his garments were not to become a source of personal pride, but were to remain as a reminder to him and the people of his position as the principal priestly servant of Israel.

The robes conferred upon Aaron a visible distinctiveness among his fellows as the spiritual leader and moral guide of the nation. Attractive though such a position might be, however, it would bring its own responsibilities in terms of consistency of witness and holiness of life, and this has presented a challenge to believers in every age. The visible seal of Aaron's dedication to his office was furnished appropriately by the golden plate on the front of the turban inscribed with the motto 'Holy to the Lord'. The Lord's priests must be certain that their way of life is in continual harmony with God's will (Heb. 13:21), and must try to exemplify the gifts of the Spirit in daily living.

8. In this verse the oracular stones are described by their official names. The word *Urim* is a plural term of unknown derivation, but it has been connected with the Hebrew noun meaning 'light', and also with the root *'ārar*, meaning 'to curse'. Equally unknown is the origin of the word *Thummim*, which is always found in conjunction with Urim in Scripture. It has been associated in meaning with the root *tāmam*, 'be perfect', and as a result some interpreters have understood these two objects to indicate 'lights' (or 'curses') and 'perfections'. At the very best, however, these meanings are highly conjectural, and could actually be misleading. It is probably best to assume that the terms designated the sacred lots without further specification. The fact that one word began with the first letter of the Hebrew alphabet and the other with the last letter, thereby indicating some sort of alpha-omega totality, is most probably purely coincidental. These two objects were used up to the period of the early monarchy as a means of ascertaining God's will (*cf.* 1 Sa. 14:41), but precisely how they were employed to obtain information is not stated. It has been suggested that they were used in the manner of dice or small marked sticks, and the way in which they fell or their appearance when on the ground revealed the divine will in some manner. A more cultic explanation has seen the objects as symbols of the high priest's authority to seek the direct counsel of God on issues that needed to be resolved. It is probably best to see the purpose of the Urim and Thummim as an oracular means of furnishing the enquirer with what was hoped would be a direct positive or negative answer. There were occasions, however, when the oracle simply did not give an answer (1 Sa. 14:37; 28:6). The first mention of these cultic objects (Ex. 28:30) assumes that the Israelites were already familiar with them, since no explanation regarding their nature and function is given. They appeared to be hereditary possessions of the high priest, since they were passed on from Aaron to Eleazar (Nu. 20:28). The last reference to them in the Old Testament is in Nehemiah 7:65.[35] In the Christian

35 On the Urim and Thummim see A. Jeremias in *H. V. Hilprecht Anniversary Volume* (1909), pp. 223–242; H. G. May, *American Journal of Semitic Languages and Literatures*, 56, 1939, pp. 44–69; R. de Vaux, *Ancient Israel* (1961), p. 352; J. Lindblom, *VT*, 12, 1962, pp. 164–178; E. Robertson, *VT*, 14, 1964, pp. 67–74;

dispensation the 'casting of lots' has been replaced by the direct guidance of God the Holy Spirit.

9-12. The vesting of Aaron was followed by the anointing and consecration of the tabernacle and its furnishings, as a prelude to Aaron's own anointing. Moses acts as officiant, and he sprinkles the altar seven times, anointing its utensils as well as the laver with the holy *anointing oil*, the use of which, as noted above, was restricted to the consecrating of priests. Then the anointing of Aaron took place, at which time Moses poured some of the sacred oil upon the high priest's head. Precisely why the head was anointed in antiquity, and not the hands, is unknown. The modern suggestion that the head was anointed as a token that the mind and intellect of the individual were being dedicated to God would have had no meaning for the ancient Hebrews, since they did not understand the nature or functioning of the brain, and instead regarded the heart as the seat of intelligence, purposiveness and will. The anointing of Aaron was an indication that he had been selected by God and designated to perform a particular function. The *golden plate* (NEB 'gold rosette') which was placed on the front of the turban was probably a band of gold which went around the headdress at the level of the forehead to comprise a *holy crown* (9), rendered variously by 'sacred diadem' (JB; NIV) and 'symbol of holy dedication' (NEB). Certainly the headdress was a highly visible symbol of the high priest's consecration to his office in Israel. The anointing procedure and the crown were emblematic of royalty, and are still part of the coronation ceremonies of British monarchs. The consecration ceremony was impressive, dignified and solemn, befitting the status and responsibilities of the recipient. There is no record of any words of institution being exchanged between Moses and Aaron, or of any blessing being pronounced upon the new high priest of Israel.

13. A less elaborate part of the consecration ceremony then followed, in which Moses took the sons of Aaron and dressed them in *coats ... girdles ... and caps*. The first two items would

---

I. Mendelsohn, *IDB*, 4, pp. 739–740; G. Fohrer, *History of Israelite Religion* (1972), pp. 83, 115.

probably be less elaborate vestments than those prescribed for the high priest, but well suited for the usual range of priestly activities, which included teaching (Dt. 33:10), the casting of lots (Ex. 28:30), and the giving of decisions at sanctuaries (Ex. 22:8), as well as officiating at the sacrificial altar. Whereas the high priest wore a turban, the lesser priests had a simple cap, probably made from a folded cloth and having ties by which it could be held in place on the head. This small item served a very important practical purpose in protecting the priest's head from the heat of the sun as he officiated outdoors, sometimes for hours at a time.

In this part of the ceremony, the anointing has implications that are of the greatest importance for the Christian reader. In addition to the priest, the prophet (*cf.* 1 Ki. 19:16) and the king (*cf.* Is. 16:13, *etc.*) were also anointed as they assumed their duties. These three functions were united ultimately in the person of the Messiah, a title which is derived from the root for 'anoint'. The term 'Christ' is the Greek (*Christos*) equivalent of the Hebrew word for 'Messiah'. To speak therefore of Jesus as 'Christ' is to recognize Him as God's chosen Servant, the long-promised Messiah, who would be annointed not merely with oil (Is. 11:2; 42:1), in the tradition of the old covenant, but more particularly with the Holy Spirit (Mt. 3:16; Lk. 4:1, 18, 21; Jn. 1:32–33), who sustained Him as He became our great High Priest.

c. Consecration offering (8:14–36)
Although the tabernacle and its contents had been anointed with the sacred oil, thus making it a consecrated place, it was necessary for three sacrifices to be offered in atonement for Aaron and his sons so that they would be cleansed completely from sin. These rites were integral to the whole ceremony of anointing and consecration, and were all of equal significance. Since God's purpose for Israel as expressed in Leviticus is that they shall be a holy nation, any suggestion of contamination either in worship or in community life must necessarily be removed if that objective is to be attained. Hence the entire tabernacle area had to be consecrated before worship acceptable to God could be offered there. Aaron was thus consecrated in a ceremonially clean place, and his sons were

installed in their sacred office in the same environment. The altar itself was purified so that no pollution of the sacrificial offerings would occur to disrupt the holiness of the sanctuary and the community. In a later age God was to censure His priests for offering polluted sacrifices on His altar (Mal. 1:7), thus invalidating the entire concept of worship. The importance of ritual propriety is again stressed here, in that the priests must first secure atonement for themselves before they can purport to obtain it on behalf of other Israelites. No priest in any age can lead his followers to a point of spiritual development which he himself has not previously attained.

14–17. The Aaronites laid their hands on *the bull of the sin offering* (14), identifying themselves with the animal that was to be slain on their behalf, after which Moses, in his capacity of officiant, followed the procedures laid down for sacrificing the sin offering (4:1 – 5:13). He smeared the horns of the altar of burnt offering (*cf.* 4:25, 30, 34), purified the altar, and then poured out the rest of the blood at the base to sanctify and atone for it. The disposal of the fatty tissues followed the normal pattern of the peace and sin offerings (*cf.* 3:9–10, 14–15; 4:8–9, *etc.*), with an appropriate verbal correspondence in the text. The remainder of the animal was carried outside the camp to a clean, *i.e.*, consecrated, place where it was burned according to the regulations governing the sin offering (*cf.* 4:12).

18–21. The burnt offering of a ram followed the directions of Leviticus 1:3–13, which the newly consecrated priests would themselves soon be observing. Moses slaughtered the animal, sprinkled its blood, and burned the head and other parts along with the fat. When the legs and entrails had been washed, they too were burned as an offering by fire to the Lord (21). In this sacrifice the priests demonstrated their complete obedience to God's will, and proclaimed their desire to renew and maintain fellowship with Him.

22. After this offering came a sacrifice restricted to an act of consecration (*cf.* Ex. 29:19–20). In this ceremony Moses took the second ram *of ordination* (22), and after the priests had laid their hands upon it he killed it and smeared some of the blood upon Aaron's right ear, right thumb, and right large toe. The same procedure was followed for Aaron's sons, after which the rest of the blood was dashed against the altar of burnt offering. The term for 'ordination' comes from a root meaning 'to fill up', and in Exodus 29:9 is rendered by the technical expression 'fill the hand'. This phrase also occurs in Mesopotamian tradition in some texts from Mari, dated about 1750 BC, where the allusion seems to have been to the sharing of booty among conquerors. The Hebrew may imply that the sanctuary priests were entitled to share in the sacrificial offerings that were brought to the tabernacle, but as has been made clear already, provision for their needs was an important element in the sacrificial system. The NEB of Leviticus 8:22 reads 'the ram for the installation of priests', and this conveys the sense of admission to rights and privileges of office. This seems rather different from the original meaning of 'fill the hand', which appears to have referred to those offerings placed in the hands of the priests at the time of their consecration that conferred on them the authority to perform priestly duties. The difference is that between the placing of a Bible in the hand of a candidate at the time of ordination, and the subsequent appointment of that person to some pastoral function with its accompanying rights and emoluments.

23–25. The smearing of blood on specific parts of the bodies of Aaron and his sons was a highly symbolic gesture, bearing directly upon the priest and his work. In a token fashion the entire body was consecrated to the Lord's service, and by accepting the smearing the priest acknowledged the obligations inherent in the symbolism. Hereafter he must listen carefully to God's pronouncements so that he can proclaim them properly. His hands must be devoted entirely to those things connected with the Lord's work, so that he will not be tempted to perform evil deeds. His feet must always be directed in such a manner that they will be walking continually in the ways of the Lord. The use of blood in this ritual separated the priest from wordly concerns and dedicated him completely to the service of God. This particular procedure is rich in meaning for the Christian priesthood of all believers, consecrated by the blood of Jesus Christ to hear the Word of God, to perform works of grace and mercy, and to walk according to the Lord's guidance.

26–29. A procedure restricted to the ordination offering occurred when Moses took all the fat of the ram, along with its right thigh (RV mg. 'shoulder'), and placed them in the hands of Aaron and his sons. This was a formal 'filling of the hands' which all could see, and the sanctity of the office to which the priests had been appointed was proclaimed by the fact that the offerings placed in their custody included the most holy parts of the sacrifice which belonged exclusively to God. In conjunction with these sacrificial portions were offerings from the *basket of unleavened bread* (26), from which were removed one unleavened cake, one that had been mixed with oil, and one wafer. These were placed upon the fat and the right thigh of the sacrificial animal, and the priests then made the presentation gesture of the wave offering in the direction of the altar before returning these choice pieces to Moses. The latter then burned them on the altar in conjunction with the burnt offering to produce, in the antiquated phraseology of the ritual, *a pleasing odour . . . to the Lord* (28).

Because Moses had for the moment officiated as a substitute for the high priest, it was necessary for him to present an offering to God on his own behalf. His *portion of the ram of ordination* comprised the front-quarter, and this too was presented to the Lord as a wave offering before being burned. The consecration offering, like the peace offering (*cf.* 7:15–18), could be eaten by those on whose behalf it had been sacrificed, but once more the rule that the priests could not eat of what had been offered on their behalf had to be enforced. The thigh represented the portion assigned to the priests, while the front-quarter was that which belonged to Moses in his capacity as a temporary officiant. Once these pieces had been burned, the rest of the sacrifice could be eaten by Aaron and his sons. As with other aspects of the ritual, these procedures were followed meticulously, *as the Lord commanded Moses* (29).

30–36. Moses had already conducted the smearing rites on the bodies of Aaron and the priests, separating them symbolically for holy things and making certain that their full strength would be devoted to the Lord's service. Still in his capacity as officiant, Moses sprinkled a mixture of anointing oil and blood upon the ceremonial clothing of Aaron and his sons as an additional act of consecration. The priests were thus spiritually secure in their office because they were protected by the blood of the sacrificial animal, just as the Israelites themselves had been when the first passover was celebrated in Egypt (Ex. 12:23). Because Christ was sacrificed as our passover lamb, His blood takes away the sins of the believers and gives them the assurance of eternal salvation as they live according to His will.

The consecration ceremony concluded with instructions by Moses to Aaron for the remainder of the sacrificial flesh to be boiled, and the unleavened bread to be eaten, outside the entrance to the sanctuary proper (31). This was a symbolic means by which the covenant established between God and the priesthood would be sealed in the presence of the whole congregation. Hereafter the priests were to devote themselves exclusively to the service of the Lord in ministering to the nation of Israel. They were not to be occupied with manual work, nor to be subjected to other mundane considerations that might divert their attention and energies from the things of God. Their support was to come entirely from the altar of the tabernacle, and they were to be separated to minister spiritual things. Paul furnished an example for believers in stating as his vocation the conviction that he was set apart for the gospel of God (Rom. 1:1). The future separation of the Hebrew priests from secular activities and their consecration to the tabernacle was symbolized by the requirement that for the next seven days they were not to leave the door of the tent of meeting (33). Only after a week had elapsed could the high priest and his sons consider themselves truly ordained. By being restricted to one small area of the tabernacle court it was impossible for the priests to become contaminated in any way, or to be distracted from the priestly pursuits which were part of the ordination process.

Verse 35 indicates that on each of the next seven days Moses was to offer the same sacrifices on behalf of Aaron and his sons as had marked the great ceremony of consecration (*cf.* Ex. 29:35–36). This procedure involved some modification in the procedures laid down for the peace or well-being offerings, which permitted the meat to be eaten on the day after it had been sacrificed (7:15–16). Under the special circumstances connected with ordination and consecration, whatever remained of the meat or unleavened bread had to be burned on

the day that it was offered (32). There is no record of any
opportunity being provided for the priests to meditate upon
the nature of the vocation for which they had been chosen, but
the character of the sacrificial rites alone would furnish them
with opportunities for repentance, confession of sin, and
adoration of a God whose mercies are continually over all His
works (Ps. 145:9). All that has been prescribed for the priests
has to be observed meticulously, lest they die for disobedience.
The office of a priest was of a very responsible nature, for those
who held it could influence the nation for weal or woe, as
became evident subsequently in Hebrew history. For this
reason the priests were warned periodically of the serious
consequences that would ensue for them if they disregarded
God's regulations. Obedience is at the heart of both the old
and the new covenant, and this, rather than love, is God's
prime demand of His followers. The Christian is urged to
bring every thought to the obedience of Christ (2 Cor. 10:5),
and to see obedience as one mark of a sanctified personality (1
Pet. 1:2). At this stage Aaron and the priests are united in a
willingness to follow divine instructions, and to initiate the
long and sometimes turbulent history of priestly service to the
nation.

d. Rules for offerings (9:1–7)

1–2. The period of consecration having elapsed, the new
Israelite priesthood entered upon its public ministry. Up to
this point the sacrifices had been offered by Moses, but now
the work is assigned to those who had been chosen and
dedicated for it. In his capacity as leader of the people, Moses
called, better 'summoned' (*cf.* 1:1), the Aaronites and the elders
of Israel, the latter having perhaps been within the tabernacle
precincts during the period of consecration even though they
were not in the same state of ceremonial holiness as the priests
themselves. At this particular time the Aaronites are respon-
sive to every command of Moses, but it would not be long
before something less than complete obedience was paid to his
instructions (*cf.* Lv. 10:16–18). Aaron's mediatorial ministry
commences when Moses instructs him to take an unblemished
two-year-old male calf for a sin offering and a ram for a burnt
offering (2), and sacrifice them before the Lord. These two

animals were to be offered on behalf of Aaron and the priesthood, and it is significant that they were sin offerings. Even the most dedicated and consecrated person still sins and falls far short of God's glory (Rom. 3:23; 5:12). The closer one lives to the Lord's will, the more one is aware of this corollary of sheer human existence.

3–5. Aaron is instructed to require from the congregation a goat, a calf and a lamb, unblemished and a year old. The consistent attention to detail which the levitical sacrificial system requires is illustrated by the mention of the lamb, which to be considered as such must be less than a year old, after which time it becomes mutton. Verses 2 and 3 comprise the only instances in the sacrificial tariff where a calf is prescribed for sacrifice. Later Jewish interpreters suggested that the calf was included here as an atonement for the events of Exodus 32, but although possible this is at best uncertain. In addition, the people were to bring animals for peace or well-being sacrifices, and provide a cereal offering mixed with oil. These requirements covered the principal forms of sacrifice, and mark the point at which the people begin to participate in the system of offerings. The demands made upon the Israelites at this stage of the wilderness sojourn are modest, and well within their abilities to meet. This illustrates an important principle of the spiritual life, namely that God does not impose upon the believer any burdens that are too heavy to bear, as contrasted with the practices of the Pharisees (Mt. 23:4; Lk. 11:46) and their spiritual successors.

6–7. The reason why the people have to be cleansed as well as the priests is now apparent. The glory of the Lord is to be revealed to the community, and His presence will add a visible seal of approval to the ceremonies of consecration that have just been concluded. For those who had experienced the shaking of Mount Sinai (Ex. 19:18), this would be at once an exhilarating and fearsome prospect.

The word *appear* is in the perfect tense in the Hebrew, being spoken of as though it had happened already, because there was no doubt in Moses' mind that it would occur. When everything was in readiness, Moses told Aaron to commence his priestly duties by making atonement for himself and the people according to the Lord's instructions. Until this had been done, the presence of God would not honour either the proceedings or the participants. His glory had already descended upon the finished tabernacle (Ex. 40:34), and now it was about to ratify the ministry to be undertaken there.

e. Aaron's sacrifices (9:8–24)

This section presents what appears to have been the normal pattern of Israelite sacrificial worship, in which the ritual of the sin offering quite naturally precedes the burnt offering,[36] and indicates the way in which God desires the worshippers to approach Him. First and foremost was the need for cleansing from sin, so that the offender could stand spotless before God. The burnt offering symbolized the obedience and submission of the person who had already identified himself manually with his sacrifice as a means of gaining divine favour, while the peace or well-being offering was intended to promote the welfare of the donor as he continued in fellowship with his Lord. There is a slight variation from the detail of the regulations governing the sin offering of the high priest (4:5–7), where all the blood was thrown at the base of the altar instead of part being sprinkled in front of the sanctuary veil and smeared on the projections of the altar of incense. This divergence can be accounted for by recalling that Aaron had yet to enter the tent of meeting for the first time (23). Again, the procedures described in connection with the peace offering (*cf.* 3:1–17) vary somewhat in that the breast, which normally became the property of the priesthood (7:31) and the right thigh, which was the perquisite of the officiating priest (7:32), were on this occasion presented as a wave offering (NEB 'a special gift') to God.

8–11. Aaron sacrificed his own sin offering first, since his purity was closely connected with that of the congregation, of which he was the exemplar. This reflects the standards of obedience, purity and holiness set by Jesus which the Christian is urged to follow (1 Pet. 2:21–24). Aaron's sons assisted in the ritual of smearing the blood on the projections of the altar of burnt offering, after which the remainder of the blood was poured out at its base and the fatty tissue burned in the normal manner. The pieces of the flesh and the skin were also

[36] W. F. Lofthouse in A. S. Peake (ed.), *Commentary on the Bible* (1937), p. 201.

burned outside the camp, according to the procedures required for the sin offering (Lv. 4:11-12).

12-14. The burnt offering having been killed, its blood was dashed against the altar, Aaron being once more assisted by his sons in this process. Their duties were to hand over to him the various sections of the sacrificial animal. These parts were then burned along with the head, the washed entrails and legs, in the prescribed manner (Lv. 1:6-9). The ceremony of handing the sacrifice to Aaron piece by piece was no doubt an impressive part of the ritual, but also indicated that as the component parts were subsumed under the whole, so the entire priesthood was represented by the officiating high priest.

15-17. The goat for the sin offering of the people was then killed and presented to the Lord. This was followed by the burnt offering, which was also sacrificed according to directions (RSV 'ordinance'). The rituals involving the cereal offerings were observed carefully, the narrative mentioning the burning of the memorial portions (*cf.* Lv. 2:2) at the appropriate point in the ceremony. While tedious recapitulation of the regulations is avoided in the procedural summaries presented here, it is obvious that the various sacrifices are offered in strict accordance with the prescribed procedures. Implicit obedience, not individualism or innovation, was what God required of the worshipper.

18-21. The peace or well-being sacrifices were killed next, and once more Aaron's sons delivered the blood of the ox and ram to him for dashing against the altar. All the organs that were covered with fat were disposed of by fire, but the front quarters and the right thigh were dedicated to God, using the appropriate presentation gestures.

The order of sacrifices described in the ritual prescriptions constitutes an important guide for Christians with regard to the principles of spirituality underlying divine worship. Of the three concepts enunciated, the one that had priority concerned cleansing from sin, denoted by the sin offering. When proper atonement had been made, the worshipper was to surrender his life and labour to God, as indicated by the burnt and cereal offerings. Finally, he was to enjoy fellowship with God within the context of a communion meal, which the peace offering furnished. There is no conflict of interest here with the rituals of Leviticus 1 – 5, since of the five types enumerated no fewer than three are concerned in some manner with the removal of sin and guilt. Opportunities are also provided through the sacrificial prescriptions for personal dedication, thanksgiving and fellowship. Some early Gentile Christians at Corinth, who were unfamiliar with the spiritual conditions governing Jewish worship, did not observe this order and so were not able to discern the Lord's body (1 Cor. 11:20–21, 29).

22–24. Aaron now exercises his priestly prerogative by invoking God's blessing upon the people. Later Jewish tradition maintained that he used the magnificent phraseology of the priestly benediction in Numbers 6:24–26, in which God's power, presence and peace for those being blessed constitute the intent of the pronouncement. After this, both Moses and Aaron entered the holy place of the tent of meeting. Perhaps at this time Moses formally transferred the responsibilities of the sanctuary to Aaron, and instructed him in the performance of those tasks which he himself had undertaken previously. When they came out into the tabernacle court, both of them prayed for God's blessing upon the nation of Israel. In response to this the glory of the Lord became visible to the people, probably in the same manner as that recorded in Exodus 40:34, in which a cloud and the 'glory' (the latter derived from a root 'to be heavy') continued to indicate God's presence. There seems little doubt that the phenomena of the cloud and fire, prominent at the time of the exodus (Ex. 13:21), descended again upon the tabernacle at this juncture. Fire flamed out from the cloud and burned up the sacrificial portions that belonged to God, thus placing an unmistakable sign of divine approval upon the procedures (*cf.* Gn. 15:17; Jdg. 13:19–20; 1 Ki. 18:38; 2 Ch. 7:1). A view widely accepted in liberal circles that this miraculous phenomenon is a later addition, inasmuch as the sacrifices had already been burned on the altar, has been dismissed by Porter as being 'too literal minded'.[37] What appears to have happened is that the fire of God consumed wholly the sacrifices that were already in process of burning. The important and startling aspect which

[37] J. R. Porter, *Leviticus*, p. 75.

commanded attention, however, was the divine origin of the fire that burned on the sacrificial altar.

In the Scriptures, fire is frequently employed as a symbol of God's presence and activities (*cf.* Dt. 4:24; Ps. 18:8–14; Ezk. 1:4; Rev. 1:14). In Malachi 3:2 the coming Messiah was likened to a silversmith's fire that would remove the dross and process the metal to a high degree of purity. John the Baptist carried this a stage further in promising that when the Messiah came He would baptize with the Holy Spirit and with fire (Mt. 3:11; Lk. 3:16). The manifestation of the Holy Spirit at Pentecost was described as 'tongues of fire' resting on the apostles, and this fulfilled in a spectacular manner the predictions of John. The imagery of Malachi is related in Paul's thought to the final assessment of the believer's activities in the day of judgment (1 Cor. 3:13–15), when they will be examined in terms of the most exacting standards. The fire that Christ came to send upon the earth (Lk. 12:49) must consume everything that is iniquitous and unworthy in the believer if the Lord's ministers are indeed to become flames of fire (Heb. 1:7).

The dramatic nature of the theophany caused the people to shout aloud, prompted no doubt by a mixture of emotions including fear, surprise, joy and thanksgiving. They *fell on their faces* (24) in prostration before God, adopting a characteristic Near Eastern method of demonstrating complete submission to an overlord. In addition to the burnt offering and the well-being sacrifice which had just been presented to God on behalf of the people by the newly ordained priesthood, the Israelites were afforded a quite unexpected opportunity for spontaneous worship and an expression of gratitude to God.

f. Nadab and Abihu (10:1–7)

Barely had the consecration ceremonies concluded with the priests entering upon their sacred functions, than an act of sacrilege was perpetrated by Aaron's eldest sons, Nadab and Abihu. Chapter 9 shows the way in which the people were to approach God in worship, and the blessings and benefits which would result. Chapter 10 makes clear how swiftly divine retribution came upon those who refused to follow the guidelines, and insisted instead upon pursuing an independent course. What had so recently been a time of happiness and splendour for the nation is suddenly marred by needless tragedy. The situation was made even more unfortunate by the privileged position which these two men had enjoyed when, along with Moses, their father Aaron and seventy of the elders of Israel, they had been allowed to see a manifestation of the God of Israel on Mount Sinai (Ex. 24:1, 10). The abuses in which they indulged were of a very serious nature, since they were prompted by disobedience.

1-2. The two men began their tabernacle duties by taking their own censers, consisting of fairly flat pans in which burning coals were carried, and putting fire in them. They then placed incense on the coals and apparently presented this *unholy fire* to God in a manner that had not been prescribed. There are several elements of this procedure that violated all the instructions for sacrifice given to Moses by God. In the first instance, there is no indication in the record that the coals had been removed from the altar of burnt offering (*cf.* Lv. 16:12), the contents of which had been set alight by divine fire when the Lord sanctified the tabernacle at the consecration ceremonies of the priests. To that extent, therefore, a significant change had been made in the sacrificial rituals, and something that was unholy, *i.e.*, not consecrated to the service of God, had been allowed to intrude upon other consecrated elements. Secondly, there is nothing in the detailed prescriptions of sacrifice which stated that anyone except the high priest himself should place incense upon a censer of coals and present it to God. Even that ceremony was restricted to the rites of the day of atonement when once each year the high priest entered the most holy place of the sanctuary to cover the mercy seat with a cloud of incense. Therefore, in behaving as they did, Nadab and Abihu were usurping in a blatant and unpardonable manner the responsibilities of the chief person in the priestly hierarchy. Their actions may have resulted from pride, ambition, jealousy or impatience, and if so their motivation was very far removed from the intent of one trying to lead a life of holiness to the Lord.

Thirdly, it is obvious that neither Moses nor Aaron had been consulted about the sudden change in procedure, and therefore the actions of Nadab and Abihu comprised a flagrant act of disobedience to the known wishes of their superiors, as expressed in the sacrificial legislation, to say nothing of constituting an act of defiance towards God. Thus the penalty of being 'cut off', prescribed in Numbers 15:30 for sins of deliberate intent against covenantal regulations, was put into dramatic effect. Furthermore, the act of placing incense upon burning coals could well have been construed as being part of a simple ritual of offering incense to a pagan god, such as was engaged in by the women of Jerusalem in the time of Jeremiah (Je. 44:25). Because being holy to the Lord involved a separation from all forms of worldliness (*cf.* 2 Cor. 6:14-17), this kind of ritual innovation was the very antithesis of what God had prescribed for His worship.

Other factors that may well have entered into the transgression included the possibility that the incense had not been compounded according to the instructions given by God to Moses (Ex. 30:34-38); that the two men used their own domestic censers rather than the ones that had been consecrated specifically for tabernacle use; or that the offering had been made improperly so that it usurped the function of the altar of incense (Ex. 30:7-8). Perhaps most important of all is the possibility that Nadab and Abihu were in a state of intoxication as they entered upon their duties, and that this condition interfered with their judgment. In this connection the prohibition of verse 9 is of great significance.

In the light of the foregoing it appears difficult to believe that the offence committed was purely accidental in nature. The reversal of values whereby what is unholy is offered to the Lord as though it were something sacred and consecrated is diametrically opposed to all for which the Sinai covenant stood. Ironically it was by fire that the offenders died (2), killed by a consuming flame that is characteristic of the nature of God (Heb. 12:29), who demands acceptable worship with reverence and awe. Precisely how the fire killed Nadab and Abihu is unknown, or whether the word 'fire' was a synonym for a flash of lightning.

Many of those scholars who assign a post-exile date of composition to Leviticus have assumed that during the exile there was a migration to Jerusalem of 'priestly groups' from the northern area, presumably in an attempt to set up a northern priesthood in the southern kingdom. Though these priests claimed to be in the Aaronite tradition, this narrative made it clear that only the obedient sons, Eleazar and Ithamar, did in fact transmit the legitimate priesthood of Aaron, to which the apostate Israelite priests clearly did not belong. For those who uphold this view, the present narrative comprises an 'aetiological story' which attempts to explain the rationale of conditions obtaining at a subsequent period. A supposition of this kind depends upon an arbitrary dating of Leviticus in the second-temple era, a proposition that has been asserted many times by liberal scholars but has yet to be demonstrated factually.

Most significant of all is the complete lack of evidence in the Old Testament for any movement of priests from shrines outside Jerusalem to the capital of Judah in order to replace those priests that had been taken into captivity. After 581 BC the area around Jerusalem lay desolate, and the city itself was a ruin, if the evidence of Lamentations is to be believed. When the captives returned from exile between 538 BC and about 525 BC, the opposition which they encountered was not from rival priestly circles, which are conspicuously absent from the relevant narratives, but from individuals or groups with political interests such as Sanballat, the Arabs, Ammonites and Ashdodites (Ez. 4:4; Ne. 4:7).

3. Moses used this incident to illustrate precisely what God meant by holiness and separation, in order that the bereaved father and the people as a whole might understand. Whereas for contemporary pagan peoples the concept of holiness meant nothing more than a person or an object being consecrated to the service of a deity, for the Israelites holiness was an ethical attribute of the divine character which had to be reflected in their own lives and behaviour, since they were bound by covenant to the God of Sinai. There are two basic aspects to this relationship which had always to be at the forefront of the Israelites' minds: the first was that the covenant proceeded from God's love (*ḥeseḏ*); the second, that it demanded a response from the Israelites of unhesitating and unqualified obedience. Since certain members of the priestly line had apparently refused to take the human response to God's covenantal love seriously, everybody had to be taught a lesson which, by its visual nature, would make a lasting impression upon individual minds. Hence Moses' statement that God will demonstrate the nature and significance of holiness.

The words of Moses do not comprise an actual quotation of pronouncements recorded in the Torah, but reflect its teachings about the requirements of sanctification for the office of priest (*cf.* Ex. 19:22; 29:1, 44, *etc.*) and the aphorism of Samuel that obedience is preferable to sacrifice (1 Sa. 15:22). Because holiness is one of God's most characteristic spiritual attributes, it is bound to be manifested among those associated with Him. The New Testament is in harmony with this proposition in its insistence upon believers in Christ living lives of consecration and holiness (Rom. 12:1; Eph. 5:27; 1 Pet. 1:15–16, *etc.*). The closer one is associated with God's work in the world, the more necessary it is to ensure that the relationship with God is not marred by spiritual blemishes, otherwise the believer cannot function properly as a channel for God's healing grace.

A situation of this sort also demands that those who are especially gifted, or who occupy positions of great responsibility in society, must be particularly scrupulous about their general conduct. Far too many people at all levels of community living imagine that social or political prominence somehow exempts an individual from the requirements of the moral law. By contrast, the New Testament teaches the judgment will be applied more rigorously to those who have been endowed richly with abilities and knowledge than to others in a less fortunate situation (*cf.* Lk. 12:48). The fact that this judgment will begin in God's household (1 Pet. 4:17) demands that each Christian should make his calling and election sure (2 Pet. 1:10). The sons of Aaron had occupied for a very brief period a privileged position as spiritual leaders of the nation, but they had not taken their responsibilities with the degree of seriousness required by a just and holy God. As a result, it was impossible for God to be glorified *before all the people*. The consistency of Christian witness by lip and life is seen in Paul's insistence upon individual believers glorifying God in their bodies (1 Cor. 6:20), *i.e.*, with their entire personalities.

The impact of this dramatic turn of events upon Aaron is seen in his silence as the lesson was absorbed. He was undoubtedly in a state of severe shock, but in any event he could hardly have justified his sons' behaviour on any grounds. If in his heart he acknowledged that the punishment had been just, though swift and severe, his only response could be that of a humble acceptance of God's will (*cf.* Ps. 39:9).

4–5. For the task of removing the corpses from the tabernacle area, Moses called upon two first cousins of Aaron, Mishael and Elzaphan, about whom nothing else is known other than that they were not priests. No consecrated person could have touched the dead without becoming defiled, and this prohibited the bereaved father from coming into physical contact with his dead sons. Presumably Aaron's cousins were the next-of-kin, and thus able to attend to the burial rites. The corpses were to be buried at some site beyond the Israelite encampment proper, because this would prevent the ceremonial defilement of any who might come upon the burial place by accident. In rocky terrain the grave would be marked by a cairn of stones heaped up over the bodies to prevent them from being mutilated by predatory animals or birds. The dead men were apparently buried wrapped up in their priestly linen tunics (Heb. *keṭōnet*) woven in chequer work (Ex. 28:39), thus indicating that whatever damage the fire had done to them at the time of death, it had not burned off their outer clothing.

6–7. Moses instructed Aaron and his two surviving sons, Eleazar and Ithamar, not to mourn the sudden death of Nadab and Abihu. Allowing long hair to *hang loose* and tearing one's garments were common indications of grief among the Israelites (*cf.* Gn. 37:29–30; 44:13). Other members of the congregation might bewail the calamity in this manner if they so desired, but for the surviving consecrated priests to do so would imply that they were not giving priority to their priestly responsibilities. This would bring upon them the same kind of punishment from God, because it would appear that they were disputing or challenging in some manner the judgment that had been executed. This prohibition must have placed an enormous strain upon the self-control of Aaron and his two surviving sons, particularly because the Israelites responded in a very emotional manner to the incidence of death. The remaining Aaronites were also forbidden to leave the sanctuary area, because they were in a state of ritual consecration. To violate this holy condition would bring death upon them, and God's punitive anger upon the people of Israel. Even in a time of great calamity the priests of the Lord must set an example to the nation of strict obedience to the will of God, and an unswerving adherence to the laws governing the tabernacle rituals. No matter what their personal feelings might be, nothing must be allowed to interfere with the work of the ministry. In fulfilling His Father's will, Jesus Christ permitted no personal considerations of any kind to stand in the way of His redemptive work on Calvary. As such He becomes a model of the dedication and devotion that a Christian is expected to exemplify.

g. Drunken priests prohibited (10:8–11)

8. This section opens with a direct statement from God to Aaron, rather than to Moses, dealing with the drinking of intoxicating beverages. In future, whatever the circumstances, officiating priests were prohibited from imbibing intoxicants prior to undertaking their sacrificial duties in the tabernacle. Disobeying this proscription would result in the death of the offender. Ceremonial holiness and self-discipline were therefore to go hand in hand. The presence of one did not guarantee that the other would be there automatically. The fact that the priest was consecrated according to the divinely revealed rituals did not prevent him from making his own decisions, for better or worse. The development of Christian character requires that the individual's will be surrendered to God's purpose for his life, following the example set by Christ (Jn. 4:34; 5:30). From the foregoing the rabbinic tradition that the two sons of Aaron committed sacrilege by officiating in the tabernacle while under the influence of alcohol seems to have considerable substance.

9. *Wine* and *strong drink* seem to have been the chief beverages for adults in the ancient Near East, since neither tea nor coffee had been introduced into the area at that time. Wine (Heb. *yayin*) was made from the expressed and fermented juice of grapes, which were quite possibly cultivated first in the Ararat region.[38] Strong drink (Heb. *šēkār*) was a term frequently used in association with wine, and both words seem to have described alcoholic drinks of varying strength. Perhaps

---

[38] *Cf.* R. K. Harrison, *NBD*, pp. 1310–1312.

the 'strong drink' was the product of distillation, and as such was a spirituous liquor rather than a fermented beverage such as wine or beer. The latter was brewed from both barley and dates, and was especially favoured by the Egyptians and Philistines. Because supplies of water suitable for human consumption were by no means abundant in the Near East, there seemed to be little else available for drinking apart from alcoholic beverages of one kind or another. Under such conditions it was far from easy to control drunkenness, and only the most disciplined, such as the Nazirites (Nu. 6:3) could abstain from intoxicating drinks for any length of time. In the days of Isaiah the priests seem to have come increasingly under the influence of alcohol (*cf.* Is. 28:7), while the book of Proverbs gives frequent warnings about the dangers of intoxication (*cf.* Pr. 20:1; 23:30–31).

Ethyl alcohol is a substance which does not occur naturally in the constituent tissues of the human body. When ingested it is distributed rapidly through the small intestine, although a small quantity passes from the stomach directly into the bloodstream. A maximum of 10% of the alcohol consumed is disposed of by normal physical processes, the balance being metabolized by certain bodily organs, principally the liver. Those who drink small quantities of alcohol regularly over a prolonged period of time do not seem to experience significant ill effects, probably because when the alocohol has been ingested it is diluted greatly by the body's own fluids as part of the absorption process. Alcohol works directly upon the central nervous system, and while its effect in large and sustained doses is that of a depressant, it can produce certain forms of exitement when ingested in small quantities. In this latter state the loss of inhibitions is clearly noticeable, indicating that the immediate effect of alcohol is upon such advanced mental functions as thinking and making judgments. Since very early times alcohol has been drunk to alleviate tension or grief, in the belief that sorrows could be 'drowned' (*cf.* Pr. 31:6–7), or to act as a carminative in cases of dyspepsia or mild gastritis (*cf.* 1 Tim. 5:23), in addition to serving as the normal beverage in various cultures.[39] Occasionally modern doctors

---

[39] One Bayblonian medical text described an all too common condition of

prescribe oral ingestion of alcohol in something approaching clinical doses, but this practice is strictly a survival from folk medicine.

Plentiful supplies of wine were regarded in the Old Testament as one of God's blessings (*cf.* Gn. 27:28, *etc.*), bringing joy to the heart and relief to the sorrowful (Ps. 104:15; Pr. 31:7). What was frowned upon, however, was the drunkenness that formed an integral element of pagan religious rites in Canaan and elsewhere, and while the Hebrew priests were permitted to drink alcoholic beverages as part of a meal, they were prohibited from emulating the drunken activities of their Canaanite counterparts, or the behaviour of such cultic prophets as the Mesopotamian *muḫḫu*, whose oracular pronouncements seem to have been inspired at least in part by alcohol.

The Nazirites (AV 'Nazarites') reflected ancient practices of separation and self-imposed abstinence in order to perform some special kind of religious duty (Nu. 6:1–21). One of the three main distinguishing features of the Nazirites was complete abstinence from wine and grapes. According to Amos 2:11–12, God had given the Nazirites to apostate Israel as spiritual examples and instructors, but the people had compromised their witness. Another group which seems to have arisen as a protest against the luxury and corruption of eighth- and seventh-century BC Judah was known as the Rechabites, an order founded by Rechab of the tribe of Judah. Rechab's descendant, Jonadab, had imposed a ban upon the drinking of wine, no doubt as part of the family tradition, and the group members were adamant about their position when Jeremiah, at God's command, tested their self-discipline (Je. 35:1–11). The prophet then used their obedience to their ancestor as an example of true fidelity, and contrasted sharply the apostasy and disobedience of the Israelites to their spiritual Father (Je. 35:12–19).

---

the time: 'If a man has drunk too much strong wine, and if his head is confused, if he forgets his words and his speech becomes blurred, if his thoughts wander and his eyes are glassy ...' F. Küchler, *Beiträge zur Kenntnis der Assyrisch-Babylonischen Medizin* (1904), p. 33, quoted by R. C. Thompson, *Encyclopaedia of Religion and Ethics*, 4 (1912), p. 745. The diagnosis indicated by the symptoms should be fairly obvious.

The Christian is similarly warned against the intemperate use of beverage alcohol (1 Cor. 6:10; Eph. 5:18), since the personality must at all times be under Christ's complete control.

10-11. Because the priests have to give counsel affecting the lives of the Israelites, they must be in full possession of their faculties when performing their duties. Nothing must be allowed to interfere with their mental processes, otherwise they will not be able to discern and mediate God's will for His people. If they are under the influence of alcohol, the distinction between holy and unholy will soon become blurred, perhaps to the point of being meaningless. This would defeat an important purpose of the covenant relationship, which was intended in part to make the Israelites the most distinctive group in the ancient world (*cf.* Dt. 7:6; 14:2). Theoretically this distinctiveness would enable the people, when asked, to testify to their faith in the living God of Sinai, who above all other deities in the ancient Near East was unique. Thus the covenant people would be able to witness to those around them as to the true meaning of holiness. As they became progressively conformed to the world of secular culture (*cf.* Rom. 12:2), their distinctiveness disappeared and their witness was compromised correspondingly.

Since the priest was also a teacher of the Torah, it was a matter of great importance for him not merely to know the ceremonial and ritual regulations, but also to be convinced in his own mind of the difference between good and evil, moral and immoral behaviour, the sacred and the profane. Jesus in His teaching had similar advice for His disciples (*cf.* Mt. 7:6), so that, being able to distinguish between holy and common, they would not profane holy things. As the result of a vision (Acts 10:10-16), the apostle Peter was reminded of God's ability to cleanse that which was common, an activity that is characteristic of the Christian gospel. The laws concerning *the unclean and the clean* are given in detail in Leviticus 11 – 15.

The duty of the priest as an instructor of the people in the ways of the Lord is impressed upon Aaron (11). The priest is not a mechanical officiant, programmed to follow automatically a series of cultic regulations, but is a self-conscious person, consecrated to the Lord's service, and charged in consequence with important spiritual responsibilities. Instead of uttering blasphemy or profanity, his lips will teach the knowledge of God. So far from being swayed by the ethos of the pagan world, the priest will delight to do the will of God (Ps. 40:8), and will know God's law so well that he will be able to indicate to others the direction that their lives should take (*cf.* Mal. 2:7). It is thus not by accident that the New Testament uses the concept of priesthood to describe the company of believers in Christ, for it speaks of commitment, dedication, holiness and close, continuing fellowship with the Lord.

h. Rules for eating consecrated food (10:12–20)

12–13. These instructions should be read in conjunction with the events described in chapter 9, since they deal with the disposition of the priestly portions of the offerings. The *cereal offering* was the one mixed with oil (Lv. 9:4), and had been presented at the time of the burnt offering. Because it was *most holy* it had to be eaten at the altar, and being part of the people's offering (Lv. 9:17), it was the perquisite of the priests alone by divine specification.

14–15. In contrast to the restrictions imposed upon the eating of the cereal offering, the priests are allowed to share with the members of their families the breast ('of the special gift' NEB) and thigh ('of the contribution' NEB), presented as peace offerings. These portions were not described as 'most holy' and therefore could be eaten in any suitable clean place. The meat had been consecrated by the special form of presentation before God (see notes on Lv. 9:18–21), and was henceforth to be restricted to the priests. It was appropriate that such choice portions should be the reward of persons who trusted God entirely for their livelihood.

16–20. The reference to *the goat of the sin offering* is obviously to the sacrifice presented by the people at the conclusion of the consecration ceremonies (Lv. 9:3, 15). From this it would appear that the latter had only just been completed before Nadab and Abihu died. The goat was supposed to have been offered according to the procedures of Leviticus 9:8–11, where the parts which were not burned on the bronze altar were disposed of outside the Israelite camp. From the narrative it is not clear whether or not two separate burnings were involved, but there were certainly other ritual irregularities. In Leviticus 9:15, Aaron had presented this offering, and was therefore technically responsible for seeing that the procedures were followed correctly. But it was probably out of respect for the high priest's great sorrow that Moses chastised the two surviving sons. According to the rules laid down in Leviticus 6:26, the sin offering had to be eaten in the precincts of the holy place. What was not stated in that passage was the reason underlying the eating of the offering by the priests, namely that they might *bear the iniquity of the congregation* by atoning for it. It is thus made clear that the priests are mediators of divine grace, assisting the populace to make atonement for sin and then partaking of the offering, indicating its full acceptance by God and the restoration to fellowship of the people. The RSV of verse 18, along with the AV, RV, JB and some other versions, renders the Hebrew as a direct statement, whereas the NEB introduces a conditional element: 'If the blood is not brought within the sacred precincts, you shall eat the sin offering there as I was commanded.' This rendering from the Hebrew is difficult to sustain.

The breach of liturgical procedures by the two sons of Aaron may not have been particularly wilful. Due to the tragedy that had befallen the family so soon after the consecration ceremonies, the surviving sons may have felt that they simply could not eat because of shock and sorrow. They might also have thought that they were tainted in some way by their brothers' offence, and therefore fearful that they too would be struck down suddenly. On the other hand they might have taken their cue from Aaron's own abstinence from the sin offering. Aaron seems to have been completely bewildered by the incidence of the calamity, particularly when procedural rules appeared to have been followed closely (19). On grounds of appropriateness he excused his own behaviour and that of his two surviving sons, an explanation that was acceptable to Moses.

With this tragic event the second major section of Leviticus concludes. The priests have been consecrated, and the three family members who are left are by now painfully aware of the stringent behavioural requirements which govern their office.

The remainder of Leviticus consists of regulations, ceremonial procedures and ritual laws, which were the responsibility of the priesthood to administer. The character of these ordinances shows that all aspects of life under God are sacred.

III. CLEAN AND UNCLEAN DIFFERENTIATED (11:1–15:33)

This section deals with the more mundane issues of daily life which would have an important bearing upon ceremonial purity. For the ancient Hebrews, to be holy, distinctive and priestly in character was not an abstract ideal, but an attainable reality that had practical dimensions in everyday living. The law, therefore, furnishes detailed guidelines for the benefit of the community, so that all possible forms of defilement might be avoided.

a. Clean and unclean species (11:1–47)
Since food is basic to human survival, it is natural for dietary considerations to appear at the forefront of practical concerns. The determining of what is clean or otherwise does not represent the accumulation of folk wisdom, but instead is received directly from God by Moses. As such the enactments carry precisely the same kind of authority as the sacrificial regulations. If the nation is to be a kingdom of priests and a holy people, the observance of these dietary rules is mandatory.

1–4. The list commences on a positive note, dealing with what is permissible for food among the land animals. A simple principle is enunciated which anyone can apply, namely, that whatever animal is completely cloven-footed and chews the cud is suitable for human consumption. Any other mammal is unclean, and must not be eaten. This rule is a comprehensive substitute for the rather more detailed enumeration of species in the corresponding material in Deuteronomy 14. In order to eliminate borderline cases, the law makes it clear that if an animal has only one of the two stated requirements for cleanness, it must not be eaten. Thus the camel is excluded because it does not part the hoof completely, having a pad of tissue on the bottom which gives it excellent traction in sand, but prevents the animal from having a completely divided hoof.

5-8. Other animals declared to be unclean in this way are the rock badger (AV, RV, 'coney'; JB 'hyrax'), the hare and the pig. The rock badger is generally agreed to be the *Hyrax syriacus*, an animal about the size of a rabbit, that has soft pads on its feet enabling it to jump safely among the rocks. Its jaws move in a crosswise manner when eating, giving the impression that it is chewing, although it is not a true ruminant. The camel is a ruminant, but as noted above it is disallowed on other grounds. According to some authorities camel meat is unappetizing, being dry and tough, although it is allegedly esteemed by some Bedouin tribes. The hare could be any one of several members of the family *Leporidae*, perhaps *Lepus syriacus*, occurring in northern Palestine, or possibly *Lepus europaeus connori*,[40] both of which resemble the English hare. As with the coney, the movement of the hare's jaw suggests a chewing (Heb. 'brought up') of the cud, but again it is not a true ruminant. While the rabbit does not have a four-part stomach, it can nevertheless ferment food. By ingesting its soft droppings, it increases its nitrogen and protein balance, and at the same time acquires extra sodium and potassium. The ingestion process provides the rabbit with 100% more riboflavin, 80% more niacin, 160% more pantothenic acid, and a little in excess of 40% more of vitamin B12. The classification of these animals is empirical rather than scientific, but would serve the purpose for which it was intended.

The pig was yet another quadruped which did not satisfy the requirements for cleanness. This animal was known and reared in Mesopotamia from at least 2500 BC, the species in question most probably being *Sus scrofa*. Remains of this variety have also been recovered from Old Stone Age levels of the Mount Carmel caves. This animal, the wild boar, was the ancestor of the domestic pig, and was one of the choice beasts of the hunt in Bronze Age Mesopotamia. The domestic pig appears to have been first reared in Egypt during the Old Kingdom period (*c.* 2700-2200 BC), although the wild boar

40 F. S. Bodenheimer, *Animal and Man in Bible Lands*, pp. 47-48.

was evidently known there from Neolithic times. Pig bones recovered from early levels at Gezer indicate that the animal was reared and eaten by the Neolithic settlers there. Excavations at other Palestinian sites make it clear that the successors to the pre-Semitic population included swine in their livestock.

There seem to be two principal reasons why pigs were raised in the ancient Near East. The first is that when the animals were turned loose in wooded areas to forage for food, they burrowed under the surface of the soil in their search for edible roots and seeds thus helping early settlers to break up the land. Secondly, and of even greater importance, the pig was able to digest and convert into meat the kinds of vegetable matter that other animals found inedible. Thus the pig was an invaluable source of protein, since it came to maturity in a shorter period than most other animals. There appears to have been only a limited use for the skin of pigs in antiquity, so it is evident that the animal was valued for its flesh.

An underground sanctuary at Tell el-Far‘ah (eighteenth to sixteenth centuries BC) contained a number of pig bones that had evidently survived from sacrificial rites. Perhaps the worshippers were being influenced by Babylonian practices, where the flesh of the pig was regarded as sacred, and could therefore be eaten only on certain festive occasions. A similar practice appears to have obtained among the ancient Egyptians also. Although the bones of a pig cannot be used as implements of any kind, some pierced bones were recovered from Taanach and also from Megiddo. To account for their presence it has been suggested that they were either used in Canaanite divinatory rites, or else were worn as amulets to confer a degree of protection from harm upon the wearer. What seems to have been a deliberate attempt to defile the corpses of Hebrews killed in battle came to light when the north-west slope of Lachish was excavated. A battle had occurred there in which between 1500 and 2000 soldiers had met their deaths, either at the hands of the Assyrians in 701 BC or at a subsequent period under the Babylonians. The bodies had been put in an existing tomb, and quantities of animal bones, predominantly those of pigs, were thrown on top of them, evidently as an act of desecration.

The reason why the rules about clean and unclean flesh

were laid down in the manner in which they appear in the Torah has been a topic of discussion for many centuries. Clean and unclean animals as such were distinguished even before the flood (Gn. 7:2–3, 8–9), but only in Leviticus 11 and Deuteronomy 14 were the various kinds specified. The concern in the present section between clean and unclean is with what may be eaten for food without any harm or penalty being incurred. The purpose of the regulations has been considered by various authors in three distinct ways. The first saw the intent of the directives as a conscious effort to avoid in Israelite life any semblance of the pagan sacrificial rites such as those that were associated with the consumption of the animal's flesh in Mesopotamia, Egypt or Canaan.[41] If this was the sole purpose of the differentiation between clean and unclean species, it is nowhere mentioned in the narratives, nor is it implied in any way, since dietary rather than sacrificial considerations are the predominant concern of the passage. Nor does such an understanding explain why the bull, a prominent feature of pagan religious rites in Egypt and Canaan, was not prohibited to the Israelites.

The second suggested purpose of the legislation as it has been preserved has envisaged the perpetuation of the separateness of the Israelites in dietary as well as in ethical and spiritual matters, presumably with the aim of relating one to the other. Adherence to a particular regimen of diet has for millennia constituted a mark of distinctiveness among religious people, and even in modern society it confers something of a special status upon an individual, as many adherents of 'diet plans' are well aware. To be forbidden to indulge in certain foods because of religious considerations would emphasize for the Israelites the need to obey God's directions implicitly, while reinforcing in their minds the conviction that they were distinctive as the people of God. This spiritual status would furnish them with an opportunity of witnessing to the nature of their faith, if anyone were to enquire as to the rationale of their behaviour. In the event, the latter consideration was never more than a possibility in the pre-exilic period, since conformity to Canaanite ways of life rather than the evangelizing of the

[41] *Cf.* M. Noth, *The Laws in the Pentateuch and Other Studies* (1966), pp. 56 ff.

pagan Near East proved to be the direction that was generally followed. Even when distinctiveness was restored to the nation in the post-exilic period, the spiritual energies of the people seemed to be concentrated inwardly on the perpetuation of a society governed by Mosaic law, and not outwardly on the wider prophetic task of being a spiritual light to the nations.

A third explanation of the significance of the distinction between clean and unclean has to do with specifically hygienic and dietary considerations. This approach is sometimes depreciated as being a reflection of current occidental preoccupation with matters of personal health, but since the passage under consideration deals exclusively with flesh which may or may not be eaten as food, questions relating to issues of hygiene and diet are obviously of great importance here. According to this approach, clean animals are comparatively safe as sources of food, whereas unclean ones are to be avoided because of the possibility that their flesh might transmit infection. These concerns have been justified amply by subsequent studies in the general area of preventive medicine. For example, it has been found that the hare and the coney carry in the bloodstream a virus which, when ingested by human beings, can result in a disease known as tularemia. North American rabbits and particularly hares have been discovered to be carriers of the virus, the pathological consequences of which include chills, fever, general malaise and swollen glands. By itself it is not a fatal disease, but it is certainly debilitating, and if complicated by other ailments could well have a serious outcome.[42]

Comparatively little is known about the effects of the camel's flesh upon the human body, apart from the fact that it is supposedly rather unpalatable to many occidental eaters. The milk of the female camel, like that of other lactating animals, was a valuable source of nourishment in the Middle Bronze Age (*cf.* Gn. 32:15), but even here it would be necessary for the milk to be drained into clean containers and drunk before it became sour, otherwise it could prove very

---

[42] For a description of a tularemia epidemic in Vermont, USA, in 1968, see L. S. Young *et al.*, *The New England Journal of Medicine*, Vol. 280, No. 23, 1969, pp. 1253–1260, and accompanying bibliography.

upsetting to the digestive system, especially where children were concerned.

As a possible source of food, however, it was the pig that presented the greatest threat to health. It is now known that the pig is the intermediate host for several parasitic organisms, some of which can result in tapeworm infestation. One of these worms, the *Taenia solium,* grows to about 2.5 m in length, and is found in poorly cooked pork containing the organism *Cysticercus cellulosae.* An unwelcome complication of this condition occurs when nodules form in the brain to produce attacks that resemble epilepsy.

Another infecting agent, the *Trichinella spirilis,* is a small organism occurring in raw or poorly cooked pork or sausages. The disease which results from this agent is trichinosis, and is marked initially by fever, gastro-intestinal disturbance and general malaise. In a developed state there occur oedema of the face and lower limbs, changes in the white blood cell count, an urticarial rash, and pains in various muscles. If the affliction progresses to the encapsuled stage, small knotlike swellings form in the muscles to cause a good deal of discomfort. Yet another disease that is the result of eating improperly prepared pork or pork products has been discovered in recent years. Called toxoplasmosis, it resembles pneumonia and is the result of infection by a vigorous organism that is found in a cyst-like form and is resistant to freezing, the action of gastric juices, or the normal range of cooking temperatures.

Apart from the possibility of contracting food poisoning from eating pork, it is not uncommon for certain persons to have an allergic reaction after ingesting pork or its by-products. To imagine that modern cooking methods have eliminated the risk of such infections entirely is to be misguided. The fact is that there is no 'safe' temperature at which pork can be cooked to ensure that parasitic organisms are killed,[43] and even if prolonged cooking is undertaken, it

---

[43] The author once had a student whose teenage son contracted a tapeworm. Exhaustive investigation revealed that the infecting organism had originated in a tin of a popular North American brand of cooked pork shoulder. This product had been processed under properly controlled conditions at high temperatures, but even these precautions were insufficient to kill the parasitic organism present in the meat.

generally renders the meat tough and tasteless. Nor can western methods of slaughtering pigs guarantee that the carcass will be safe for human consumption, since the toxoplasmosis organism, for example, survives without effort the hygienic procedures prescribed by the various food laws. It is sometimes maintained that wild pigs are much less liable than domestic ones to be the intermediate host of parasitic bodies, but at best this is a rather empirical judgment and cannot be relied upon in practice. Interestingly enough, the liver of the pig is the only kind of animal liver to be completely free from germs, making it the only part of the pig safe enough for humans to eat.

The separation of clean from unclean meats should not be taken to imply that the true ruminants are completely free from parasitic organisms. Thus the ox is the intermediate host for a worm known as *Taenia saginata*, which has about 2000 segments and can grow to 6 m in length. The emphasis upon not touching the carcasses (8) of the unclean animals is very important for hygienic living. The transmission of infection from decaying animals through contagion is fairly obvious, but sometimes parasitic worms can be acquired from nothing more sinister than close contact with some animals, including pigs. In this connection the latter are intermediate hosts of a small tapeworm, the *Echinococcus Granulosus*, which in a larval or cystic form results in small tumours in the brain, lungs and other organs.

9–12. Marine species are also to be differentiated in terms of clean and unclean as with animals, so that the Israelites would know what was permissible for food. Clean species are those that have fins and scales, whether such fish occur in salt or fresh-water sources. The clean varieties mentioned usually swim at various depths in the water, whereas the unclean species tend to have their habitat in shallow water. Unclean fish would include the edible crustaceae such as lobster, crab, shrimps and similar species that feed upon decaying flesh where it happens to be available, and can transmit infection readily.[44] Some of the warnings given above about clean meats

44 Bilharziasis (urinary schistosomiasis), though known among Egyptian and other Near Eastern river cultures from a remote period, has become a particular menace to health in Egypt since the construction of the Aswan High

are appropriate here also. However careful one might be in the preparation and serving of the edible crustaceae, there can be no guarantee that the food will not produce such adverse effects as allergic reactions of varying severity, or even more serious complications involving food poisoning or parasitic infestation. Even the 'clean' species of fish are only relatively so, since tape worms can be contracted from eating raw or imperfectly cooked varieties. Thus the parasitic worm *Diphyllobothrium Latum* frequently grows to about 24 m in length, having as many as 3,000 segments, and the infecting organism occurs in many species of fish, clean and unclean alike. Nevertheless, if various kinds of fish form part of a diet, those with fins and scales present the least potential hazard to health. Once more the differentiation is empirical, but it is nevertheless suited admirably to the needs of those for whom the regulations were made, and who, like a great many moderns, might scarcely know one variety of fish from another. Thus recognition of the forbidden species by sight alone would enable the Israelites to be healthy in body and pure in ceremonial or ritual matters. The effects of contact with dead and putrefying fish were not defiling in nature, as were those associated with the carcasses of unclean animals. Perhaps this was because blood was not involved to any significant extent.

13–20. A list of unclean birds is given for the guidance of the people (*cf.* Dt. 14:11–18), and it names some species as well as individual birds. Many of those mentioned were birds of prey, or birds which fed on carrion. The *eagle* was most probably the powerful griffon vulture (*Gyps fulvus* L.), a distinguished-looking bird with a head of cream-coloured down which gave it a bald appearance. The *ossifrage* (NEB mg.)

Dam. This disease is contracted through the eating of infected snails and the drinking of water contaminated by trematodes (*flukes*). Before the dam was built the rise and fall of the Nile cleansed the irrigation channels and killed off the infected snails periodically. Now they remain in stagnant water for most of the year, and the peasants who eat the snails are much more prone to infection than formerly. The disease, which is also known as schistosomiasis, occurs in forms which affect the intestines and urinary system, as well as the spleen and liver, in a painful and disabling manner.

and *osprey* were related species, the former being an obsolete name for the latter. NEB reads 'black vulture' and 'bearded vulture' respectively, while JB has 'griffon' and 'osprey'. Two species of *kite*, a red and a black variety, were known in ancient Palestine but were mostly migratory. As many as ten species of *falcon* also existed there in Bible times. The *ostrich* (NEB 'desert owl') is more correctly translated 'owl' (so AV) since a bird of prey seems indicated, although ostriches were familiar sights in the ancient Near East and were hunted eagerly.[45] The *night-hawk* (NEB 'short-eared owl'; JB 'screech owl'), a bird of uncertain identification, was probably a species of owl, while the *sea gull* (AV 'cuckow'; RV 'seamew') may have been the long-eared owl (so NEB). The *owl* of verse 17 was perhaps the tawny owl (NEB), while *cormorant* (NEB 'fisher-owl') seems to be a reasonably correct rendering of a rather obscure term. It is clear that a bird which fished in marshes or along the coastline of the ocean is meant, since it is grouped with other marsh birds such as the *ibis* (AV 'great owl'; NEB 'screech-owl'), the *water hen* (AV 'swan'; NEB 'little owl') and the pelican, the latter being a bird which migrated annually to Palestine from its winter home in central Africa. The *stork* (*Ciconia alba*) was another familiar migrant, as was the heron (NEB 'cormorant'), of which there were several varieties. The *hoopoe* (AV 'lapwing') was known in Palestine from early times, and its elegant appearance contrasted sharply with the insanitary conditions which marked its nesting place. The *bat* was included at the end of the list of birds, although technically it is a mammal. About twenty varieties of this creature have been found in Palestine. It has to be remembered that some of the terminology in this list is quite obscure, to say the least, and therefore certain of the translations are understandably conjectural and possibly quite erroneous.

20–23. The unclean winged insects were not specified in the manner of the mammals and birds, but were classified by the description of those that *go upon all fours*. This phrase can hardly describe insects as having four legs, since the *Insectae* as a class normally have six legs. The reference is evidently to their movements, which resemble the creeping or running of

45 *Cf.* A. Parmalee, *All the Birds of the Bible* (1959), p. 141.

the four-footed animals. The clean insects are members of the group *Orthoptera*, and could be identified from the jointed hind legs, which are longer than the others and enable the insect to leap about (21). It is very difficult to identify the species mentioned here, although some translators attempt the task. Thus JB reads 'migratory locust, solham, hargol and hagab locusts', the last three terms merely transliterating the Hebrew. The *bald locust* (NEB 'long-headed') may belong to the *Tryxaline* species, which have long smooth heads giving the appearance of baldness. The *cricket* (AV 'beetle'; NEB 'green locust') is not easy to identify, but with the *grasshopper* (NEB 'desert locust') appears to be some variety of locust.

All insects that did not jump about because they did not possess the elongated hind legs of the locust family were to be regarded as detestable. This unclean group would include all those insects that fed upon filth, rubbish or carrion, and were therefore potential transmitters of disease.

As a food, locusts have been eaten in the Near East for millennia. A royal banquet scene from the palace of Ashurbanipal (*c.* 669–627 BC), the last great Assyrian king, depicted servants bringing locusts on sticks for the guests to eat. Some modern African tribes derive much of their protein from boiled, roasted or pulverized locusts, and the insects can still be found in bazaars in some Arab lands, devoid of their wings and ready to be eaten. While somewhat deficient in vitamin content, locusts contain upwards of 50% of protein and as much as 20% of fat, along with mineral salts and some calories. Poor people, or desert hermits such as John the Baptist (Mt. 3:4), could enjoy a reasonably balanced diet by eating locusts along with honey. It must be remarked again that these rules relating to clean and unclean species have dietary considerations in view primarily, and the simple though entirely rational character of the rules enables those who are familiar with them to recognize harmful kinds of potential food quite readily.

24–28. Defilement thorough contact with dead animals (*carcass*) is of concern here, since working with animals such as camels that were unfit for food did not result in uncleanness. Any person who became defiled through touching the bodies of unclean animals had to *wash his clothes* and remain defiled until the evening, when a new day commenced. At that time he would wash his body also, and until this had been done he could not participate in tabernacle worship or in any personal sacrificial rites. Clothes that had been in contact with such carcasses had to be washed also, for they too were defiled. Clearly the legislation is aimed at the control of disease by minimizing the possibility of infection through germs, viruses and other organisms that might be associated with putrefying animal carcasses. This is an especially important health precaution in tropical and semi-tropical climates, and is typical of the prophylactic emphasis of the Mosaic health regulations.

Attention to one's state of physical well-being is a matter of some concern if for the Christian the body is indeed the temple of the Holy Spirit (1 Cor. 6:19). Even more desirable is the necessity for the believer to be free from dead works to serve the living God (*cf.* Heb. 9:14). A celebrated example of one who touched the carcass of an animal that went on its *paws* (27) is seen in Judges 14:8-9. Such animals were unsuitable for food when alive, and produced ritual uncleanness if they were touched when dead. Cats and dogs would come under this heading, and hence would be eaten only under the greatest possible conditions of deprivation, if at all. There are no references to cats in Scripture, and in consequence it is difficult to estimate the extent to which cats were domesticated by the Hebrews. Such animals were a popular feature of ancient Egyptian life, however, being sometimes used by their owners as fowlers during game-hunting in papyrus marshes. The Egyptian goddess, Bastet, usually represented in the form of a cat, may originally have had a lioness, not a tame cat, as her cult animal.[46] While dogs were domesticated at a comparatively early period, particularly in Egypt, they were generally despised as outcasts and unclean animals in Bible times. Savage, ravenous and ruthless by nature, they lived by scavenging and prowling around, looking for prey. Of the forty or so references to dogs in Scripture, few are polite and none is complimentary (*cf.* Pss. 22:16; 59:6; Is. 56:10-11; Je. 15:3; Rev. 22:15).

---

[46] J. Černý, *Ancient Egyptian Religion* (1952), p. 25.

29-38. In addition to the detestable insects of verses 20–23, several kinds of creeping or *swarming things* are described specifically as unclean for food while alive, and defiling to the touch when dead. As with the insects there are problems of identification, but in general the list seems to be that of reptiles, with the occasional rodent included. The *weasel* (NEB 'mole-rat'; JB 'mole') may be correctly identified, since such animals were common in ancient Palestine, while the *mouse* (NEB 'jerboa') is more probably the rat, and is thus rendered in JB. The *great lizard* (AV 'tortoise'; LXX 'land crocodile'; NEB 'thorn-tailed lizard') was perhaps some species of lizard or gecko, while the *land crocodile* (NEB 'sand-gecko'; JB 'koah') was doubtless another of the numerous varieties of lizard. The *chameleon* (30) was well known in ancient Palestine, and if the translation is correct this is the only reference to it in Scripture.

These animals when dead defile anything they touch, and such articles or objects have to be soaked in water to remove any impurities, and be regarded as unclean until the evening, by which time any infectious organisms should have dissipated with the drying process and exposure to sunlight. If an earthen vessel was contaminated by the presence of a dead animal or reptile, it had to be broken, since it would be very difficult to remove all germs from the surface, especially if the latter was unglazed. There can be no doubt that hygienic factors are the only considerations here, since a variety of serious diseases could be spread by infected or contaminated containers or food. The scriptural correlation between physical and spiritual health is not always either noticed or followed by the Christian. To do God's work best, and to be an example of Christ's saving and healing power, the believer has to maximize the potential of body and spirit, and this requires careful attention to both aspects of the human personality.

Even cooking equipment (35), such as ovens or stoves, was defiled by the carcasses of the unclean species. The *stove* (Heb. *kîrayim*) or range was an earthenware potstand with two compartments in which cooking pots could be placed. The only exception to the rules about contamination consisted of the *spring* or *cistern* (36), the latter being an artificially constructed container for domestic water supplies. Numerous examples have been recovered from Palestinian sites, indicating that by the Iron Age the cisterns were lined with plaster. Similar structures were also used for the underground storage of grain. The legislation provided that, where water collected naturally, it was not polluted by the carcasses of unclean species of animals or insects, although whoever or whatever touched the carcass was thereby rendered unclean. Presumably the fact that such water would be in a fairly continuous state of movement, thereby dissipating any sources of potential or actual infection, would account for this exception to an otherwise stringent and highly desirable hygienic regulation. Seed that was ready for sowing was not polluted when in contact with the carcasses of unclean species as long as the seed remained dry. If it became wet when it was contaminated, it became unclean because the moisture, whether water or some excretion from the defiling agent, would act as a vehicle for infection.

39–41. Contact with the carcasses of clean animals that had died from natural causes was also forbidden, otherwise temporary defilement would result. Eating such potentially dangerous meat was strictly prohibited for the Israelites on ceremonial grounds (Dt. 14:21), although it was quite permissible for aliens and foreigners to purchase and consume such meat if they so desired.

42–45. This section comments further on the dietary regulations of verses 1–23, and enlarges the class of the *swarming things* to include insects, snakes, lizards, worms, caterpillars and the like. All of these would be well known to the Israelites, and therefore extreme care was necessary if defilement was to be avoided. The rationale of these laws concerning cleanness and uncleanness is now made explicit. The Israelites are instructed not to have any dealings with anything that would make them impure. Instead, they were to concentrate upon a positive approach to living, the principal feature of which was a conscious attempt to imitate the holiness of the covenant God. In a characteristically propositional manner the Lord informs His people of His high moral and ethical character, and demands that they consecrate themselves accordingly to His service. He also reminds them of the great deliverance which He achieved for them at the time of the exodus, and makes it clear that the Israelites are to be a distinctive spiritual body, of which He is the undisputed head. Holiness must therefore be the watchword of personal and national life alike.

While these laws go into great detail about the day-to-day existence of God's people, they also have an important spiritual purpose. They demonstrate that all aspects of life come within God's purview, since He is concerned both with the material and spiritual well-being of His followers. There is thus no detail of daily living that is too small to be regulated by the will of God (1 Cor. 10:31). To become holy involves a complete submission of one's total personality to the sanctifying work of the Holy Spirit. Sanctification cannot be acquired through periodic contact with 'sacred' objects, but is essentially a matter of personal spiritual growth, requiring a great deal of consistent effort. But the same God who delivered His ancient people from Egypt, and who raised Christ from the dead, can empower the Christian to follow a life of holiness as a member of that great community of which Jesus is the head (*cf.* Eph. 1:22; 4:15; Col. 1:18). Translating these lofty spiritual concepts into everyday life quite naturally involves the distinction between clean and unclean, as well as a positive emphasis upon individual well-being, provided for in the dietary enactments. God's people must be seen to be distinctive in their way of life, and as free as possible from any evil pollution of body or spirit.

46–47. These verses summarize the purpose of the legislation under two main headings, and are somewhat reminiscent of a colophon in that the 'title' of the chapter ('These are the living things which you may eat') is repeated in verse 47, making the entire chapter a complete legislative unit. The prophylactic character of the hygienic enactments is unique in the ancient world, and the underlying principles form an important part of modern preventive medical practice.

b. Purification following childbirth (12:1–8)

Some commentators have found difficulty with this section of purification laws, since it appears to designate as unclean the act of childbirth that resulted from God's command to be fruitful and multiply (Gn. 1:28). Since children were regarded as a divine heritage and gift (Ps. 127:3), and a fruitful woman was esteemed as blessed of God (*cf.* Ps. 128:3), it would appear somewhat surprising for the birth of a child to be regarded as a circumstance that was sinful, and therefore needed atonement. The legislation, however, deals with the secretions that occur at parturition, and it is these that make the mother unclean. Thus the chapter should be read within the context of chapter 15, which also deals with bodily secretions.

1–4. When a woman *bears a male child* she is unclean with respect to her home for a seven-day period, as was the case with her menstruation. On the eighth day the child was circumcised (*cf.* Gn. 21:4), but another thirty-three days had to elapse before the mother could participate once more in the worship of the sanctuary. Circumcision had been instituted by God as a sign of His covenant with Abraham (Gn. 17:12). It was also practised for different reasons among the west Semitic peoples, including the Ammonites, Moabites, Arabs and Edomites, but it did not occur among the Philistines, Canaanites, Assyrians or Babylonians. The rite was normally performed with a flint knife by the father, but on occasions the mother officiated (Ex. 4:25). By this act the male child was formally initiated into the body of the covenant people. In the Christian dispensation, baptism has been regarded by many as constituting the New Testament equivalent of circumcision, but the parallels are too superficial and narrow to be entirely convincing or valid.

Circumcision *on the eighth day* is ideal medically, since after that period the nervous and vascular development of the child makes resection a more painful affair. Furthermore, newborn children are susceptible to haemorrhage up to the fifth day of life, due to inadequate levels in the body of vitamin K and prothrombin, both of which are important elements in the clotting process. By the eighth day the prothrombin level has stabilized at 100%, making it a suitable time for circumcision. Certain medical benefits are also held to accrue to those who practise circumcision. For example, the resection removes the cause of phimosis, a painful and embarrassing condition, and prevents any accumulation of smegma which would normally be deposited between the *corona glandis* and the prepuce. *Smegma praeputii*, produced by adult males, has been found to be a powerful carcinogenic agent, and is frequently blamed for the incidence of uterine cancer. Circumcised males supposedly experience a more controlled rate of sexual excitation than others, and are seldom, if ever, troubled by the rare cancer of the male organ.

The act of circumcision did not purify the child, since the infant was already ceremonially clean when born. The purification which the mother underwent was strictly the result of the secretions which accompanied the birth. The discharges involve tissue debris, mucus and blood, and are known as the lochia. Two stages are normally experienced after parturition, the first (*lochia cruenta*) being stained with blood, while the second (*lochia alba*) has a paler appearance and is free from blood. Unless there is some retention of the lochia in the uterus, the discharge is often of comparatively short duration, but it can last as long as six weeks in certain circumstances. The laws of purification after childbirth thus cover the maximum amount of time that the lochia could be expected to continue.

5. When a female child was born, the mother was ceremonially unclean for twice as many days as were required for a male. No reason is given for this disparity, and explanations that suggest the influence of pre-Israelite taboos or the fear of attack by demons[47] are entirely speculative and devoid of any actual basis. The suggestion that the female foetus was considered more defiling than that of a male is not borne out by the nature of the purificatory rites, which were the same for both male and female offspring. Perhaps the difference has to do with the comparative status of the sexes in a patriarchal society (*cf.* Lv. 27:2-7), and the fact of the female child's future menstrual functions. The presence of blood in the discharge is clearly the defiling agent and merits special procedures, since blood and life are intimately connected in the levitical legislation (Lv. 17:11). The cleansing ceremonies would give proper dignity to the purely hygienic aspects of the post-natal period.

6-8. The completion of the purification was to be marked by sacrificial offerings, which are given here in a reverse order from that prescribed in the list of sacrifices in earlier chapters.

---

47 *Cf.* C. J. Vos, *Woman in Old Testament Worship* (1968), pp. 62-69; K. Elliger, *Leviticus* (1966), pp. 167-168.

A *young pigeon or a turtledove* comprised the sin offering, which was primarily of a purificatory nature, while the *burnt offering* was a year-old lamb, and this when sacrificed by the officiating priest restored the new mother to the fellowship of the holy place. The woman who could not afford a choice lamb had to provide two doves or two young pigeons for the sin and burnt offerings. It was important for the Israelites to have a choice between these two closely related species, since the former was migratory (*cf.* Song 2:12), spending its winters in Africa and occurring in Palestine only between April and October. By contrast, the nests of the pigeon could be found locally at any time of the year, and so these birds were suitable for sacrifices occuring during the winter. When Joseph and Mary came to the temple for the purification ceremonies at the time that Jesus was presented, they followed the ancient rituals prescribed in Leviticus (*cf.* Lk. 2:22–24). The mention of birds in the narrative indicates that our Lord's parents were poor at the time, otherwise they would have provided a lamb.

There is little doubt that this chapter takes extremely seriously the birth of a child. For the women of antiquity the occasion was frequently fraught with danger, but when mother and child survived the ordeal it was a time of happiness in the family. The agonies of childbirth would certainly impress themselves upon all who witnessed them, and would help to deepen the parents' own sense of responsibility towards each other and their offspring.

c. Regulations involving leprosy (13:1 – 14:57)

An extremely important section of Leviticus deals with the topic of what is rendered in most English versions as 'leprosy'.[48] The Hebrew term *sāraʿat* comes from a root meaning 'to become diseased in the skin', and is a generic rather than a specific description. In Old Testament usage it was extended to include mould or mildew in fabrics, as well as mineral eruptions on the walls of buildings, and possibly dry rot in the fabric of such structures. In the LXX the Hebrew was rendered by the Greek word *lepra*, which itself appears to have

---

[48] An experimental translation of Leviticus 13 into semi-technical English is contained in Appendix A, p. 241.

been rather indefinite in nature and meaning. The Greek medical authors used the word to describe a disease that made the surface of the skin flaky or scaly, while Herodotus mentioned it in connection with an affliction known as *leukē*, a type of cutaneous eruption which seems to have been the same as the Greek *elephantiasis*, and thus similar to modern clinical leprosy (Hansen's disease). The Romans adopted the Greek word *lepra*, and seem to have used it both to designate the disease known to them as *elephantiasis Graecorum*, and, in somewhat later Christian circles, to describe the affliction in Leviticus, as in the Vulgate. There is obviously considerable confusion in terminology, and a breadth of usage which increases the difficulty in understanding the meaning of the original Hebrew term. If its root, *ṣrʿ*, is related to the Akkadian *sinnītu* ('eruption'), it would describe any form of cutaneous lesion, of which clinical leprosy would be one. Since *ṣāraʿat* is descriptive of a class of ailments, it is important to keep the designation as broad as possible and to include Hansen's disease, which some modern diagnosticians seem bent on excluding.[49]

Deciding upon a word, or a group of words, with which to translate *ṣāraʿat* is the principal problem here, as it is with the other diseased conditions described. The Hebrew is technical in character, and the passing of time has obliterated the original meaning of the terms used. This is true, however, of other comparable ancient Near Eastern medical texts, so the difficulty is not unique to Scripture. Unfortunately no translation is particularly satisfactory, whether it be *hautkrankheit* ('skin disease'), or the NEB 'malignant skin-disease.' The latter is a particularly unhappy choice, since 'malignant' can hardly describe accurately some of the cutaneous conditions mentioned in this section. Perhaps 'suspected skin disease' would be a better rendering for the purposes of the NEB, since it would avoid prejudging the nature of the diagnosis. Anything that is malignant is either resistant to treatment, has a tendency to recur and become degenerate, or occurs in an already serious

---

[49] *E.g.*, R. G. Cochrane, *Biblical Leprosy: A Suggested Interpretation* (1961), p. 3; S. G. Browne, *Leprosy in the Bible* (1970), pp. 5–6; J. Wilkinson, *Scottish Journal of Theology*, 31, 1978, pp. 153–166

form. None of these three qualifications can be applied properly to an ailment such as ringworm or psoriasis, both of which seem to be described in this chapter. The present writer prefers to use the traditional term 'leprosy' for *sāra'at*, regarding it as a general designation of a class of skin afflictions of varying severity. An analogy can be drawn between this and the use of 'cancer' as a pathological designation. 'Cancer' is actually a lay term employed to describe malignant growths, but doctors think more specifically of two principal types of neoplastic tumours according to the site and the kind of tissue involved. As a result there are numerous specific forms of 'cancer', some of which respond to treatment while others remain intractable, but all of them can be covered acceptably both for the layman and the doctor by the one generic term.

Of the ailments to be discussed, clinical leprosy has a long history, being supposedly in evidence in India and China by about 4000 BC. The disease was known in Mesopotamia in the third millennium BC, and at least one instance of leprosy has been demonstrated on an Egyptian mummy. One would have expected to find many other instances of leprosy in Egypt if the statement of Lucretius is to be believed that the disease originated there. Some authorities have adduced reasons for believing that the mummified Egyptian leper had originally been an immigrant from Syria-Palestine. It thus appears that clinical leprosy was familiar to the ancient Near Eastern peoples by the beginning of the second millennium BC, and thus there is no ground for the supposition, common to certain authors, that leprosy was probably unknown among the Hebrews until they had been settled in Canaan for some time.

Hansen's disease, to use the modern euphemism for leprosy, is the result of infection by a tiny bacillus, *Mycobacterium leprae*, which Hansen discovered in 1871. The disease has a slow onset, and has been described in terms of two principal types. The nodular or lepromatous form is characterized by the emergence of spongy lumps in the skin and a general thickening of local cutaneous tissues. Where the lumps occur painless suppurating ulcers sometimes form, a condition which is usually the result of neglect. The mucous membranes of the nose and throat frequently exhibit degeneration also, and in its more advanced stages the disease often involves internal organs. The anaesthetic or tuberculoid variety of leprosy is less severe, and is marked by a degeneration of nerves in the skin. This results in the appearance of discoloured or depigmented patches of skin in which there is no sensation at all. Ulcers sometimes occur on these anaesthetic areas, and in severe cases portions of the extremities necrose and fall off (*lepra mutilans*). Despite the sometimes forbidding appearance of those afflicted with this form of leprosy, it seems to be virtually non-infective. It is chronic in nature, and has been known to last as long as thirty years. Unfortunately this kind of leprosy can develop into the more serious nodular form. Sometimes a third variety of Hansen's disease is described in medical text books, consisting of all the foregoing symptoms combined in varying degrees. Chaulmoogra oil, derived from the seed of an Indian shrub, was the medication favoured for leprosy and some other chronic dermatoses until the advent of antibiotics. Astonishing therapeutic success has been reported in connection with the use of thalidomide.

1. Diagnosis and treatment of skin afflictions (1–46)

1. The procedures to be undertaken are revealed by God to Moses and Aaron, and are not the product of folklore or adaptations of pagan therapeutic procedures. As with some of the narratives dealing with the sacrifices, the descriptions of clinical cases tend to follow a stereotyped form. This actually constitutes the clinical method to be adopted by the Hebrew priest-physicians when examining persons exhibiting various forms of skin disease. The diagnosis must not be intuitive in nature, but must be the product of certain standard examining procedures of a strictly rational order. Initially the patient would present certain symptoms such as a rash, a burn, or a skin eruption, after which the priest-physician made a visual examination. His diagnosis had to be based upon the presence of specific disease symptoms, and once he was satisfied that such was the case he prescribed a form of treatment. This did not involve the use of therapeutic substances in any way, but required a declaration of cleanness or uncleanness for suspected persons, and for clothing or property necessitated certain sanitary precautions. If the patient did not exhibit the disease in a sufficiently developed form, he could be quarantined for a period of time until a proper diagnosis could be established.

2. Symptoms that would lead a person to seek the aid of the priest would include any suspicious swelling of the skin (Heb. *śᵉʾēt;* LXX *oulē*), a rash, spotting or some other skin lesion (Heb. *sappaḥaṯ;* LXX *sēmasia*) or a swollen spot, whether pinkish or red (Heb. *baheret;* LXX *tēlaugēs*). When any one of these was present it could be the precursor of a variety of ailments, of which Hansen's disease could be one. Both forms of clinical leprosy commence with pink or white discoloured areas of skin, and these frequently occur on the head. A fairly well-developed pathology seems to be indicated by the phrase *it turns into a leprous disease*, and this would facilitate diagnosis. If the ancient 'leper' was at all similar to many moderns, he would delay being examined by the priest-physician as long as he could, if only because he did not want to hear the devastating news about his condition.

3–4. The examining priest would be looking for changes in the cuticle or epidermis, including the possibility of subcutaneous penetration and a change in the colour of any hair in the vicinity of the eruption. If these conditions existed, the sufferer was pronounced leprous and unclean. But if the glossy area of the skin was pinkish-white instead of being inflamed, and if there was no subcutaneous penetration and no depigmentation of local hair, the priest placed the person in quarantine for a week. The Hebrew priest-physicians appear to have been the first in the ancient world to isolate persons suspected of infectious or contagious diseases. This procedure would allow a reasonable incubation period for most of the afflictions dealt with in this chapter, although it certainly would not be long enough for clinical leprosy, which develops more slowly. It would be a suitable interval, however, in instances where the sufferer had not consulted a priest until the prodromal symptoms were well advanced. In the ancient world, where even the physicians were generally abysmally ignorant of the nature and cause of disease, many sick persons would neglect their symptoms until a cure was impossible. Thus king Hezekiah of Judah would most probably have died from a carbuncle if Isaiah had not intervened (2 Ki. 20:7; Is. 38:21). Symptoms are warnings that all is not well with the body, and those who extend the attributes of wholeness and holiness to the physical aspect of personality will not neglect indications of somatic disorder. Jesus Christ, the holy Son of God, brings healing to the body as well as the spirit, since His work of salvation involves the entire person.

5–8. After a week in quarantine the patient was re-examined, and if the disease seemed to be checked a further quarantine period was ordered, lasting seven days. If after that time the affected area was resuming its normal appearance, the priest would declare the person clean and diagnose *an eruption*. This condition could include anything from a maculo-papular rash to the wheals of an allergic reaction. The patient could then resume normal life after all clothing had been washed. In the event of a relapse, the sufferer submitted to re-examination, and if the lesion was found to have spread in the skin itself, leprosy was diagnosed. The extent to which the cutaneous tissues had been infiltrated was basic to the recognition of clinical leprosy, and in proper diagnostic fashion other pathological possibilities were included in order that they might be excluded ultimately in favour of the considered diagnosis.

9–11. Where a chronic form of leprosy was suspected, an examination by the priest was a necessity. If it revealed a distinct white vesicle in the skin that had turned any associated hair white, and if the lesion was characterized by ulcerating tissue, the diagnosis of leprosy was confirmed without the necessity of a quarantine period being imposed upon the sufferer. An instance of well-established (RSV, NEB, NIV 'chronic') Hansen's disease seems indicated here, since the hairs growing in an anaesthetic patch of skin on a patient's body break off, or split and become depigmented.[50] Furthermore, one of the early symptoms of *elephantiasis Graecorum* is the development of shiny white vesicles which rupture and discharge a white-coloured substance. Nodular or lepromatous leprosy would probably constitute the disease in question, which could be recognized at that stage of development. It is important for the reader to bear in mind that advanced forms of the disease are not described in this chapter, since the

[50] A. R. Short, *The Bible and Modern Medicine* (1953), p. 78.

predominant concern of the legislation is with early diagnosis and isolation, that the community might be protected to the fullest extent.

12–17. A different type of *ṣāra'aṯ* involved a cutaneous condition which covered the person's body from head to foot. Its distinctive feature was not cutaneous penetration by swellings or sores, but rather what seems to have been a depigmentation of the skin over most of the body. No ulceration, rash or lesion was associated with this particular form of skin condition. The affliction which corresponds most closely to these symptoms is vitiligo (*acquired leucoderma*), in which patches of skin lose their normal colour and become white. The condition is due to a simple loss of pigment in the skin, and occurs more frequently in black races than among whites. Apart from the presence of ivory-coloured or white patches, the skin is normal, and this condition would therefore justify a diagnosis of *clean* (13). A great many skin diseases exhibit various degrees of ulceration, but any person with vitiligo who developed sores subsequent to his discharge by the priest was immediately suspected of having a more serious ailment. The presence of ulcers rendered the person unclean and resulted in a diagnosis of *ṣāra'aṯ*. If the sores healed quickly, however, and the flesh assumed its normal tinge, the condition was regarded as benign and the diseased person was once again pronounced clean. The care and concern which are required to be exhibited by the priest-physician where individual well-being is involved are noteworthy features of this hygienic legislation. For the nation to be truly representative of God's holiness, its physical blemishes were to be treated as seriously as its moral and spiritual ones. Many common skin diseases are frequently psychosomatic in nature, and as such they point to established emotional conflicts that are demanding recognition and treatment.

18–23. The extent of skin penetration and the degree of localization of the lesions are important considerations for a diagnosis of the most serious forms of *ṣāra'aṯ*. A white swelling or a pink papule which suddenly erupted at the site of a healed boil or ulcer had to be scrutinized by the priest. If it was seen to have fulfilled the conditions of cutaneous infiltration and the discoloration of local hair, it was regarded as a highly dangerous condition and would most probably be the clinical form of leprosy, but if the swelling was pale and had not penetrated the skin, the afflicted person had to be quarantined for one week. If the disease had spread in the meantime the individual was pronounced unclean, though not leprous. If the swelling or papule remained localized, it was held to be a minor inflammation of old scar tissue. The precise nature of the condition described is uncertain, but it may have been a keloid. This is a skin disorder characterized by whitish or pale yellow patches of hardened tissue surrounded by a darker coloured border. Sometimes known as *circumscribed scleroderma*, it has been described in terms of white, atrophied, or pigmented patches. The Hebrew term *š^{e}hîn*, normally rendered 'boil', could well be a designation of an ulcer. The latter is a cutaneous lesion which may suppurate to a greater or lesser degree, while a boil (*furuncle*) is an inflammation of tissue surrounding a skin follicle and is the result of infection by staphylococci. The mature boil has a well-defined core which suppurates and breaks down by necrosis. A more severe staphylococcal inflammation of an area of skin and subcutaneous tissue is known as a *carbuncle*. This generally forms into several distinct heads, and when they rupture there is liquefaction and necrosis of the tissues involved.

24-28. A burn that has become infected and has produced a pustule is also a potentially unclean condition. If the local hair had changed colour and the corium was infiltrated, the sufferer was pronounced unclean since the priest would suspect a degenerative skin condition. If there was no whitening of the hair at the site of the spot, and the lesion itself was pale, a seven-day quarantine period was imposed. On re-examination the affected person was declared unclean if the condition had spread in the skin, but if the pustule remained pale and localized, the case was diagnosed as being *a swelling from the burn* (28), and the person was pronounced clean. The modern doctor would doubtless object that the quarantine period for suspected cases was much too short for discerning morbid changes in a patient where a slowly developing condition such as Hansen's disease was concerned. While this may be true, it has to be remembered that the Israelite priest-physician had his own recognized diagnostic guidelines, and any incorrect diagnoses that resulted certainly erred on the side of caution. Even modern practitioners have been known to follow this pattern in the interests of public health where communicable or infectious diseases are involved, in the conviction that such matters should not be left to chance.

29-37. An itching *ṣāra'at* is now described which afflicted persons on the head, and in the case of men could spread down into the beard. The condition of the skin and hair at the site was checked for early signs of morbidity, and if skin penetration had occurred and the surface hair was discoloured the ailment was diagnosed as *an itch* (30). The entire condition was regarded as serious, being rendered by the Hebrew *nega'*, which is often used of 'plague'. In instances where the skin had not been broken by the itching disease, a seven-day quarantine period was imposed, and if there were no further degenerative indications a man would be allowed to shave areas other than those infected. After an additional period of isolation a person could be declared clean if the condition had not spread. If a relapse occurred subsequently, that eventuality was sufficient for the priest to declare the individual unclean, whether there was any yellow hair present or not. The growth of new dark hair was one indication that healing had taken place (37).

The nature of this condition is rather uncertain, but it may have been one of the *Tinea* or ringworm group of afflictions, perhaps *tinea tonsurans* or *tinea favosus* (favus). Ringworm is normally a childhood disease which can be contracted merely through proximity to infected cattle, and is caused by a fungus, *Achorion schönleinii*. This organism invades principally the scalp, penetrating the skin and forming yellow saucer-like crusts around the hair follicles. Scar tissue can develop, and in older persons sometimes results in bald patches. The affliction is both irritating and debilitating, and being infectious requires careful treatment.[51] An alternative diagnosis might be that of psoriasis, which is a non-infectious disease. It erupts in the form of rounded red patches covered with white scales, and while it is found chiefly in the head it also occurs on the elbows, knees and other parts of the body. Psoriasis is commoner in colder climates than in warmer ones, and once

[51] *Cf.* E. V. Hulse, *Palestine Exploration Quarterly*, 107, 1975, pp. 96-97, 100.

acquired it is difficult to remove. The control of communicable diseases among people who are living in close contact under semi-tropical or tropical conditions requires careful management and continuous insistence upon hygienic procedures. While the Israelite priest did not prescribe medicaments as such, he was able to exert some control over the spread of infection by isolating suspected cases during the incubation period.

38–39. The presence of white spots or speckles on the skin called for an examination by the priest. If they were pale in colour, and not the inflamed white vesicles of clinical leprosy, they were described as *bōhaq*. Precisely what disease is meant by this term is uncertain. The RSV preserved the obsolete English word 'tetter', which was a term applied to such skin disorders as eczema, impetigo and acne. The condition referred to may have involved papules or herpes simplex.

40–44. Ordinary baldness (*alopecia*) was not an unclean condition, but a leprous disease was suspected when a reddish-white vesicle was present. If the eruption bore the characteristics of clinical leprosy as seen on other parts of the body, the person was pronounced unclean.

45–46. A diagnosis of *sāra'at̲* was as much of a death sentence to the ancient Israelites as tidings about an advanced malignancy would be to a modern patient. The diagnostic guidelines furnished for the priest-physician would prevent him from bringing unnecessary sorrow and hardship to his countrymen while at the same time ensuring the health of the community. Once a man was branded as a 'leper', he had to adopt the posture of a mourner by tearing his clothes, allowing his hair to become unkempt, covering his beard or moustache, and crying 'unclean'. He had to live outside the camp, or perhaps in company with other 'lepers' (*cf.* 2 Ki. 7:3), but his existence was nothing more than a living death. Unless there was a quick remission of the disease, the victim of clinical leprosy knew that his condition would be of lengthy duration, and that its loathsome nature would prohibit significant contact with society. Most of all, the 'leper' would be cut off from spiritual fellowship with the covenant people, and in a real sense would be without hope and without God in the world.

2. Unwholesome conditions of clothing (47–59)

The principles of the transmission of disease by contact, which underlie the legislation of Leviticus 11:24–40, are applied to articles of clothing or other garments that might have been infected by victims of the diseases classified as *sāraʿat*, or might seem to be exhibiting degenerative changes of their own. The occidental mind regards as bizarre the notion of a 'leprosy of garments', but it is worth remembering that the Greeks used the term *lepros* to describe the roughly textured skins from which the best quality straps and reins were made.[52] Both people and their clothing can be amenable to physical agents that deface or disfigure the exterior. The resulting processes of deterioration are abnormal in both instances, and in each situation they cause the surface to swell, flake, or peel off. Finally, both persons and garments can be affected in this way by bacterial organisms or fungi.

47–58. The *sāraʿat* of woollen or linen clothing would be indicated by the presence of a greenish or reddish mould in the warp or woof. Skin garments could also exhibit such moulds, and in that event they too would be diseased. Moulds are fungous growths on dead or decomposing animal or vegetable matter, and occur in patches of various shades. If eaten by accident they can provoke violent toxic reactions. The significance of the phrase *warp and woof* in this connection has puzzled commentators. Apart from this chapter (verses 48, 49, 51, 52, 53, 56, 57, 58, 59), the expression occurs nowhere else in Scripture. Some have thought that it described two different types of yarn employed in the weaving, but this is improbable since the Hebrews were forbidden to mix yarns or materials in garments (Dt. 22:11). Another view thought of the spun yarn and the woven material as different stages in the manufacturing process.[53] The present writer prefers to see it as a comprehensive expression denoting the totality of a woven garment. The fungous growth affects the entire article by its presence, just as the taint of original sin reaches to all areas of the human personality.

---

[52] R. K. Harrison in C. Brown (eds.), *The New International Dictionary of New Testament Theology*, 2 (1976), p. 464.

[53] N. H. Snaith, *Leviticus and Numbers* (1967), p. 98.

The principles of isolation which were employed for persons suspected of one or other of the *sāraʿat* afflictions were also applied to garments. The affected articles were inspected by the priest, and because doubt exisited at that stage they were *shut up* (50) for a week. On re-examination, the garment was declared unclean if the mould or mildew had spread, and was burned. If the mould appeared to have stopped growing, the article was washed and shut up for another week. After that time the priest conducted yet another examination, and if he found that the mould or mildew had not changed colour, he condemned the garment as unclean, even though the fungous growth had not spread. Under these conditions ironmould would obviously make any article unclean, and would necessitate its being burned. If the affected area of the garment appeared to fade after being washed, that part of it could be torn out and the remainder of the article preserved. If, however, the mould recurred, the whole garment was obviously infected by bacterial bodies and had to be destroyed (57).

59. The concluding verse recapitulates the basic theme of the chapter ('leprous disease', 13:2) with reference to the laws of cleanness and uncleanness. The priest was furnished with the requisite information, which he would no doubt pass on to the people as part of his teachings on covenant living, although he is not instructed to do this here. His main concern was to preserve the spiritual uniqueness of the covenant people, and one aspect of their separation to God involved a distinctive way of life. This was characterized by an emphasis upon holiness, which had practical as well as ethical and spiritual dimensions. Separation from physical defilement was just as important for the Israelites as the punctilious observance of sacrificial regulations.

The law did not make an artificial distinction between physical well-being and spiritual vitality, exalting one at the expense of the other, but required that the true Israelite should be an integrated person whose spirituality involved all areas of his life. Holiness was thus expressed negatively in the avoidance of those things that might defile a person, and positively in the concentration of the personality upon a relationship with God that was marked by obedience and faith. Unless both aspects of holiness were being exemplified, the Israelites could not expect God to dwell in their midst, for His presence was incompatible with uncleanness of any kind. Christian life makes the same demands upon the believer, with the added difference that defilement can result from the motive as well as the act (Mt. 5:28; 15:19–20). The pursuit of holiness under the guidance of God's Spirit is mandatory if the Christian is to grow truly into the fullness of Christ.

3. Cleansing rituals (14:1–32)

The occasion on which a person was cured from a malignant form of *sāra'at* was of considerable significance. It marked his unexpected restoration to fellowship with his family and the community as a whole, and brought him back into a relationship with God's sanctuary. The outcast was now able to pick up the threads of his earlier existence, having been admitted formally to the congregation of Israel. The seriousness of the disease and the marvel of the healing were reflected in the cleansing ceremonies, which were elaborate and of a deeply spiritual nature.

1–3. The fact that the former 'leper' was now free of his disease was announced to the priest, who then went outside *the camp* to verify the situation by conducting his own examination. Nothing must be allowed to compromise the ceremonial purity of the congregation; hence the first stages of the ceremony take place at some distance from the community proper. Once the priest was satisfied that the disease had in fact been cured, he could then order the purification rituals to be initiated. The ceremony lasted for eight days, and involved elements of the four principal forms of Hebrew sacrifice as well as symbolic procedures reminiscent of the consecration of priests and of the annual day of atonement ceremony.

4–7. The rituals are marked by great emphasis upon cleansing, in which the person concerned not merely offered sacrifices with a view to receiving a priestly declaration of cleanness, but actually washed his whole body and his clothes as a token of his renewed existence. The priest's approval having been secured, the purification ceremonies began with the presentation of *two living clean birds* (4), along with some cedarwood, scarlet material, and hyssop. These items were procured on behalf of the 'leper' by relatives or friends, since the person to be declared clean would not normally have access to such things.

Those who brought the offerings were ordered to kill one of the birds in an earthenware container *over running water* (5) in such a way that its blood would be preserved. The remaining bird, along with the other materials, was then to be dipped in this blood, after which the healed person was to be sprinkled seven times before being pronounced clean. While there are overtones of the sacrificial system in this ritual, it is important to realize that the bird was not intended as a sacrifice in the usual sense, if only because no pieces of its body were offered on the altar of burnt offering. Instead, a different kind of symbolism is involved, indicating that the ritual is not intended to secure purification so much as to declare publicly that the formerly diseased person was now ritually clean.

The selection of two clean birds typified this renewed state of cleanness in the healed person, who was shortly to re-enter the community life of the nation. Clean animals were characteristic of the holy Israelites, who were exhorted continually to remain in this condition of body and mind. The bird's blood, when sprinkled on the individual undergoing the rite, identified him once again with the community, and was therefore symbolic of his restoration to fellowship. In precisely the same manner, the shedding of Christ's blood on the cross reconciles man to God and makes it possible for the sinner to join the household of faith. The bird's death also served as a graphic reminder of the fate that would have overtaken the former 'leper' if the Lord, the supreme and only healer of Israel (Ex. 15:26), had not intervened and restored him to health.

At the end of this part of the ceremony the other living bird was released into the open countryside, presumably so that it could return to its nest. This has been seen as symbolic of the new life which the cured 'leper' would now experience, and which would enable him to resume his former existence. Some interpreters have also understood the ritual in the less arcane sense of release and cleansing. Other authors have drawn a parallel between the release of the bird and that of the scapegoat in the day of atonement ceremonies (Lv. 16:21-22). The latter carried in a token fashion the national sins of inadvertence and omission away from the people to the outside world, and thus preserved the purity and integrity of the encampment. At the very least it points to the removal of a disability, and to the consequent new beginnings.

The purpose of the wood and the scarlet material is not easy to understand. Cedar is an extremely durable substance because its oil content makes it highly resistant to decay. Perhaps it was intended to symbolize the resistance which the 'leper's' body would have towards future serious diseases, in which case it would be an early indication of the principle of acquired immunity. The piece of scarlet material would probably have been made of wool, but apart from its colour being that of blood itself, its purpose is uncertain unless it was used to hold the bunch of hyssop.

This latter has proved difficult to identify because there were several varieties of hyssop in ancient Palestine. One of the Labiate family, either thyme (*Thymus capitatus* L.), mint (*Mentha sativa* L.) or sage (*Salvia triloba* L.) has been suggested, though many botanists think that the small grey-green marjoram plant (*Origanum maru* L.) was the hyssop commonly used in antiquity. This would certainly accord with Samaritan passover traditions, since they still use the marjoram plant in their rituals.[54] Whatever the true nature of the plant, it seems to have been able to be bunched together so that it would absorb liquid quickly and dispense it freely when shaken. In Psalm 51:7 it was employed as a symbol of cleansing from sin, which was a natural outcome of the function of hyssop in ceremonies of purification. When Christ was dying on the cross, His thirst was quenched by means of hyssop dipped in vinegar (Mt. 27:48), which indicates the ability of the plant to retain fluid in its leaves and stems.

8–9. Before the former sufferer can be declared clean, he must wash all his clothes so as to remove any lingering traces of infection, shave off all his hair, and wash his body. If shaving involved the removal of all bodily hair and any accompanying lice, the person awaiting a declaration of cleanness would be comparable to a newborn baby, ready to

---

[54] On the identification see R. K. Harrison, *Evangelical Quarterly*, 26, 1954, pp. 218–224.

enter upon a fresh phase of existence. Once these procedures, which resemble modern pre-operative preparations, had been followed, the person concerned was permitted to enter the camp, but could not go directly to his dwelling for another week. At the end of this period all the hair had to be removed from the head, while the person's clothes and body were washed once more. The shaving and washing were undertaken as preliminaries to the consecration ritual, and this was comparable to the shaving which the Levites underwent prior to their ministry at the tent of meeting (Nu. 8:7).

10–13. On the eighth day the former 'leper' offered three unblemished lambs successively as a guilt offering, a sin offering and a burnt offering. The first of these sacrifices always had to consist of a ram (*cf.* verse 21). A *cereal offering* comprised about one-third of a bushel basket of fine flour mixed with oil, and one *lōg* (almost one pint) of oil. All these were to be placed before the entrance to the holy place. The ram of the guilt offering was 'waved' before the Lord, as was the oil. Having been cut off from contact with his people, the restored 'leper' now had to renew his relationship with the God of the covenant. The guilt or reparation offering (*cf.* Lv. 7:1) was closely connected with the sin offering, but was not expiatory in nature, being instead an act of restitution for offerings and sacrifices which he had been unable to make while ceremonially unclean.

14–20. An impressive part of the cleansing ritual involved the smearing of blood by the priest on the right ear, the right thumb, and the right large toe, a procedure that formed part of the consecration ceremonies of the Aaronites (Lv. 8:24). The symbolism was also identical: namely that the cleansed man should hear God's voice, should perform works of righteousness with his hands, and should walk in God's ways. The reason why the smearing was performed on the right rather than the left side of the body is that, for most people, the right side is used rather more frequently than the left, and is therefore somewhat stronger. For the people of the ancient Near East, a person's strength required that the limbs be intact and functional, and this was especially important where the Hebrew priesthood was concerned. A man could be disabled humanely by the simple expedient of removing both his thumbs (*cf.* Jdg. 1:6) so that he could not grasp properly, and his mobility impaired by the amputation of his large toes.

Another smearing took place with some of the *lōg of oil* (15), and this was placed on top of the blood that had been applied previously. The balance of the oil was then poured on the head of the person being cleansed. While the symbolism of the anointing was comparable, the oil used in the consecration of the priests was compounded specially (Ex. 30:23–25) for that particular occasion. Having formally dedicated the 'leper' to the Lord's service, the priest then made atonement for him by means of the sin, burnt, and cereal offerings. The last of these would be understood as representing an expression of gratitude for healing on the part of the cleansed 'leper'.

21–32. The fact that the 'leper' would have been deprived of the opportunity of employment while his disease lasted was recognized in a provision relating to a reduced sacrificial tariff for those of very limited means. Poor persons were permitted to present a guilt or reparation offering consisting of a ram and fine flour mixed with oil for a cereal offering, along with a lōg of oil (21). In place of lambs, the impoverished person could substitute two doves or two young pigeons for the sin and burnt offerings. This procedure follows the option available for poor mothers at the time of their post-natal purification ceremonies (Lv. 12:8). The description of the ritual follows very closely that of verses 12 to 20, with the formal cleansing taking place at the entrance to the tent of meeting. The restored sufferer is smeared with the sacrificial blood (14) and subsequently anointed with oil in exactly the same areas of the body (17). The birds are offered in the accustomed manner, together with the cereal offering, and at the end of the ceremony the priest declares that atonement has been made.

Many expositors over the centuries have understood leprosy to be typical of sin in the individual's personality. Like leprosy, the onset of sin is so insidious that it is frequently well established before the individual is aware of what has transpired. In serious cases it can become a lifelong condition, causing misery, degeneration, and ultimate spiritual death. While this may well be a graphic comparison, it is important to remember that nowhere in the Bible is *ṣāraʿat* regarded as symbolic of sin. Instead, the clinical form was feared as a devastating physical condition which a person could contract without any awareness of causative factors. Even less serious types were matters of great concern because of the fact that they might be the precursors of the dreaded chronic disease. When the biblical authors wished to describe sin in metaphorical terms, they spoke of blindness, hardness of heart and obduracy of will ('stiff-necked'), not of a person being afflicted with *sāra'at*. Even the 'bruises and sores and bleeding wounds' of Isaiah 1:5–6 do not characterize this disease accurately.

While it is true that leprosy was sometimes imposed as a special punishment by God (*cf.* Nu. 12:10; 2 Ki. 5:27, *etc.*), the same was also true of blindness and other physical conditions (*cf.* Gn. 19:11; 2 Ki. 6:18; Acts 12:23). Leprosy was not therefore the indication *par excellence* of sin in an individual's life, but merely one form or other of cutaneous disorder which could result in the priest giving a verdict of uncleanness if the clinical condition was serious. The tragedy of leprosy lay not so much in personal sin as in isolation from community life and worship. While any one of the various forms of *sāra'at* comes to fruition only in a minuscule proportion of the human race, all mankind has sinned, and all fall short of God's glory (Rom. 3:23). The real message of the legislation is that any type of uncleanness separates the believer from God, of which leprosy is one representative.

The elaborate purificatory rituals are as impressive spiritually for the Christian as they were ceremonially for the person who had experienced a cure or a remission of symptoms. Restoration to fellowship with God must be based upon a sense of need for cleansing from all defilement. In the light of man's natural condition sin must always necessarily be involved, and until this has been forgiven a person cannot experience a proper sense of communion with God. The act of worship by which the 'leper' was declared clean was a communal one. The believer is not meant to live in spiritual isolation, for it is within the fellowship of Christ's body, the church, that faith grows and individuals mature spiritually.

The legislation prescribed the offerings that were to be used in the cleansing ceremonies. The 'leper' had no part in providing them, since he was unable to help himself in this respect. In the same way, people cannot save themselves from their sin, since salvation is by divine grace through faith, and not of human works (Eph. 2:8–9). The priest commenced the cleansing rituals by going to the former sufferer outside the camp, just as Christ did in atoning for human sin (Heb 13:12). The bird that was killed and the one that remained alive are graphic illustrations of the Saviour who was put to death for our trespasses and raised for our justification (Rom. 4:25). The smearing of blood on the 'leper' was a token of cleansing through life that had been offered up vicariously, and was accepted as such in faith by the person being cleansed. The washing and shaving of the body pointed to a fresh beginning for the former 'leper' in the society of ceremonially clean people. His sin offering showed that before restoration to fellowship was achieved he had to dissociate himself from all known sin in his life, using procedures established as part of the normal sacrificial system. Where forgiveness was concerned, innovations or deviations were not permitted. While provision was made for differences in economic circumstances, a person still had to approach God in penitence and trust before the priest could make atonement for him.

The New Testament also directs the penitent sinner along the 'narrow way' of eternal salvation through faith in the atoning work of Christ. The exclusive and distinctive nature of the Christian fellowship is made abundantly clear in Peter's pronouncement that there is no salvation in anyone else, for there is no other name under heaven given among men by which we must be saved (Acts 4:12). The smearing of blood on representative parts of the person's body indicates that atonement touches every area of one's life, and warns the individual concerned against hearing, doing or walking in the ways of anything that would separate him from spiritual fellowship with God. Just as the blood signifies justification, so the anointing with oil on top of the smeared blood shows that the truly sanctified life of the believer needs the sustaining presence of God's Holy Spirit. The penitent sinner, whether a former victim of *ṣāraʿat* or not, is not cleansed in order to enable him to pursue a life of self-will and wantonness. His cleansing is intended to enable him to live in continued righteousness and holiness before God, and exactly the same objective is in view for the believer in the age of grace.

33-36. The designation of *sāra'at* is here extended to houses, in the same way that the Greeks used *lepros* to describe anything that was rough, scaly or encrusted. This type of eruption on the surface of property could perhaps have been caused by some form of fungus if the condition approximated to that of dry rot in wood. Where stones were involved, the scaly deposit would probably be the result of mineral efflorescence. The fact that the incidence of this condition was attributed consciously to God merely reflects the consistent monistic philosophy of the Old Testament writers. God was the ground of all existence, and therefore everything took its rise from Him. This thought is made explicit by Isaiah in a magnificent poetic passage (Is. 45:7) in which, employing the familiar idiom of paired opposites to denote completeness of totality, he credits God with all the facets of physical life ('light ... darkness'), and also with complete responsibility for man's metaphysical existence ('weal ... woe'). The present legislation looks forward to the sedentary occupation of Canaan by the Israelites, and for that reason is dealt with in a separate section.

37-42. If the eruption was red or green in appearance, and if it seemed to have penetrated the surface of the material, the house was ordered to be closed for one week. On reinspection, if the condition had spread into the walls of the building, radical treatment of the affected area was deemed necessary. It should be observed that the same degree of care was to be taken in excising a 'diseased' part of a house as in removing a similar condition from clothing (Lv. 13:56). It was not necessary to demolish the structure if less drastic remedies would suffice, the most probable reason being that a house in the period of sedentary occupation of Palestine always represented a vastly greater investment of time and money than a tent did.

An intractable condition required complete removal of the affected masonry, which then had to be thrown in a place that was used as a repository for unclean articles. In later times the valley of the sons of Hinnom, to the west and south west of Jerusalem, was one location that served such a function. The settlements in which God's people lived must be free from anything that might pollute, or cause epidemic disease. Once the stones of the structure had been removed, the lime plaster that had been put on the walls had to be scraped off and taken to an unclean place *outside the city* (41). Plastering was common in the ancient Near East, being found in Mesopotamia from the Chalcolithic levels of such sites as Tell el-Obeid and Tepe Gawra. The ancient Egyptians plastered their buildings in order to provide a smooth surface on which frescoes could be painted. As in Mesopotamia, the peasants of Egypt frequently used a mixture of straw and mud for their plaster, daubing it on the exterior of their dwellings. On larger buildings an undercoating of gypsum and red clay or potash was generally followed by a finishing mixture of slaked lime and white sand, to which chopped straw was often added to increase the strength and plasticity of the finish. Stone houses of the Israelite sedentary period in Palestine often had an exterior coating of clay, most of which generally fell off during the spring and autumn rainy seasons. The kind of plaster used from about the eleventh century BC for lining the interior of Palestinian houses was made of limestone, to which a little sand was sometimes added to produce a mixture closely resembling cement. Cisterns or domestic reservoirs, which came into general use in Palestine about the thirteenth century BC, were also lined by the monarchy period with a covering of lime plaster.[55] This helped to make the structure watertight (*cf*. Je. 2:13), thus safeguarding precious supplies, and also enabled the cistern to be cleaned out more easily when the occasion required. Once the deteriorated material had been taken out of the fabric of the dwelling, it was replaced with other stones and fresh plaster, after which the house was considered fit for reoccupation.

43–47. Just as the remission of symptoms in the unclean person could be followed by a resurgence of the disease (Lv. 13:7–8), so the possibility of a fresh outbreak of scaly incrustations on previously affected property had to be recognized, and appropriate procedures prescribed. When such an eventuality occurred, the house was declared unclean. Since previous measures had obviously proved ineffective, the priest had no alternative but to order the demolition of the property. In the case of termite infestation or the presence of dry rot, the

---

[55] W. F. Albright, *The Archaeology of Palestine* (1960 ed.), pp. 113, 210.

premises would pose the danger of collapse at points where the infestation was well advanced. The entire fabric of the dwelling had then to be taken to an unclean place, from which the materials would not be salvaged and re-used, thereby spreading the particular condition. The uncleanness of the house extended under such conditions to people who had entered it while it was closed. Anyone who had taken up residence in it had to *wash his clothes* (47), which were also defiled by contact, and be unclean until the evening.

48–53. If following a quarantine period the eruption had not spread in the house after repairs had been made to the infected area, the priest would pronounce the house ceremonially clean, since the organism that had been causing the trouble had been treated successfully. Then a ceremony of ritual cleansing could take place, the format of which was parallel to the preliminary phase of the healed 'leper's' cleansing (Lv. 14:4–7). Just as the latter was restored whole to the congregation of Israel, so the house was returned in a ceremonially clean condition to its owner. The *atonement* (53) is of a purificatory nature, of course, since sin as such is not involved, and is comparable to the procedures in Exodus 29:36, where the priests were instructed to atone for the altar.

54–57. The repetition of the title in this section ('this shall be the law of the leper') recapitulates the entire body of material (Lv. 13:1 – 14:53) relating to unnatural exterior conditions of people's bodies, their clothing, and their dwelling-places. A distinct legislative unit is thus indicated, which is dignified by the designation of *tôrâ* or law. The regulations governing the subject of the section are thus authoritative because they have been revealed by God. There is not one element of the enactments that is even remotely connected with folklore, magic, or any form of paganism. The diagnostic procedures are thoroughly rational, and suited to the conditions under which the nation would be living. The instructions were not of an esoteric order, known only to the priests, but were the property of the people, as all of God's law was. The clinical situations involved were described in such a manner that the priest-physician would have no ultimate doubt about the diagnosis. As is the case with other medical enactments in the Mosaic law, there is great emphasis upon prophylaxis. The necessity for such precautions in community life will be apparent immediately to anyone who has lived in, or even visited, the Near East. Insect-borne and water-borne diseases can arise and spread with amazing rapidity, and the primitive conditions under which many people still live do little to ease apprehensions about epidemics of contagious or infectious diseases such as cholera, smallpox, typhoid fever, typhus and bubonic plague.

While sanitation, personal hygiene and physical cleanliness are prominent in this legislation, there is a consistent emphasis upon the rationale of cleanness in terms of the holiness of God as it is to be reflected in both individual and community life. While cleanness and holiness are obviously not synonymous terms, since the clean is not necessarily that which is holy, they are closely related in these enactments and in the whole cultic life of the nation. Cleanness, of which physical washing forms a small part under ceremonial conditions, is a reflection of that dynamic holiness which constitutes God's nature. When an individual is clean, his condition is a consequence of being obedient to the various ordinances of the law. It is this state of obedience that produces the end-result of holiness in both the individual believer and the community as a whole. Uncleanness separates persons from God, and on occasions when it comes within the range of God's holiness it immediately falls under judgment. It can either be cleansed by the contact, for which appropriate rituals were prescribed in Leviticus, or it can be destroyed where the unclean person refuses to seek ceremonial cleansing along the approved lines. The emphasis upon states of uncleanness makes the individual conscious of alienation from God. The response of the participant indicates whether the basic condition of obedience to the revealed will of God has any place in his life, and whether in the end he will know God as the Holy One of Israel. The obedience and holiness of Jesus Christ are models for the Christian to follow in the quest for conformity to His image.

d. Purification following bodily secretions (15:1–33)

An important section dealing with personal hygiene is written in the 'case-law' fashion. There are four principal subdivisions of the material, each of which is introduced by the formula, 'If a man ...' or 'If a woman ...'. The literary style has the same objective character as that of other legislation dealing with cleanness and uncleanness. While the material has obvious importance as a diagnostic and ritual guide for the Hebrew priesthood, it was meant to be available generally for those in need. As with the regulations concerning leprosy, this material would most probably be included in the kind of instruction that the priests gave to the Israelites. The subject of the section is the kind of physical secretions that would render a person ritually unclean, and would therefore prevent such an individual from participation in sanctuary worship. The nature of this legislation is quite unique in ancient Near Eastern literature, and while it was obviously important from a hygienic standpoint, the overall purpose was to preserve the purity and ceremonial holiness of the community.

The literary structure of this chapter balances two types of discharge, chronic and intermittent, against both sexes, making for four specific cases. Thus a chronic discharge in the male (verses 2–12) is followed by regulations governing an occasional ejaculation of semen (verses 16–18). For females, the intermittent discharges associated with menstruation (verses 19–24) come first, and these are followed by the rules governing a chronic emission (verses 25–27). It will be seen, therefore, that the discharges affecting females are dealt with in the reverse order to those characterizing males. This type of pattern is known technically as *chiastic*, and was a favourite literary device among the Hebrews for demonstrating the fundamental unity of a double-sided phenomenon.[56] This unity also extends to the relationship between the sexes, reflecting the affirmation of Genesis that male and female were made in the divine image (Gn. 1:27). A final touch of literary artistry has been seen in the mention of coition at the central point of the case discussions. In this act both male and female can express their sense of physical and emotional unity as they demonstrate the oneness of their humanity.

1–12. Since these regulations proceed from the *Lord* (1), they carry precisely the same authority as those dealing with other legislative matters. A chronic male emission is the first

[56]*Cf.* F. I. Andersen, *The Sentence in Biblical Hebrew* (1974), pp. 120 ff.

matter to be considered. The discharge is described in terms of the *body* (2), the Hebrew word being *bāśăr*, which is frequently rendered 'flesh' or 'meat' (*cf.* Lv. 4:11). It also describes the physical structure of the person as a whole (*cf.* Gn. 2:21), while under other circumstances it is used euphemistically of the primary sexual characteristics of both male and female. In this passage the emission seems to be related to the male sexual organ. The Hebrew term for emission (*zôb*) is rare, occurring only in Leviticus, and this suggests a technical hygienic usage. The meaning is amplified somewhat in verse 3 by the statement that the discharge *runs* periodically. This word (Heb. *rār*) is not found anywhere else in the Hebrew Bible, but is related to a noun, *rîr*, meaning 'slimy juice' or 'saliva' (*cf.* 1 Sa. 2:13; Jb. 6:6). The expression *stopped from discharge* (3) seems to mean that the emission has ceased, not that it has blocked the male urethra as some commentators have thought. Were the latter true, the sufferer would be in a serious condition. That the discharge is from the *urethra virilis* and not from the rectum, as would occur in the case of haemorrhoids, diverticulitis, and other intestinal disorders, seems most probable, since in the latter instances the presence of blood would undoubtedly have been mentioned in the narrative.

From the information given it is far from easy to be certain about the nature of the emission. The most obvious diagnosis would be that of gonorrhoea, which is an infection of the genital tract by the organism *Neisseria gonorrhoeae*. The disease is acquired normally through sexual contact with an infected person, although *ophthalmia neonatorum* results when the newborn baby comes into contact with its mother's gonorrhoeal discharge. A purulent secretion follows an incubation period varying from two to ten days, and unless the condition is treated it can result in arthritis of one or two joints. Other complications such as endocarditis and skin lesions are rare, and the mortality from the disease is negligible. Spontaneous recovery can occur in an otherwise healthy male within a period ranging from a few months to a year. Another form of secretion or 'issue' which must be borne in mind is that of infectious pus from a tubercular lesion.

The fact that a discharge has been present makes the person unclean (3). This is stated as a proposition, and as with other declarations of uncleanness the Old Testament does not attempt to suggest why discharges should produce this result. In the instance of blood, the vehicle of life and the agent by which cleansing from sin was secured, the defilement seems to arise because the blood is not emitted in the course of ritual functions, but instead belongs to a particular person's physiology and is not offered on behalf of sin. Some writers connect wholeness and holiness in a way that is not immediately evident when such Hebrew terms as *hay, hāyyeh, kôl*, and the like, representing wholeness, are compared philologically with *qādôš* and *qōdeš*, the usual words for holy or holiness. As a result, anything that is not completely whole is thereby considered to be unclean.[57] This view overlooks the fact that Israelites who had various deformities could still be properly accredited members of the congregation and share in its condition of ceremonial holiness, although Aaronites afflicted with a physical disability could not become priests.

Most probably the reason why discharges were defiling was that they contained dead matter within themselves. This, as is now known, includes white blood cells that have succumbed in the attempt to halt the spread of the infection, as well as actual necrosed tissue on many occasions. Separation from dead matter in order to prevent the transmission of disease was one of the most important means of controlling infectious and contagious conditions among the Israelites. That which is dead defiles both physically and spiritually, and those who have been in contact with it are unclean. If the diagnosis of gonorrhoea for the male discharge under consideration is correct, it was appropriate for the legislation to regard this condition as particularly defiling, since it involved the kind of sexual irregularity that was to bring so much calamity upon the nation subsequently.

Not only did the discharges make the affected individual unclean but contaminated other persons and objects that came into contact with him. Pallets, seats and clothing were particularly vulnerable, and had to be washed thoroughly, indicating that the discharge was infectious. Gonorrhoea can be contracted occasionally from clothing and towels, which absorb

57 So M. Douglas, *Purity and Danger* (1966), p. 51.

and transmit the contagium of the affliction. Ceremonial uncleanness lasted until the evening, by which time the hygienic precautions would have helped to dissipate the infectious organisms. Rather than being selective, the legislation was enacted on the basis that it was safer as far as community health was concerned to regard whatever had been in contact with the afflicted person as unclean, lest the various items quite inadvertently became secondary sources of infection.

One of the most interesting prescriptions concerns a ritually clean individual upon whom the infected person had spat (8). The victim of such an unfortunate incident was defiled, and had to wash both his body and his clothes before he could be regarded once more as clean. Modern medicine, especially in the field of public health, is extremely sensitive to the concept of the sputum as a vehicle for infection, and accordingly it is instructive to find the principle contained in literature which many consider to have emerged from the 'pre-scientific age'. The washing of the hands in water or other cleansing agents is now so common a hygienic procedure as to be thought quite unexceptionable, but once again it was enunciated on precisely these grounds as far back as the Late Bronze Age, in Israel. If the infected peron did not wash his hands before touching someone, he conveyed the pollution of the infectious condition to the person touched (11). Earthenware vessels thus affected had to be broken, but wooden containers could be washed and then reused (12).

13–15. Remission or cure of the discharge enabled a person to undergo the cleansing rituals, thus allowing him to renew his fellowship with God and man. The ceremonies were by no means as elaborate as those prescribed for the cleansing of the leper, suggesting that the discharges were of a far less serious nature. One week after the emission had ceased, the person concerned was required to wash his clothes and present to God the least expensive of the offerings, that of turtledoves or pigeons (14). When the rituals for the sin and guilt offerings had been completed, the person was declared clean. The ceremony reminded all concerned that there was nothing in life that was purely secular, for even things that might seem to have no connection with spirituality were indeed amenable to such an interpretation, since all life was lived under God. The Christian must strive to glorify God in all facets of existence, making no distinction between sacred and secular, but integrating all experience under the guidance of the Holy Spirit.

16–18. Temporary male discharges were discussed in terms of the emission of semen, principally in relationship to sexual activity, though other situations including spontaneous nocturnal emissions (*cf.* Dt. 23:10) could have been envisaged. Contact with semen made persons and clothing unclean. The remedy for this was to wash the body and any contaminated articles with water and be unclean until the evening. The notion that ejaculated semen was a pollutant seems to have been widespread in the ancient Near East, being found among the Babylonians, Egyptians, Greeks and Romans, as well as in some Semitic groups. In the Old Testament the idea is referred to in Exodus 19:15, Leviticus 22:4, Deuteronomy 23:10, 1 Samuel 21:4–5 and 2 Samuel 11:11. Anything that was deemed unclean could contaminate the ceremonial purity of the individual. Even though no purificatory sacrifice was necessary in the instances mentioned here, the prescribed ritual procedures had to be undertaken because whatever had come into contact with the emission was unclean for that day. The intent was to keep a legitimate but 'unclean' biological function from defiling that which was holy.

19–24. The normal intermittent discharge of a woman was legislated for on a hygienic basis, and reflects the common understanding of most ancient peoples that it was defiling cultically. Menstruation made a woman unclean for seven days, at the end of which time the discharge would have ceased under normal circumstances. Anyone who touched her during that period would become defiled for the day (19), while everything upon which the woman sat or lay was also unclean, and could convey the pollution to those who touched such articles. If a man was intimate with a woman at some point during her menstrual period, he became ceremonially unclean for an entire week, and contaminated any bed upon which he lay (24). This verse does not seem to imply that if a man had intercourse with a woman up to seven days after menstruation had ended he was unclean, as some expositors have thought. In terms of family relationships, contact by the husband with his menstruating wife could be quite accidental in nature. By contrast, some moderns deliberately restrict coition to the interval when the woman is menstruating, on the ground that this constitutes the most effective form of contraception. To what extent the woman derives emotional satisfaction from the experience under such conditions is a matter of some conjecture. Contact with menstrual blood during coition is supposed to be a cause of non-specific urethritis in the male.

Apart from their obvious hygienic importance, there is a humane aspect to these legislative provisions. The hormonal cycle which governs menstruation often affects women in different ways. For some, the two days prior to the onset of menstruation are times of considerable emotional tension which sometimes reacts upon family members. During menstruation itself some women experience painful abdominal cramps, profuse bleeding, migraine, low backache and associated irritability, while others pass through the period with few if any noticeable side-effects. By placing the woman in what amounted to a state of isolation, the legislation made it possible for her to enjoy some respite from her normal duties, and gave her an opportunity of renewing her energy. The life of the woman in the ancient Near East was normally very arduous, and these regulations enabled younger females in Israel to rest legitimately during the menses.

25–27. With respect to a woman whose discharge did not conform to the usual menstrual pattern, her state of uncleanness lasted until the discharge had ended. In menostaxis the menstrual flow is prolonged unduly, and this would be one of the conditions covered by the provisions relating to her uncleanness. Bleeding that was not associated with the menses could result from a uterine fibroid or some other morbid condition of the reproductive system. Whatever the cause of the abnormality, the woman along with her garments and her bed were unclean for as long as the bleeding continued. Once it ceased she could become ceremonially clean after an additional waiting-period of one week. This interval would be long enough to assure her that it was proper for her to proceed with her cleansing. Whereas for normal discharges it was sufficient for a woman to wash after waiting seven days to see if the bleeding resumed, in instances of abnormal bleeding she followed the ritual procedures prescribed for men with chronic discharges (29). Having made the necessary sacrifice, the woman was declared clean, and remained so until her next discharge.

31–33. These verses summarize the contents of the regulations governing emissions, and make it clear that the purity of the community, and especially that of the tabernacle, has to be safeguarded. It is important to notice that there is a difference established between physical uncleanness and sin in this legislation. While coition is a ceremonially defiling process, it is not regarded as a sinful one when undertaken with a lawful spouse. It is instructive to contrast the purification rites of the ancient Hebrews with those current in contemporary pagan society. In the latter, uncleanness was associated with demonic influences which needed to be countered by means of incantations, spells and magical charms. For the Hebrews, all that was necessary for cleansing from impurity was a sense of need, an expression of complete trust in the mercies and forgiveness of God, and a willingness to obey implicitly the regulations that He had enacted for the cleansing process. This is a wonderful paradigm of God's great salvation in Christ, which requires exactly the same responses from the one who desires cleansing from sin and a new life of fellowship with the Lord.

It is quite clear that hygienic considerations are prominent in these laws,[58] and that there is distinct provision biologically for the woman as a female. She is to be given due consideration as such, and thus honoured by the members of her household instead of being exploited at times of indisposition. It must be remembered that the Hebrew woman would not menstruate with quite the regularity experienced by some of her modern occidental counterparts, due to a succession of pregnancies, breast feeding, the weaning of the child after two or three years of nursing, during which time intercourse with the spouse was not encouraged, and a generally shorter life-span.

One valuable feature of this legislation that had an impor-

---

[58] *Cf.* R. E. Clements, *Leviticus*, Broadman Bible Commentary, 2 (1970), p. 43.

tant bearing upon Israel's cultic and social life was the rule which made partners in coition unclean for the whole day. This contingency separated sexual activity from cultic worship in a unique manner, and thus precluded the orgiastic fertility rites that were so much a part of religion among peoples such as the Canaanites. Furthermore, the continuous state of ceremonial uncleanness experienced by the prostitute in Israel would remove any possibility of her participation in Hebrew worship, and take away anything approaching respectability from her way of life, if, indeed, she was at all sensitive to the requirements of the sanctuary.

This material also illumines the New Testament account of the haemorrhaging woman whom Christ healed (Mk. 5:25–34). Her belief in His healing power obviously had a firm foundation, based perhaps on others who had experienced miraculous cures at His hands. Whether this was so or not, her action in touching Him surreptitiously seems to have resulted from her confidence that Jesus would not be defiled by such an action. For her, holiness had a contagious quality from which she could receive special benefit, and her faith was such that she expected complete healing just by touching the border of Christ's robe. The shock attached to being discovered and called to account is well portrayed in the narrative. Christ was not concerned to chastise her, however, but to hold her up as an example of faith. His love transcended all the procedures and strictures of the law, although like the woman He was thoroughly familiar with them (Gal. 4:4). Clearly it was the woman's faith in Christ's ability to heal her that brought about a recovery which the physicians had been unable to effect. This sense of trust was consistent with the Hebrew tradition which thought of God as the supreme healer (Ex. 15:26). For this woman Christ was indeed God, and her faith was confirmed by the sign that followed (*cf.* Mk. 16:20, AV).

IV. THE DAY OF ATONEMENT (16:1–34)

This chapter comprises the ceremonial and theological pivot upon which the entire book of Leviticus turns. Previous legislation has dealt with the different kinds of sacrifices and the conditions under which they were to be offered, the

emphasis being upon the provision for individual needs. Now the focus is upon the making of atonement for all the uncleannesses and sins of inadvertence of the entire Israelite congregation, beginning with the priesthood. Six months after the passover had been celebrated, the people were instructed to 'afflict themselves', after which the high priest would make atonement for them. Like the passover, this ceremony had to be observed annually, and it marked the occasion when the entire religious community was mobilized before God in a joint act of confession and atonement. It was a time of great solemnity, unlike the annual feasts, and if fasting was involved in the preparatory self-discipline, as many interpreters think, it was the only ceremony that demanded such a communal exercise. By its nature it was a distinctive religious observance and was central to the worship-life of the nation. The importance of the high priest is made clear in the position which he holds in the rituals as the mediator between God and man. The ritual is given in its entirety, which is fitting in a manual of public worship.

Some scholars have questioned the logical nature of the arrangement of Leviticus in terms of the position of chapters 11 – 15 in the text. Since Leviticus 10:20 concludes the narrative of the events associated with the death of Aaron's sons, Nadab and Abihu, and the historical material recommences in Leviticus 16:1 at that same point, it has been maintained that the latter chapter logically follows Leviticus 10:20. This conclusion then leads to questions about supposed documentary sources, the dislocation of the text, redactional processes and the like, depending upon the predilection of the scholar concerned.

While chapters 11 – 15 certainly disrupt the flow of the historical narrative, and to that extent could well be regarded as an interpolation, the fact remains that they have been integrated firmly into the book as a whole by means of the references in Leviticus 5:2 and 7:21. The antecedent passage in Leviticus 10:10 prepares the reader for the detailed distinction between clean and unclean species in chapter 11, while chapters 12 – 15 apply the same theme to social situations. In the process of compilation it was deemed proper for a block of material dealing with special topics to be inserted into the historical narrative. The section is clearly in harmony with the concerns for holiness and ceremonial purity expressed elsewhere in Leviticus, and while a modern compiler might have placed chapters 11 – 15 elsewhere in the text, their present position does not damage the organizational unity of Leviticus to any appreciable extent.

a. Priestly preparation (1–4)

The fact that the Lord instructed Moses in the procedures to be followed on this solemn day indicates the exalted status of the leader of the nation. It was his responsibility to pass this information on to the Aaronites, who still appeared to need specific guidance, judging by the events of chapter 10. To safeguard the sanctity of the most holy place, Aaron was forbidden to enter it *at all times* (2). The latter phrase has been understood by some to mean 'not . . . at any time', but in all probability the intent was to forbid indiscriminate or casual entry to the most sacred area of the tabernacle and its successors. This seems indicated further by the provisions made for the time and circumstances under which entry was permissible. The regulations were intended to prevent a recurrence of the tragedy which overtook Nadab and Abihu, and to make the annual appearance of the high priest in God's presence a solemn and awesome occasion. The *veil* which separated the holy place from the most holy place was actually a curtain on which cherubim were embroidered in red, purple and blue, and which hung from four supports made of acacia wood (Ex. 26:31–32).

The most important sacred object in Hebrew worship was the ark of the covenant and its surmounting mercy seat. The specifications for the ark occur in Exodus 25:10–20, and indicate that it was a rectangular box of acacia wood overlaid entirely with beaten sheet gold. It was transported from place to place by means of gold-covered acacia poles which fitted into golden rings placed on the side of the ark. On the basis of some modern attempts to reconstruct the ark, it has been suggested that the original was highly charged with electricity. This seems doubtful, if only for the reason that no-one would ever have been able to transport the ark without receiving a serious, if not a fatal, shock through contact with the metal on the poles. The rendering 'mercy seat' (Heb. *kappōret*) is not altogether felicitous. The notion of a seat was derived presumably from Psalm 99:1, which spoke of God sitting between the cherubim as on a throne. A possible etymological connection with *kipper*, to make atonement', may have suggested the idea of mercy to the English translators, supported to some extent by the LXX rendering *hilastērion*, 'propitiation'. If *kipper* means 'to cover', *i.e.* sin, as some authorities maintain, there seems no reason why *kappōret* should not be translated 'lid' or 'cover', as in some modern English versions. The lid with its surmounting cherubim served as a cover for the ark, and also as the locale of God's glory and the place where the annual atonement for the inadvertent sins of the congregation was made by the high priest. Most important of all, it was supremely a place of meeting and communication with God (Ex. 25:22).

Before he could enter the holy place, the high priest had to sacrifice as a prerequisite a sin offering and a burnt offering to the Lord, the former to be presented in order to secure atonement for himself and his family. Elaborate preparations were needed before the high priest could be considered fit to appear before God at the mercy seat. He had to bathe his body completely, thereby cleansing himself symbolically of all impurity, but instead of wearing the highly decorated garments of his consecration ceremony he was to be attired in simple duty clothes, comprising a coat, breeches, a linen girdle and a turban. While the linen is not described as 'white', it would most probably have been bleached to accord with priestly traditions in the ancient Near East. As such it would depict the purity and state of ceremonial cleanness required for an approach to the most holy God of Israel. This ritual furnishes a dramatic contrast between the holiness and purity of God and the sin of man, emphasizing the need for atonement if the people are to be holy as God is holy.

b. The two goats (5-10)

The sin offering of the people comprises two male goats, while a ram is presented for a burnt offering. Aaron commences the formal ceremonies by sacrificing the bullock as a sin offering for the priests. Only when he had been cleansed from sin and had made atonement for his house could he begin to secure forgiveness for the congregation (*cf.* Heb. 7:26). Aaron's sacrificial offerings were his own property, with which he had to identify in the usual manner. Having presented the two goats to the Lord, Aaron *cast lots* upon them (8) as a preliminary to the purificatory rites for the community. The casting of *lots* (Heb. *gôrālôt*) probably involved the use of the sacred stones known as Urim and Thummin, and were cast in such a way as to determine which goat was to be sacrificed to the Lord, and which was to be assigned to *Azazel*. The meaning of this word is far from certain, which is all the more unfortunate since the ritual is otherwise preserved in a clear and straightforward manner. It was evidently such a familiar term in the wilderness and later periods that it was not thought necessary to preserve its meaning by the addition of an explanatory gloss. The word may perhaps signify 'removal' or 'dismissal', but since it occurs only in this chapter in connection with specific ritual functions, this explanation is both circumstantial and inferential. The AV and NIV 'scape-goat', which follows the Vulgate, describes quite adequately the animal that was allowed to go free, but whether the expression *leʿazāʾzēl* can have this meaning is far from certain. The translation of this word has varied considerably, and includes such renderings as 'that shall be sent out' (Wycliffe), 'for discharge' (Knox), 'Azazel' (RSV), and 'for the Precipice' (NEB). The idea of 'precipice' seems to have been derived from Talmudic tradition, where *ʿazāʾzēl* was translated by 'steep mountain'. The allusion appears to have been to the precipitous slope or rock in the wilderness from which in the post-exilic period the goat was hurled to death.

Three principal explanations have been suggested: firstly, that the term describes the abstract concept of removal; secondly, that the word is a proper name synonymous with the powers of evil to which the sin-laden goat quite properly went; and thirdly, that it was the name of a wilderness demon which needed to be propitiated in some manner. Any mythological explanation can be dismissed immediately as having no place whatever in the most sacred ordinance of Hebrew cultic worship. The notion that the Israelites ought to make propitia-tory or other offerings to such supposed wilderness demons as satyrs was repudiated in the following chapter (Lv. 17:7), and thus it cannot be associated with the unique character of the day of atonement. Probably the best explanation is that the word was a rare technical term describing 'complete removal', *i.e.*, of communal guilt, and that later personifications brought about myths and legends concerning Azazel in Jewish writings.[59]

An interpretation of this kind accords with the general usage of the LXX ('the one to be dismissed') and the Mishnah. But whatever the precise meaning of the term, the purpose of this very dramatic portion of the day of atonement ritual was to place before the eyes of the Israelites an unmistakable token that their sins of inadvertence had been removed from their midst. It was a symbol of the fact that both people and land had been purged from their guilt, since a confession of communal sin would be made over the goat's head by the high priest before it was driven out into the wilderness. The other goat, chosen by lot for the Lord, was presented as a sin offering for the people (9) and sacrificed subsequently (15). Both animals preserve the Old Testament concept of sin being taken away by an agent other than the sinner. This principle of vicarious atonement finds its fullest expression in Christ, the divine Lamb, who takes away human sin by His death (*cf.* Jn. 1:29). From levitical usage the term 'scape-goat' is still employed to describe a person who takes the blame for some misdemeanour committed by another individual or group.

c. The sin offerings (11–22)

This section furnished the detailed ritual procedures which are mentioned in summary form in the preceding verses. Once Aaron had slaughtered the bull of the sin offering, he began the most serious and responsible part of the annual liturgy of communal atonement. A censer had to be filled with burning embers from the bronze altar, and carried along with two handfuls of finely pulverized incense into the most holy place. The incense was then placed on the embers so that the resultant smoke covered the ornate lid on the ark of the

[59] J. H. Hertz, *The Pentateuch and Haftorahs* (1960) p. 481.

covenant, where God's presence was revealed. Because of this the high priest was unable to see the Lord, and this fact saved his life (13). Punctilious attention to the observance of the regulations governing entrance into the most holy place was clearly of the greatest importance, and the interval during which the high priest was out of sight of the congregation would be filled with tension and drama, relieved only when the Israelites saw him emerge periodically at different stages in the ritual.

Having gained access to the dark cubicle where the sacred ark was placed, the high priest sprinkled some of the sacrificial blood which he had now brought with him towards the front of the ornate lid covering the ark. This act was followed by a sevenfold sprinkling of blood in the air at the front of the ark itself. This was the only occasion on which the high priest was permitted to enter the most holy place for any purpose, and the only time that such a sprinkling was carried out in that sacred location. In the sin offerings described in Leviticus 4, the priest was instructed to sprinkle blood seven times in God's presence (verses 6, 17), but this had to be performed in front of the decorated curtain, not beyond it. The sprinkling on the cover of the ark brought the sacrifice into unique contact with God's presence, and made expiation for the high priest and other members of the priestly line. Jesus Christ, the sinless High Priest, had no need to make atonement for Himself before he could die for human sin (Heb. 7:27 28).

Yet another entrance into the inner part of the sanctuary was required for blood from the goat of the people's sin offering to be sprinkled in front of the sacred ark (15). This act was necessary in order to purify the whole tabernacle area from uncleanness caused by the very presence of the ceremonially defiled Israelites. Their *transgressions* and *sins* (16) were those of accident, neglect or inadvertence, and not the rejection of covenant love, for which there was no forgiveness (Nu. 15:30). During these acts of atonement the high priest had to be entirely alone, and was not permitted to have any assistance in his duties. In the same sense Christ was also uniquely alone when He was atoning for the sins of the world (*cf.* Mt. 27:46; Mk. 15:34).

Atonement for the altar *which is before the Lord* (18) was the next step in the cleansing rituals. Both bull and goat blood were used to smear the horns of the altar, and to sprinkle it as a means of purification and reconsecration. The rather vague nature of the wording has led to questions as to which altar was meant. Jewish commentators have taken the reference to indicate the golden altar of incense in the holy place (*cf.* Ex. 30:10; Lv. 4:7, 18), but most Christian writers think that the passage refers to the altar of burnt offering, on which sacrifices were also offered before the Lord (Lv. 1:3, 5; 4:24, *etc.*). The former interpretation seems more probable, however, since the altar to be atoned for is intimately related to *the holy place and the tent of meeting* (20). The altar was smeared with blood as part of the ritual for the sin offerings (Lv. 4:7, 18), and would therefore need to be purified.

Once this had been done, the high priest was to bring the goat to an open area in the tabernacle court, and confess over it all the manifold transgressions of the Israelites, which were then transferred symbolically to the animal by the imposition of Aaron's hands. The *iniquities, transgressions,* and *sins* of the people represented the consequences of ignorance or inadvertence. But this was not all. Because the Hebrew term *peša'* (21) not merely means 'transgressions', but also carries with it a consistent sense of revolt or rebellion against an overlord, some of the offences for which atonement was to be made would have been committed despite the known will of God. These latter would be regarded as sins of error or accident if the sinner by true penitence showed that his misdemeanours were mostly the product of ignorance. The goat was then sent out into the wilderness area beyond the camp from which it could not return, typifying the complete removal of the nation's sin and guilt. The rituals are entirely correct psychologically and spiritually in connecting the forgiveness of sin and the removal of guilt. The antiquity of this passage is indicated by the fact that in later periods of Israel's history, the goat was hurled to its death from a steep cliff in the wilderness. God's loving nature is such that He delights in being able to cleanse the sinner and effect complete removal of the sin, whether in the old dispensation (*cf.* Ps. 103:12; Mi. 7:19) or the new (1 Jn. 1:7, 9).

d. Rituals for cleansing (23–28)

After the goat had been dispatched to the wilderness, Aaron had to take off his linen attire and wash his entire body in a specially reserved area of the tabernacle court. He was then required to wear his normal priestly vestments while he offered burnt sacrifices for himself and the people (24). The person who had conducted the goat into the wilderness was ceremonially unclean as a result of contact with the sins of the people, and he had to bathe and wash his clothes before being readmitted to the community (26). The same was true of the individual who carried out the carcasses of the bull and goat sacrificed for a sin offering. The rituals of the sacrifices are not described in detail here, since they followed the normal pattern. As always, all the fat was reserved as God's special portion (25). Through the entire ceremony the emphasis is upon the holiness of God as contrasted with the sin of man, and the necessity for the worshipper, whether high priest or not, to follow scrupulously the directions for approaching God in worship. Only when all has been done in accordance with God's will can forgiveness be expected to follow. The ritual of the day of atonement contained a definite sense of drama, as indeed all ancient Hebrew rituals did, but it also made clear the responsibilities of the worshipper in the whole process of cleansing from sin, especially at the climactic moment when the high priest entered the most holy place and stood in God's presence. The Christian, whose life is hidden with the Saviour in God (Col. 3:3) has nothing to fear when he comes to stand before the judgment seat of Christ (Rom. 14:10).

e. Enactment of the day of atonement (29–34)

This section confirms that this special day shall be an institution amongst the Israelites for ever. The ceremony was to be observed on the tenth day of the seventh month, that is to say, six months after the passover had been celebrated. The permanence of the statute is indicated by the fact that to the present day this solemn ceremony, with appropriate modifications, is conducted on the tenth day of the seventh month, following the traditional calendar. The seventh month, known in the post-exilic period as Tishri (September-October), was in the autumn when the early rains fell and the land was ploughed ready for sowing in the following month. Such old Canaanite or Phoenician names of the months (*cf.* Ex. 13:4; 1 Ki. 6:1, 38; 8:2) had been replaced by the end of the kingdom period (*cf.* 1 Ki. 6:1; 8:2) with traditional ordinal numbers, as in verse 29, and the beginning of the year was placed in March-April, when the barley harvest began. The self-affliction which was a preparation for the ceremony has been interpreted traditionally in terms of fasting, though this is not stated here. It seems at least possible that affliction included some distinctive penal variation from routine behaviour such as the wearing of sackcloth. The Hebrew verb *'anâ* in the intensive form carries the sense of 'humbling oneself', but without further specification in Leviticus. In Isaiah 58:35 the same verb occurs within the context of fasting, but appears to refer to some other activity, perhaps the wearing of ashes. While the native and alien alike were forbidden to work, the alien was not required to 'afflict' himself.

In the Old Testament fasting was sometimes undertaken to avoid calamity (*cf.* 1 Sa. 7:6; 1 Ki. 21:9, 12; Je. 36:9, *etc.*), but always seems to have carried with it an awareness of human sin, with the object of averting God's anger or winning His compassion. While Jesus Himself fasted periodically, He did not impose it as a discipline upon His followers. Instead, He warned them against using fasting as an exhibition of piety as the Pharisees did, stressing that fasting must be an act of devotion to God, proceeding from a pure and honest motive (*cf.* Mt. 6:16–18; 9:14–17; Mk. 2:18–22; Lk. 5:33–39). The *sabbath of solemn rest* (31) would enable the Israelites to reflect upon their destiny as the chosen people, and the extent to which they were living as a spiritual community. The permanence of the legislation regarding the day of atonement is reflected in the instructions for succeeding generations of high priests to continue the solemn observance as a means of making annual atonement for national sin (32). In view of this injunction it is curious that no specific reference to the day of atonement occurs elsewhere in the Old Testament, despite the periodic occurrence of certain significant events in the seventh month (*cf.* 1 Ki. 8:2, 65–66; Ezr. 3:1–6; Ne. 8:17–18).

The ceremonies of the day of atonement made abundantly clear God's detestation of sin, which if it was continued resulted in defilement and death (*cf.* Rom. 6:23). The chosen people were required to reflect the holiness of their covenant God, and the day of atonement provided a new beginning each year for the fulfilment of that ideal. It also demonstrated the universality and omnipresence of sin. High priest and layman alike had offended against God's holiness, and therefore atonement was needed by everybody. Not even the material objects of cultic worship could escape the suspicion of being tainted by communal sin; hence the emphasis in the rituals on the cleansing of the whole tabernacle area. The entire ceremony was conducted with a solemnity and an attention to detail that was characteristic of the levitical sacrificial system, in the knowledge that the slightest violation of divine propriety could result in instant death for the offender.

As well as stressing the contagion and dissemination of sin, the rituals demonstrate that no person can make atonement for his own sins. Blood was to be shed (Heb. 9:22) by a substitute, for which under the old dispensation a variety of animals sufficed. The offering of two goats for the sins of the community was obviously out of all proportion to the need for atonement. This, however, appears to have been a deliberate indication of the temporary and typical nature of the ceremony. One of the weaknesses of the levitical sacrificial system was that it could make no provision for full and final forgiveness of the sinner. The various rituals had to be repeated periodically, and a human mediator, who himself needed atonement, was required to declare God's absolving grace.

For the Christian, the solemn day looked forward to the time when a representative human being would bear the sins of the world (Is. 53:6) as the Lamb of God (Jn. 1:29). This was necessary since the blood of bulls and goats could not possibly remove sin (Heb. 10:4). Only God as manifested in the person of Jesus Christ could reconcile the world to Himself (2 Cor. 5:19). The blood is the life of the flesh (Lv. 17:11), and it is through the atoning blood of Christ that the believer receives redemption (1 Pet. 1:18–19), forgiveness (Eph. 1:7), justification (Rom. 5:9), spiritual peace (Col. 1:20), and sanctification (Heb. 13:12).

As Christ was dying on the cross, the highly embroidered veil of the temple was torn in half, signifying that from that time forward mankind was living under the new covenant of grace. Its institution by the perfect sin-bearer has made it evident that the ceremonies of the old covenant were but symbols, types and shadows (*cf.* Col. 2:17; Heb. 8:5; 10:1). The way into the most holy presence of God has been opened for the sinner by the shed blood of Christ (Heb. 10:20). The Saviour is now the great High Priest over the household of faith, the Christian church, and it is through Him alone that we approach God in penitence and trust for the forgiveness of our sins. The Christian looks back to the events of Calvary as the one great occasion (Rom. 6:10; Heb. 7:27; 9:12) when the day of atonement was celebrated. Unlike the Israelite high priests who were subject to human mortality, Jesus continues for ever as our High Priest (Heb. 7:24) because of His eternal nature. Being sinless, Jesus Christ had an immense moral advantage over the priests of the old dispensation, who first had to atone for themselves before being able to atone for the people. The covenant of grace which Christ introduced means that the individual no longer has to relate to God on the basis of legalism (Heb. 7:18–19), for now man can have unhampered access to God. Unlike the Hebrew priests who presented animal sacrifices as a means of atoning for sin, Jesus made the supreme sacrifice by offering Himself (Heb. 7:27), making a once-for-all-time atonement for human wickedness. By contrast with the work of the Israelite high priests, the priesthood which Christ exercised is supreme.

V. RITUAL LAWS (17:1 – 25:55)

a. Sacrificial blood (17:1–16)

The material in this chapter forms a supplement to the legislation contained in the first seven chapters of the book, and it is also connected very closely with chapter 16. Since the formulation of the Graf-Wellhausen theory of pentateuchal composition towards the end of the nineteenth century, literary-critical scholarship has uniformly regarded Leviticus 17 – 26 as comprising a so-called 'holiness code' which according to the theory was added to the priestly 'document' a little after the time of Ezekiel.[60] Unfortunately this view cannot be supported by any form of objective evidence, and has the undoubted demerit of separating this ancillary material governing ritual laws from the concerns of the book as a whole, which is unquestionably a manual of holiness. While it is fashionable in literary-critical circles to see 'late' elements in the second half of Leviticus, it is nevertheless true that there is not one aspect of this legislative material that is inconsistent with a date of origin in the second millennium BC.

The chapter begins with a formula that is typical of Leviticus (*cf.* Lv. 1:1; 4:1; 6:1; 7:28, *etc.*), after which it deals with four situations in which the sacrifice and consumption of meat are involved. Its unity with preceding chapters is seen in its recapitulation of matters discussed previously (*cf.* Lv. 7:26-27 and 17:10-15; 11:39-40 and 17:15-16), with particular emphasis upon the meaning of blood in sacrificial usage. Another reason why this chapter is hardly likely to be part of a separate priestly 'holiness code' is that is says virtually nothing about the place of the priests in the matter of sacrifices. Instead, it focuses on the part of the ordinary worshipper in the sacrificial system, dealing with correct slaughtering procedures and the penalties that accrue when blood is misused. Hygienic concerns are also very much part of the legislation relating to the ingesting of blood.

1-2. An introductory formula indicates that this material, like other sections before it, bears the authority of divine revelation. It is to be part of the priestly corpus of teaching, and has to be communicated to the entire nation as a commandment from God. If kept, the injunctions will ensure the continuity of Israel's distinctive way of life; but if they are disregarded, the nation is warned of the punishment that will follow.

3-7. The first situation involving sacrifice prohibits the killing of animals without offering them to the Lord. The penalty for such an offence ('bloodguilt') is to be *cut off* (4). Bloodguilt was a legal term which was normally used in the Old Testament with reference to manslaughter or murder. This reference has been seen as reflecting man's ancient kinship with the animal creation with the implication that,

[60] *HIOT*, p. 21.

until mankind began to eat animals for food, killing them was tantamount to murder.[61] Whether this is so or not, the purpose of this enactment was to encourage those who slaughtered animals, whether in the *open field* (5) or in the camp, to bring them as peace offerings to God. In this way the Lord would receive His appointed portion (Lv. 3:1–17), as would the officiating priest (Lv. 7:11–18). Once the needs of the sanctuary had been met, and the donor reminded that his food came ultimately from God, the flesh of the animal could be eaten by the donor's family, and perhaps also by friends.

This requirement points to a primitive phase in Israelite life, when domestic animals were too valuable for milk and milk by-products to be slaughtered for food. This would be particularly applicable to a wilderness milieu, where the maintaining of livestock in however meagre a fashion was fundamental to the existence of the semi-nomadic Israelite community. Indeed, during that period the livestock resources were conserved by the fact that the people lived on manna, and only on comparatively infrequent occasions would an animal be killed as a peace offering. This early legislation was modified subsequently in Deuteronomy 12:20–28, in preparation for the dispersion of the Israelite community throughout the land of Canaan, and the consequent logistical difficulties involved in bringing to the central sanctuary animals that had been slaughtered at some distance.

All sacrifices were to be under the supervision of the sanctuary priests for another reason, namely to ensure that the Israelites avoided any form of idolatry. The Hebrew term for sacrifice (*zebaḥ*) is from a verb meaning 'to slaughter', which would indicate that in the ancient Near East the killing of domestic animals was at one period held to be a form of sacrifice. If all sacrifices were to be performed within the sanctuary area, there could be no possibility of a person making a private, idolatrous offering to some imagined denizen of the countryside. This legislation was timely, for even from the beginning of the wilderness wanderings idolatrous tendencies were never very far from the minds of the Israelites (*cf.* Ex. 32:1–6).

---

[61] J. R. Porter, *Leviticus*, p. 139.

The reference to *sacrifices for satyrs* (7) is another indication of an early phase in the life of the nation. The word 'satyr' (RV 'he-goat'; NEB 'demons') referred superstitiously to demons that were supposed to haunt areas of the wilderness (Is. 13:21; 34:14). The allusion here is to the kind of goat worship practised in Lower Egypt, a form of idolatry with which the Israelites had evidently had some contact (*cf.* Jos. 24:14). The cult in question flourished in the eastern Delta region, and part of its abhorrent rituals involved goats copulating with women votaries. Quite understandably the Israelites were prohibited from practising such worship, either in the wilderness period or subsequently in the promised land, lest the idolatry and superstitious beliefs of pagan nations should compromise their spirituality. It is extremely difficult for the modern western mind to conceive of the overpowering influence that evil spirits and demons exerted over all areas of life in the ancient world. If the Israelites could remain free from bondage to such crippling superstitions, they would indeed be unique as a people in antiquity. The intent of this legislation is to direct their activities to that end.

8–9. The second section of legal material deals with the prohibition of sacrifices made outside the tabernacle area. This reinforces the purpose of the previous verses by dealing with an offering that is meant to involve worship. Both the slaughtering and the presentation of the animal must be on holy ground, otherwise the offering would be polluted from the very beginning. The application of this prohibition to aliens living among the Israelites is meant to discourage them from sacrificing to pagan gods, and perhaps attracting the Israelites to such worship as a result. The emphasis upon ritual propriety is particularly noticeable in this section, since the *burnt offering* (8) belonged exclusively to God and was not eaten in the context of a sacrificial meal. Levitical legislation teaches repeatedly that the sinner's approach to God in worship must follow certain specified guidelines, otherwise the result will be disastrous. Christians in general need to have a greater sense of awe and reverance as they come to the Creator of the world and men.

10–12. This passage explains the rationale underlying earlier prohibitions against the ingestion of blood. In Genesis 9:4,

Noah and his family were instructed in the connection between flesh, blood and life, where life and blood were equated.
The penalty for any Israelite, or any alien living in an Israelite
family, who was caught ingesting blood in any way was to be
cut . . . off from among his people (10), presumably by a divinely
instigated act. Any animal meant for human consumption had
to be killed in such a way that all the blood was either drained
or washed from its body, a principle that results in what the
Jews call *kosher* meat. The blood is a highly complex fluid
which contains cells, various forms of nourishment for the
tissues, disease antibodies, hormones, and other substances,
which when in balance maintain health and well-being. Thus
the life of the flesh (*i.e.*, the whole body) is indeed *in the blood*
(11), or better, 'the life of every living creature is the blood'
(NEB, verse 14), following the LXX, which seems to preserve a
superior manuscript tradition here. It is given particular
sanctity because God has appointed the blood of clean animals
as the means of atonement.

The word *souls* (11) is misleading, since it involves a
metaphysic that the situation does not warrant. *Nepeš* commonly means 'life', and is so rendered at the beginning of the
verse. In a personal sense it means 'one's life', and thus
'oneself'. This was the way in which Jesus understood it when
He asked what an individual could give in exchange for
himself (Mt. 16:26; Mk. 8:37). Consequently atonement is
made 'for yourselves' (so NEB). This principle of substitutionary atonement, as has been mentioned previously, was carried
to its highest level by Jesus Christ on Calvary, through whom
we have now received atonement (Rom. 5:11). His life, as
represented by His shed blood, gives eternal life to the sinner
by cleansing him from iniquity and bringing him into a new
state of fellowship with God. The nature of Old Testament
sacrifices was such that whenever cleansing from sin was
required there had to be a blood ritual, since the relationship
with God could not be renewed without it.[62] Considerable
debate has taken place concerning the meaning of the term
'blood' in this context. The most frequent use of *dām* in the Old
Testament is in relationship to death by violence, whether in

[62] D. Kidner, *Sacrifice in the Old Testament* (1951), p. 14.

terms of the sacrificial rituals or not. Over the last century some writers have interpreted passages such as Genesis 9:4, Leviticus 17:11 and Deuteronomy 12:33 to imply that life somehow subsisted in the blood, and remained there when the animal was sacrificed. The offering of blood, therefore, was in fact an indication that life had been released in order to be offered to God.[63] By contrast, the extent to which blood was linked with death in the Old Testament has led other writers to think of blood as meaning life given up in death.[64] In view of the consistent Old Testament tradition that sin was a most serious matter in God's sight, and merited the most drastic punishment, it is difficult to see how the slain sacrifices could be interpreted in any other than penal terms, with the animal acting as a substitute for the sinner. As though that were insufficient, the sacrificial procedures mention the death of the victim frequently, while remaining silent about its life. Shed blood constituted visible evidence that life had indeed been offered up in sacrifice. In order to set in proper perspective the notion of life subsisting in the blood, it is worthy of note that the correct translation of Leviticus 17:11 is 'the life of the flesh is the blood'. Only as atonement is linked with death, represented by shed blood, and not life set free, would it appear to become efficacious in the covering of human sin.

13–16. The final legislative section has to do with the blood of clean game caught in the hunt. Although such creatures could not be offered in sacrifice, their blood must nevertheless be treated circumspectly. It was to be drained on the ground when the victim was killed, and then covered over with earth. The life had thus returned to the ground from which it had come, and the hunters and others who chanced to be in the vicinity were protected from the possibility of communicable

[63] So, *e.g.*, B. F. Westcott, *Commentary on the Epistle to the Hebrews* (1889), pp. 288f., 294; *idem, Commentary on the Epistles of St John* (1892), p. 34; A. Cave, *Sacrifice and Atonement* (1890), p. 103; V. Taylor, *Forgiveness and Reconciliation* (1941); *idem, The Atonement in New Testament Teaching* (1958 ed.), p. 123. None of these writers, or others who adhere to this view, has offered factual evidence to support it.

[64] So, *e.g.*, A. M. Stibbs, *The Meaning of the Word 'Blood' in Scripture* (1954), p. 30 *passim*; L. Morris in *Baker's Dictionary of Theology* (1960), pp. 99–100; *idem, The Cross in the New Testament* (1965), p. 219.

disease or infection. While reverence for life is indicated to some extent by this legislation, there is also an obvious hygienic concern to be borne in mind.

Animals that had died from natural causes, from suicide, or as a result of being mauled by wild beasts, were forbidden for food to Israelite and proselyte alike (*cf.* Lv. 11:39). A stranger or an alien, however, was permitted to eat of such meat (*cf.* Dt. 14:21). If the instructions regarding ceremonial cleanness were not observed, the offender would suffer the consequences of disobedience were he to participate in sactuary worship. The eating of such tainted meat would undoubtedly be done in ignorance in the majority of circumstances.

The regulations concerning the sacredness of blood are full of spiritual meaning for the Christian. In addition to justification and forgiveness through the blood of Christ (Rom. 5:9; Eph. 1:7), the Christian gains access to God in faith (Heb. 10:22), experiences victory over evil (Rev. 12:11), and obtains eternal glory (Rev. 7:15). The death of Christ has brought new life into being for mankind by atoning for us in a manner completely beyond our own abilities to perform.

b. Various laws and punishments (18:1 – 20:27)

The attention of the enactments now shifts from the matter of ceremonial defilement and its removal to the question of moral impurity and its consequences. Being a holy nation is not just a matter of obeying mechanically certain cultic presciptions or following elaborate ceremonial procedures. Holiness is a moral attribute, and thus affects behaviour and character. Jesus warned against the kind of pharisaism that made persons appear attractive outwardly, whereas within they were full of hypocrisy and wickedness (Mt. 23:28). In the same way Paul reminded his readers that the real Jew is one who has a special kind of character, not one who depends upon external appearances (Rom. 2:28). A life of holiness involves moral purity as one of its aspects, and the rules given in this section are guidelines for holy living in the midst of an evil and adulterous generation.

The literary structure of chapter 14 is interesting in that it resembles the basic shape of the vassal or suzerainty treaties of the Hittites, which in turn appear to have derived their own form from Mesopotamian sources. This pattern can be seen elsewhere in the Old Testament, especially in the book of Deuteronomy, which exhibits the various features with great clarity. The vassal treaties were made between a great Hittite king and a people whom he wished to subject to his rule. After identifying himself in a preamble and stating his beneficence to previous vassals in a passage dealing with historical retrospect, the king laid before the intended vassal the basic and detailed stipulations which comprised the agreement. A list of blessings and curses was always part of such a treaty, describing the benefits which the vassal would obtain by keeping the agreement, and the punishments that would come upon him for breaches of it. In chapter 18 the preamble is *I am the Lord your God* (2), while the historical prologue is the phrase *Egypt, where you dwelt* (3). The basic stipulation is covered by the injunction *do my ordinances and keep my statutes and walk in them* (4), while the detailed stipulations comprise the material in verses 6 to 23. The blessings occur in a shortened form in verse 5, *a man shall live*, while the curses are found in verses 24 to 30. This latter situation is typical of Hittite vassal treaties, where the curses always greatly outnumber the blessings. Other elements of Hittite covenant-forms such as the placing of the treaty in a sacred place, the ratification by witnesses, and the celebration of the occasion by means of a feast, are absent from this section but occur mostly in the book of Deuteronomy, which is a far more elaborate composition structurally.[65] This format was well known in the second millennium BC, and thus it is not surprising to find it used in writings from this period such as Leviticus and Deuteronomy, as well as in Exodus 20.[66]

1–5. The basic principles of covenant morality are set out, and are contrasted with the practices of certain contemporary nations. The Israelites can expect God's blessing upon their lives only as they obey implicity the statutes and ordinances of the covenant (*cf.* Dt. 30:15–20). The word *ḥuqqîm* ('statutes') comes from a root 'to engrave', thus describing per-

---

[65] For the latter see P. C. Craigie, *Deuteronomy* (1976), pp. 22–23, 38–45.

[66] It is interesting to note that in the second-millennium BC texts recovered from Alalakh, the treaty which founded the city (#1) was accompanied by another tablet (#126), in which the same scribe set out the sacrificial arrangements which the city deity required to be observed.

manent behavioural rules prescribed by authority and recorded for the instruction and guidance of the individual or
society. An *ordinance* (Heb. *mišpāṭ*) was a judicial decision
arrived at by properly constituted authority or on the basis of
tradition, which would serve as a precedent for the future
guidance of judges under specific circumstances. Such statutes
and ordinances as proceeded from the God of the covenant
were to be the only authoritative basis for the behaviour of the
Israelites. As long as the chosen people kept the prescribed
statutes and ordinances, they could expect to *live* (5). The kind
of life which the law brought would be one of divine blessing
and material prosperity, consonant with the covenantal promises, but contingent always upon implicit obedience to the will
of God.

Any indulgence in the immoral practices of the land from
which God had delivered them would result in punishment, as
would an espousal of the abhorrent cultic worship current in
the land which God was about to give them. The comprehen-
siveness of this legislation shows that for the covenant people
there was no aspect of their existence that could be regarded as
being out of God's control, a proposition already made clear
by earlier enactments. The people of faith and holiness
obtained their behavioural precepts and standards from God,
unlike the pagan nations of antiquity who were guided as
much by self-interest as anything else. Paul summarized the
approach which the Christian should adopt towards the new
covenant and its obligations in the phrase, *not I but Christ* (Gal.
2:20). He knew that to be carnally minded resulted in death,
but to be spiritually motivated issued in life and peace (Rom.
8:6). In this important respect both the old and new covenants
are one.

6–18. This passage lists the kinds of sexual union that are
illegal according to covenant morality. It is not without
significance that these laws form the basis of permitted degrees
of relationship within Christian marriage. In a nomadic
society where family members are necessarily in close contact
on regular occasions, it is fundamentally important for guidelines of this sort to be enunciated if illicit sexual activity is to be
prevented. By listing what is prohibited, the enactments leave
no doubt in anyone's mind about what is unacceptable **moral**

behaviour in the sight of God. The explicit nature of the passage reflects the unselfconscious attitude of the Hebrews, and indeed of all ancient Near Eastern peoples, towards sexual activity.

Marriage as a social institution is regarded throughout Scripture as the cornerstone of all other structures, and hence its purity and integrity must be protected at all times. The basic means of attaining this objective in the regulations is to forbid sexual relationships between close relatives. The Hebrews *šᵉ'ēr bᵉśarô* is literally 'flesh of his flesh', and in this chapter describes a blood relation. The various prohibitions embrace six relationships of consanguinity (verses 7, 9, 10, 11, 12, 13), and eight of affinity (verses 8, 14, 15, 16, 17, 18). These are representative cases, of course, and do not exhaust all the possible illicit combinations. They show without question that nearness of relationship is an impediment to sexual relations, affecting all ascendants and descendants, but only the nearer cases of collaterals. The regulations interpret relationships of affinity (connection by marriage) in terms of the principle that man and wife are 'one flesh' (Gn. 2:24), *i.e.*, kin or blood relations.

There has been considerable discussion among commentators as to whether or not these regulations concerned marriage, or casual sexual relationships outside the marriage bond. A careful reading of these verses makes it apparent that both situations were envisaged by the legislation. The expression *uncover the nakedness* is a synonym for sexual intercourse, particularly for relationships that cannot be regarded as genuine marriages. A union between mother and son, for example, is something that defiles the parental relationship (7), while a stepmother comes into the same general category, since she was regarded as a very close relation (8). Sexual activity, whether within marriage or outside of it, was forbidden with a sister and a half-sister (9), whether the person concerned had been brought up in the family or in another household (so NEB). The meaning of this last phrase is obscure, but it may well be a euphemism to distinguish the legitimate child from the illegitimate one. Marriage or coition with a granddaughter (10) or a stepgranddaughter (17) was forbidden, as were relationships with such close relatives as aunts

(12–14). The prohibition against marriage with a sister or a half-sister was an innovation in Israelite life, since Abraham had married his half-sister (Gn. 20:12). The injunctions of Leviticus were designed to prevent further unions of that sort, however well intended the male participants might have been. Some scholars have assumed that David's anger on learning that Amnon had violated Tamar (2 Sa. 13:21) was an indication that such Middle Bronze Age marriages were deemed illegal by the time of the early monarchy.[67] It is possible, however, that the action of Amnon resulted not so much from lust as from a carefully planned scheme to usurp his father David's kingship.[68] The enactment regarding marriage with aunts was also new in Hebrew life, as indicated by the union of Amram and Jochebed (Ex. 6:20), which was apparently acceptable in the pre-exodus period.

Marriage or sexual unions involving affinity included coition with a daughter-in-law, whether after divorce from her husband or subsequent to his death, since she was in effect a daughter of the family (15). An exception to the legislation regarding marriage with a brother's wife (16) was made in Deuteronomy 25:5–10, where the point at issue was the perpetuation of the deceased husband's family name. This levirate law, as it is called, made provision for the married man who happened to die childless, and permitted a brother of the deceased to marry the widow and endeavour to raise male progeny who would continue the line. Normally the first male from such a union was recognized as the descendant and legal heir of the dead man. For a man to have sexual relations with a woman and her daughter or granddaughter under any circumstances was considered *wickedness* (17), literally 'harlotry', since the women were held to be near relatives. Men were also spared a great deal of family strife by being prohibited from taking sisters as rival wives, and having coition with them while both were alive. This regulation did not prevent a woman from living in the same household as her brother-in-law, however, nor did it expressly prohibit the marriage of a man with the sister of his deceased wife. With respect to the

---

[67] *Cf.* G. J. Wenham, *VT*, 22 (1972), pp. 342 f.
[68] *Cf. HIOT*, pp. 56 f, 716 f.

marriage of king Herod to Herodias, the divorced wife of his brother Philip who was still alive, the rebuke of John the Baptist (Mt. 14:4; Mk. 6:18; Lk. 3:19) indicates that, while under current Jewish traditions divorce was admissible, marriage with the wife of a living brother was not.

In view of the fact that many societies have laid down rules of varying severity to deal with the matter of incest, it is rather disappointing to discover that anthropologists and others have discussed the origin of such legislation without, however, arriving at very firm conclusions. In general the anthropologists think that the laws governing incest seem to have arisen either to prevent the disastrous results of inbreeding, or as the outcome of limitations on such activity by the population.[69] As far as the levitical regulations are concerned, the rationale is not explained in terms other than those involving divine holiness. The general aim of the legislation appears to have been to encourage the avoidance rather than the actual prevention of incest. It would seem at least possible that a very small percentage of the Israelite population would, for one reason or another, indulge occasionally in sexual activity with close relatives. In order that the behaviour of possible sexual deviants might be regulated, the sanctions contained in this chapter had to be instituted.

These enactments had as their stated purpose the preservation of community holiness in the area of sexual conduct, and to this end they outlined the broad conditions under which sexual activity was forbidden. Certain other Near Eastern legal enactments such as that of Hammurabi mentioned some penalties for incest, but in general they were mild, with the threat of death in one instance as the maximum punishment. By contrast, the Israelites would be quite distinctive in their way of life as long as they obeyed these injunctions. That there were lapses in this respect, however, is indicated by the complaint of Amos about contemporary violations of covenant morality (Am. 2:7), the result of which was the profanation of God's holy name. But moral and spiritual considerations do not exhaust the intent of the legislation, for here as in other areas of leviticial law there is an underlying concern for

[69] *Cf.* R. Fox, *Kinship and Marriage* (1967), p. 75.

individual and communal well-being. Had the marriage of close relatives been permitted, it would have resulted in land and property becoming concentrated quite quickly in the hands of a few families. This in turn would have brought about serfdom for the Israelites, thereby destroying any sense of community and individual equality under the law that the covenant ideal represented.

Another important matter involved the genetic factors of the incestuous relationships, the majority of which consisted either of first or second degrees of consanguinity. The former would comprise parent-child and brother-sister unions, while the latter would include the grandparent-grandchild and nephew-aunt type of relationship. Surveys in different parts of the world where inbreeding occurs have shown that it is accompanied by an increase in congenital malformations and perinatal mortality,[70] for which recessive genes and environmental factors respectively would be responsible.

In those instances where the parents are siblings, or where the relationship is one between parent and child, the resultant offspring incur approximately a 30% risk of retardation or some other serious defect. This can emerge from the presence of detrimental genes in the parents that have been inherited from a common ancestor. The closer the relationship between those who marry, the more frequent is the incidence of harmful or lethal genes. For parents who are first cousins, there is about a 4% possibility that the offspring will experience a birth defect. Marriage between a man and his niece doubles this percentage risk of malformation because of the danger that the child will exhibit harmful recessive genes inherited from one of the couple's common ancestors. In animal husbandry, smaller litters generally result from inbreeding, as do deformed or abnormal species. Inbred racehorses exhibit neurotic tendencies that can be most disconcerting to patrons of the supposed 'sport of kings'. Despite these obvious disadvantages, close inbreeding confers certain benefits on the species by removing recessive lethal genes from the genetic pool, as experiments with many generations of mice have shown. The

[70] *Cf.* J. V. Neel, *American Journal of Human Genetics,* 10, 1958, pp. 398–445; S. Kumar, *et al., Annals of Human Genetics,* 31, 1971, pp. 141–145.

drawback to this process is that the highly inbred species, though purged of harmful recessive genes, does not exhibit the vitality or vigour of outbred species,[71] thus demonstrating the wisdom of the levitical legislation.

19-20. Carnal relations with a woman during her menses had been prohibited earlier on the basis of ceremonial uncleanness (Lv. 15:24), but here are regarded as a moral offence, and would be punished accordingly (Lv. 20:18). Adultery was expressly forbidden in the Ten Commandments (Ex. 20:14), as were other offences against individuals and property. In verse 20 the emphasis is not so much upon the disruptive effects of adultery on the fabric of the covenant community as upon the defilement which the offender will himself occur. Adultery in the Old Testament was regarded as coition between a married or engaged woman and a man who was not her husband, and was a capital offence (Lv. 20:10).

21. One of the particularly abhorrent practices of the Canaanites was selected for special condemnation (*cf.* Lv. 20:2-5; 2 Ki. 23:10; Je. 32:35). Precisely what Molech-worship involved has been a matter of debate, but the reference to devoting children by fire to this deity suggests either sacrifice or the burning of a child while still alive.[72]

The god was worshipped particularly by the Ammonites of Transjordan, although the rituals involved are of uncertain character. Evidence from North Africa might suggest that the children were flung into the flames alive, although some authors maintain that a metal image of the god Molech was made very hot and the bodies of sacrificed children were placed in its arms.[73] Excavations at the site of a Late Bronze Age temple at Amman, ancient Rabbath-Ammon, capital of the Ammonites, have revealed evidence of child sacrifice in territory whose patron deity was Molech (1 Ki. 11:7). This

---

[71] I am indebted to my daughters, Charmian Felicity and Hermione Judith, for checking the accuracy of this and other remarks involving genetics in the present work.

[72] The NEB of Lv. 20:5 has a marginal note relating to 'in his wanton following after Molech', which reads, '*Or* in his lusting after human sacrifice', indicating that the worship of that particular diety most probably involved human sacrifice.

[73] See R. de Vaux, *Studies in Old Testament Sacrifice* (1964), pp. 56–90.

inhuman practice was abhorrent to God because it profaned His holy name, partly through violating the commandment forbidding murder, but also because such an act defaced the image of God in man.[74] 'God's command to Noah to sacrifice Isaac (Gn. 22:2), an event that occurred earlier in the Bronze Age, was intended as a test of the patriarch's obedience and faith. The order of the Hebrew and the presence of the definite article as part of the word for 'God' suggest that this undertaking was of more than ordinary significance.'[75] The explanation commonly suggested, that the episode had as its aim a protest against contemporary practices of human sacrifice, is less satisfactory than the one which sees the testing of Abraham's faith in the ultimate promises of God as the real purpose of the incident.

22. Homosexuality was known and practised in the Near East as a form of carnal indulgence from very early times. Such activities between individuals of the same sex seem to have played some part in Mesopotamian cultic worship, as suggested by the duties of the *assinnu* and *kurgarrû* priests of the love and war goddess Ishtar. These priests, however, may merely have become eunuchs in order to serve Ishtar in what was thought to have been a proper manner. The regulations of Leviticus condemn certain aberrations found among the Egyptians and Canaanites, who went far towards deifying sexual activity, and assigned the title 'holy ones' to cultic prostitutes. Sacro-homosexual practices and female prostitution within the context of the cultus was probably well established throughout the ancient Near East long before the Israelites occupied Canaan. Homosexuality of a non-religious variety is poorly documented in Mesopotamian texts; and in general Mesopotamian legislation paid little attention to any kind of homosexuality, although the Middle Assyrian laws prescribed castration for a convicted homosexual.[76] The Hittites evidently did not prohibit homosexuality except where a man violated his

---

[74] On the subject of human and child sacrifices see A. R. W. Green, *The Role of Human Sacrifice in the Ancient Near East* (1975).

[75] E. A. Speiser, *Genesis* (Anchor Bible, 1964), p. 162.

[76] J. B. Pritchard, *Ancient Near Eastern Texts relating to the Old Testament* (1955), p. 181.

son, an act which was regarded as a capital offence. While the ancient Egyptians disapproved of pederasty, there is some ground for thinking that they would occasionally inflict sexual abuse on an enemy defeated in battle.[77] In the Ugaritic texts there are no pronouncements on homosexuality as such, but in Canaanite religious life the male prostitute (*cf.* Dt. 23:17; 1 Ki. 14:24, *etc.*; AV 'sodomite'; RSV 'male cult prostitute'; NEB 'male prostitute') was prominent with his female counterpart.

Interpreters of Scripture have been accustomed to trace the incidence of homosexuality to the activities of the inhabitants of Sodom (Gn. 19:5), based on the supposition that their intent, like that of the dwellers at Gibeah (Jdg. 19:22), was to indulge in an act of sexual depravity. Interestingly enough, the Talmudic authorities placed little stress on a homosexual interpretation of Genesis 19:5, preferring instead to regard the Sodomites as having violated the normal canons of hospitality and justice (*Sanhed.* 19*a*; *Bab. Bath.* 12*b*, 59*a*). The relationship between David and Jonathan has been held to suggest homosexuality, despite the obvious heterosexual character of David, and even the rabbinic scholars questioned the nature of the interest that Potiphar (described in Gn. 39:1 NEB as a 'eunuch') had in Joseph (*cf. Sotah* 13*b*). Some modern lesbians have purported to find biblical authority for their behaviour in the deep affection that existed between Naomi and Ruth. Homosexuality was uniformly condemned in the Old Testament as *an abomination*, for which the punishment was death (Lv. 20:13). It violated the natural order of sexual relationships, and catered to perverted lust rather than to procreation of the species. The term 'dogs' appears to have been applied in Deuteronomy 23:18 to male cultic prostitutes or to homosexuals generally, and this may also be the sense of the allusion to 'dogs' in Revelation 22:15. In the New Testament, homosexuals were condemned by Paul for their behaviour (*cf.* Rom. 1:27; 1 Cor. 6:9; 1 Tim. 1:10), without any reference to the incident at ancient Sodom. Jude 7, however, decidedly and unceremoniously interpreted the fate of the inhabitants of Sodom as a punishment for sexual depravity and perversity. The (second edition) RSV of 1 Corinthians 6:9 described what

77 M. H. Pope, *IDB Supplementary Volume*, pp. 416.

Moffat rendered as 'catamites and sodomites' by the general designation of 'sexual perverts', an interpretation reinforced by the NEB.

23-30. Bestiality, which was practised intermittently among the Hittites, Babylonians, Egyptians and Canaanites, was thought of in this verse as involving actual coition with animals, and not merely their manual stimulation. For a man to indulge in such behaviour was defiling, but for a woman it was regarded as a sexual *perversion*. The penalty for such an offence under Hebrew law was death (Ex. 22:19; Lv. 20:15-16). This legislation said nothing about one woman lying with another woman, either because the practice was unknown to Israelite mores, or because no sexual function, and therefore no perversion, would be attributed to such an eventuality. Mankind was created in order to have dominance over the beasts of the field, and any attempt to mate with such creatures was categorized as a deviant form of sexual behaviour which attempted to introduce confusion into the established order of sexual relationships (*cf.* Gn. 2:24; 4:1, *etc.*). These pronouncements against bestiality are the most specific statements of their kind in the whole of ancient Near Eastern legal literature, and establish the most advanced kind of moral standards. Bestiality may have been one of the sexual aberrations condemned by Paul in Romans 1:26,[78] and its very nature provided a challenge of the most fundamental kind to the ethos of the covenant nation. The possibility that the Israelites might be lured into sexual behaviour that transgressed the statutes and ordinances of God is faced squarely, and a solemn warning is given that any offenders will be *cut off* (29) from among the nation. In this instance as in others, a direct act of God seems to be contemplated. A final word of exhortation is designed to maintain the purity of the nation in the face of current sexual deviations in Canaan.

In this passage it is made clear that any deviation from the sexual norms that have been proclaimed will not merely defile

---

[78] For discussions of homosexuality and bestiality in antiquity see R. W. Wood, *One Institute Quarterly*, 5, 1962, pp. 10-19: B. L. Smith, *Christianity Today*, 13, 1969, pp. 7-10; J. Z. Eglinton, *Greek Love* (1971), pp. 50-55; W. B. Parker, *Homosexuality: A Selective Bibliography of over 3,000 Items* (1971); H. A. Hoffner in *Orient and Occident* (1973), pp. 81-90.

those who indulge in them, but will also pollute the land. Once the Canaanites had been subjugated by Israel, the country would be under the control of a ceremonially clean people, living as a holy nation in the land provided for them by God. The terrain itself was His property, but would produce its fruits for the benefit of the chosen people as long as they obeyed His laws and did not pollute their inheritance by violating the covenant stipulations. Moral uncleanness, however, would disrupt the relationship between God and His people and result in their ultimate expulsion from the land, a fate that overtook the twelve tribes at a much later period in their history.

This extremely important chapter emphasizes implicit obedience to God's commands as the only way by which the distinctiveness of the nation in terms of sexual relationships can be established and maintained. The regulations governing sexual behaviour towards primary kin prohibit casual coition as well as marriage but, as with so many other elements of the levitical legislation, the rationale is not disclosed. Many of the incestuous unions condemned in these laws were practised amongst the cultured people of antiquity. Thus the Persians, for example, encouraged marital unions with mothers, daughters and sisters, on the ground that such relationships had special merit in the eyes of the gods. But for the covenant nation, self-discipline and the control of carnal appetites were alone pleasing to God, and the sexual exploitation of dependents living in a close relationship was prohibited. While sexual activity between legally married persons is quite proper according to this legislation, no form of perversion, whether inside or outside of marriage, is to be countenanced. Persons are to have control over their own bodies, so that if they transgress the covenantal enactments they become personally accountable to God for their misdeeds. Sexual purity is a small aspect of that larger morality (*cf.* Rom. 13:13; 1 Cor. 6:9–10, 13, *etc.*) which is mandatory for those who would aspire to the nature of a holy and perfect God. By obeying the guidelines governing sexual relationships, the Israelites would come to know at first hand something of the essence of holiness at a practical level. Laws relating to incest are found in various forms in human society, but those contained in this chapter

194

are by far the most detailed written material of their kind. The wisdom of the regulations is borne out increasingly by modern genetic studies which show that the offspring of the forbidden degrees of relationship are more prone to inherited disabilities and other genetic ailments than are children from non-related parents.[79]

Additional regulations (19:1-37)

The concluding words of the preceding chapter, *I am the Lord your God,* serve as a natural transition to this particular body of legislation, which also regulates the holiness of community life. Although this section deals with a wide variety of moral, legal, ceremonial and spiritual precepts in such a way as to appear disorganized, it is actually arranged in terms of sixteen distinct paragraphs, each of which ends with the phrase, *I am the Lord (your God).* These passages are arranged in three principal sections (2b-10; 11-18; 19-37) of four, four, and eight units respectively. Jewish scholars have seen in the material a counterpart of the Ten Commandments, the precepts of which are recapitulated as follows: I and II in verse 4; III in verse 12; IV and V in verse 3; VI in verse 16; VII in verse 29; VIII and IX in verses 11 to 16; and X in verse 18.[80]

1-2a. An introductory section reiterates God's demand that His people shall be holy. This injunction, like all other covenantal laws, is to be made public and observed by all. The emphasis upon *the congregation* indicates that all members have to play their part in maintaining the covenantal ethos, and no-one is exempt from responsibility in ensuring that holiness is a regulative principle of daily living.

2b-10. Religious obligations

2b. God's holiness is to be taken as a model for individual and community life. This principle can well be regarded as the watchword of the covenant people. The personal characteristics of holiness as reflected in God's nature include the perfected state of such ethical attributes as righteousness, love, goodness and purity. But holiness also describes His infinite

[79] A more general discussion of sex and its theology is to be found in Appendix B, pp. 249 ff.
[80] J. H. Hertz, *The Pentateuch and Haftorahs*, p. 497.

power, greatness and sublime exaltation above His creation, which causes man to appear by contrast as lost and wholly unworthy. Consequently those who revere God as Holy regard Him with fear and awe (*cf.* Ps. 96:9; Is. 8:13) because of His judgments upon mankind (*cf.* Ps. 119:9; Ezk. 36:21–24; Heb. 10:31; 12:26–29). God's holiness is the antithesis of human imperfection, and revolts against everything that is impure or evil (Hab. 1:13). In urging the Christian to be perfect (Mt. 5:48), Jesus was making the same demands for holiness of life as those found in the Torah. Holiness is one result of implicit obedience to God's will. It should be noted that obedience is stressed repeatedly in Leviticus, and not man's love for God, which is not mentioned in the book, though noted elsewhere (Ex. 20:6; Dt. 6:5; 10:12, *etc.*).

3. Reverencing parents is an act of piety towards God, since the parents are substitutes for the heavenly Father as far as their children are concerned. In Exodus 20:12 the father precedes the mother, and the verb is 'honour' instead of the Hebrew 'fear' (so AV) in this verse, however, a term which elsewhere is used of reverence for God. The meaning with respect to filial duty, however, is clear. One's parents, whatever their status in society or their physical or mental condition, are to be treated with respect and love. This is one of the most important of all human duties and responsibilities. The honouring of the sabbath, which has been replaced by the first day of the week (*cf.* Mt. 28:1; Mk. 16:1; Lk. 24:1; Jn. 20:1) in Christian teaching, furnishes a regular opportunity for the believer to worship God in the company of others, and to contemplate the extent to which his or her life accords with the demands of divine holiness. The reverencing of one's parents as surrogates of God is but one step away from the venerating of God himself.

4. Indulgence in any form of idolatry is expressly forbidden, the *idols* (Heb. *ᵉlîlîm*) literally being 'things of nothingness', 'non-entities' (*cf.* Is. 44:10). The word for 'idols' is similar in sound to that for 'God' (*ᵉlōhîm*), and the two are contrasted to show the fullness of God as against the emptiness of stone or wooden idols. In the end the Israelites succumbed to •he blandishments of Canaanite idolatry, for which they were punished by exile.

5-10. Ritual propriety is again emphasized here, for while the sacrifice is voluntary it must be offered in complete conformity with the prescribed procedures, lest innovations result in punishment rather than acceptance. The rules are given in Leviticus 3:1; 7:15-18, and provide a distinctive method of sacrificing peace offerings, free from any taint of heathenism. Christians should be scrupulous in ensuring that their forms of worship are thoroughly scriptural, and are not contaminated by superstition or purely human values. Otherwise what is holy to the Lord will be profaned, and punishment will follow instead of blessing (8). God's own concern for the poor among His people must be reflected by the Israelites in the practice of leaving a small amount of grain and fruits for them at the time of harvest. The sense of community among the Israelites was such that the poor person was considered to be a brother or sister, and was treated accordingly (*cf.* Acts 4:34-35).

The very fact that they were regarded by God as being members of a holy nation involved the Israelites in a sense of responsibility towards their fellows, especially the underprivileged. The sense of brotherhood is expressed strongly in this chapter, as well as in corresponding legislation in Deuteronomy. Thus it was forbidden for an Israelite to advance a loan at interest to another member of the holy people (Dt. 23:20), since a loan would normally only be needed in an emergency of a kind that would make the payment of interest a difficult and embarrassing matter.[81] Millstones were not to be taken in pledge, since that amounted to taking away a person's livelihood (Dt. 24:6). Indeed, the taking of pledges was governed by strict rules (Dt. 24:10-13; *cf.* Ex. 22:26-27). Exploitation of needy persons was prohibited (Dt. 24:14-22) because it violated the principle of brotherhood which, in a holy nation, meant that all persons were equal before God, whatever their social status. Thus members of the body corporate must be treated in a just and humane manner.

11-18. The love of one's neighbour
   11-12. Rules for good social relationships are stated speci-

---

[81] *Cf.* S. Stein, *Journal of Theological Studies*, N.S., 4, 1953, pp. 161-170; H. Gamoran, *Journal of Near Eastern Studies*, 30, 1971, pp. 127-134.

fically here. Stealing, false dealing, and downright lying (11) are forbidden because they are alien to the covenant ethic. They breed suspicion, mistrust and hatred, and by their very nature they weaken seriously the fabric of society. The children of the new covenant are urged to avoid such evils also (*cf.* Eph 4:28; Col. 3:9, *etc.*). Swearing falsely in God's name may be no part of the process of cheating or lying, but in any event it profanes the holy name of God by associating it with some impure, immoral, deceitful or unrighteous act.

13–14. A man must not exploit his fellow-Israelites in any way, because they are brothers and sisters. The *neighbour* (13) becomes *a hired servant* in Deuteronomy 24:14, but the principle is the same. His wages must be paid at the proper rate, without any portion being withheld ('rob him'). Where servants are hired by the day they must be paid before nightfall (*cf.* Mt. 20:8), since the poor would have immediate need of the day's wage. In the New Testament masters are exhorted to treat their servants fairly (Eph. 6:9; Col. 4:1). Whereas handicapped persons in the ancient Near East tended to be exploited and abused, among the Israelites they were to be treated with consideration, since they bore the image of the God whom Israel was commanded to reverence. Cursing the deaf was actually taking unfair advantage of persons who could not rise to their own defence. Since both Leviticus (19:14) and Deuteronomy (27:18) prohibited Israelites from placing obstacles of various sorts before the blind, or leading them in directions that they did not wish to follow, it would appear that this sort of activity was not unknown in other nations. The fact that the deaf and blind were legislated for as classes in society indicates the prevalence of these two afflictions in the Mosaic era. The restoring of sight and hearing was among the wonderful attestations of Christ's supernatural ministry (*cf.* Lk. 4:18).

15–16. Justice must not be perverted through consideration of social or economic circumstances. The judge or elder at the gate must be impartial in his decisions, which are to be based solely on righteousness. People who spread malicious gossip come under the condemnation of this legislation, as do those who stand by idly or indifferently, not wishing to become involved when *the life* (16, Heb. 'blood') of a neighbour is in danger. These straightforward humanitarian provisions were by no means always observed in Near Eastern society, or even among the Israelites.

17–18. Responsibility towards one's neighbour involves a positive attitude of heart and mind. Hatred is an emotional response which should only be employed against evil (Am. 5:15), and least of all against one who is a fellow-member ('brother') of the covenant community. Where reproof is thought necessary, the matter should be discussed openly with the offender, not behind his back, lest anger should lead to resentment and hatred, thereby resulting in sin. Paul encouraged Timothy to reprove erring members of the church with love and patience (1 Tim. 4:12). Taking revenge after the manner of a blood-feud merely perpetuates an injustice, and sometimes magnifies it out of all proportion. Vengeance as such belongs solely to God (Dt. 32:35; Rom. 12:19; Heb. 10:30), who will repay in due season. The course for the Christian to follow in such cases was exemplified by Jesus Christ (1 Pet. 2:23). The law of love for one's fellows is enunciated only here and in verse 34, and appears to embrace members of the covenant community ('sons of your own people') along with aliens and strangers who lived among them. Indeed, the terms 'love' and 'neighbour' seem to have been as comprehensive in scope then as now. This so-called 'golden rule' was quoted by Christ (Mt. 19:19; 22:39; Mk. 12:31; Lk. 10:27, *etc.*) as an ideal of altruistic behaviour in society. The sentiment underlying this aphorism was unique in the ancient world, and represents one of the Old Testament's most outstanding moral precepts.

19–37. Miscellaneous regulations

19–25. The holiness and purity of the congregation were to be enhanced by observing the principle of separateness, embodied in the divine *statutes*. The breeding of different kinds of cattle to enrich the blood-line and produce hybrid species was forbidden, even though selective mating was known and practised among the Hebrews from the Middle Bronze Age (Gn. 30:37–40). Perhaps the reason for such a prohibition was the fear that the Israelites might imitate such abnormal sexual unions and ultimately indulge in the orgiastic rites of Canaanite religion. Different kinds of seed could not be sown in the same piece of ground, perhaps because by adopting that method instead of rotating the crops the land would become impoverished more quickly. Garments made from two different types of material (19) readily produced static electricity in tropical climates, and are uncomfortable to wear. Some modern mixtures of wool or cotton with synthetic fibres sometimes provoke an allergic reaction in the wearer. Considerations of personal comfort appear to be in mind in this instance. Whatever explanations are adduced for these injunctions, it seems clear that the emphasis was upon maintaining a state of holiness to the Lord. When God began His work of creation, He separated light from darkness and dry land from ocean. Man can follow in God's footsteps by observing the same general principle of separation. The chosen people had been taken out of all the other nations to be God's special possession, and if they were to fulfil their destiny it was incumbent upon them to maintain their spiritual, moral and social distinctiveness.

Another form of improper mixture, this time in the moral realm, has to do with a man who had coition with a slave woman betrothed to another man (20). The offence is not a capital crime, since the slave was not a free woman. Despite this, the offender had to sacrifice a guilt offering to the Lord after an enquiry had been made, and only then could proper atonement be effected for the transgression. Had the woman been seduced within the walls of a city, she and the offender would have been put to death (Dt. 22:23-24), presumably because she could have secured help which would have prevented the attack. While the female slave (Heb. *šiphâ*) normally belonged to her mistress, she could still be used by the patriarch of the household as a concubine, or violated by some other man as circumstances permitted. The passage shows that, although a woman might be a slave in Israel, she was still entitled to the protection of covenantal law.

The legislation forbidding the fruit of new trees to be eaten is based on sound horticulture principles. For the first three years the fruit is regarded as *forbidden* (23), described by the Hebrew in terms of 'uncircumcision'. By the fourth year the fruit would be more mature, and was reserved as *an offering of praise* to God. Thereafter the yield would increase and could be eaten freely by the people. Among the ancient Babylonians, trees bearing fruit were seldom utilized for food until after the fourth year.

26-28. Pagan customs forbidden to the holy congregation included eating meat which still contained blood (*cf.* Lv. 17:10-14), as well as the practice of *augury or witchcraft*. Augury, better 'divination' (so NEB), involved the use of charms, incantations and certain objects such as goblets (*cf.* Gn. 44:5, 15), though precisely how it was accomplished is unknown. Witchcraft, better 'soothsaying' (so NEB), seems to have consisted in this instance of the prognostication of favourable times for specific forms of action. The ancient world was burdened unbelievably by gross superstition of this sort, which had absolutely no place in the life of a nation dedicated to obey the one and only true God. He made His will known directly to His people through revelation to Moses and others, and indirectly by means of such divinatory cult-objects as the Urim and Thummin (Ex. 28:30; Lv. 8:8). No other means by which God's will might be ascertained was provided, but in any event the righteous man lived by his faith (Hab. 2:4). The shaping of the hair on the temples and beard (27), or the incising of patterns on the skin, formed part of pagan mourning practices and as such were prohibited. The disfiguring of the skin, which probably included some emblems of pagan deities, dishonoured the divine image in a person, and was forbidden because it did not reflect God's holiness (*cf.* Dt. 14:1-2). Bereavement must be accepted as part of God's will for the individual's life, and no attempt must be made to propitiate the deceased in any way.

29-30. Individuals as well as God can be profaned by immoral behaviour. Sexual relations are only to be undertaken within the sanctifying context of marriage, and under any other circumstances they become as unholy as the offenders themselves (Heb. 13:4). A man's daughter must not therefore be hired out as a prostitute for gainful purposes, since this debases the sacredness of her womanhood and denies her the control of her own body. Some commentators have understood verse 20 as a prohibition against cultic prostitution which was very common in the ancient world, but the allusion appears too general for such an interpretation. As elsewhere, it is moral rather than ceremonial offences that defile the land. Its sanctity will be preserved as the Israelites observe sabbath worship and reverence the Lord's sanctuary. Because the Hebrews failed to observe this injunction consistently in their subsequent history, the land was filled with wickedness and they themselves were taken into exile (*cf.* Ezk. 23:37-42).

31. Necromancy, which is the attempt to gain contact with the spirits of the deceased, is specifically prohibited to the Israelites. The medium (Heb. *'ōḇ*; NEB 'ghosts') was usually a woman who was able to obtain a materialization of certain deceased persons on request. The most notable attempt in Israel was in connection with the spirit of Samuel (1 Sa. 28:8-25), but the medium's technique was not described other than that she 'saw' an old man's shade coming 'up' out of the ground. In some Near Eastern societies such mediums would dig a small hole in the earth to symbolize a grave, and then put offerings in it to attract the attention of the person whom the medium desired to contact. The word translated wizards (Heb. *yiddᵉ'ōnî;* NEB 'spirits) comes from a root 'to know', perhaps referring to the occult information which the practitioner of necromancy purported to have. Contact with such persons resulted in spiritual defilement, partly because they had been in touch with the dead, but also because of the superstitious and demonic influences attending necromancy.

32. Respect for the aged was a prominent feature of ancient Near Eastern societies, on the ground that age and wisdom went hand in hand. That this was not always the case is seen in the comment of Elihu to Job (Jb. 32:9), which constitutes the only criticism of its kind in the Old Testament. The insolence of young people towards their elders is usually regarded as presaging misfortune (*cf.* 2 Ki. 2:23-25; Is. 3:5).

33-34. Aliens or visitors are not to be oppressed or exploited in any fashion by the Israelites, since such actions would not exemplify God's holiness. The Israelites have to remember always that they themselves were once aliens in Egypt, and only by God's power was their freedom and its accompanying individuality restored. Although the stranger is a temporary resident among the covenant people, he must be treated as a regular member of the community ('the native among you'), and loved as a neighbour. This distinctive mark of Israelite piety would not be lost upon the alien visitor. Christians are also urged to adopt a similar attitude towards strangers (Heb. 13:2).

35-37. Fairness and equity are important aspects of God's moral nature, and these qualities must also be reflected in the life of the covenant nation, particularly where legal and business decisions are concerned. Equitable decisions by those in authority are consonant with God's own righteousness, and work for the immediate benefit of society as a whole. More specific instructions are provided in Deuteronomy 16:18-20. Unfair trading practices were evidently very common in antiquity, compounded by the fact that there were no standard weights and measures. The *ephah* (36) has been estimated at about 15 litres (4 gallons), while the *hîn* was perhaps about 3 litres (6 pints), although exact quantities are far from certain. Deuteronomy 25:13-15 attempted to regulate fair trading also, and those who did not observe such regulations were condemned (Dt. 25:16; Pr. 20:10; Am. 8:5; Mi. 6:10-11). The freedom that merchants and others have to trade exists because God at one period in Hebrew history liberated His enslaved people and provided an environment in which they could live and work without being oppressed. But these blessings will only continue as long as they keep His commandments. Obedience to the divine will is the key to blessing in life.

Penalties for disobedience (20:1-27)
This section forms a natural appendix to the contents of chapters 18 and 19, and continues the emphasis upon holiness. Whereas the two preceding chapters specify behaviour positively or negatively, chapter 20 describes the punishments that will result should the ordinances be broken. This is done in order to demonstrate the extreme sinfulness for Israel of behaviour that was all too common amongst other Near Eastern nations. The ultimate penalty was prescribed for indulgence in Molech worship, the cursing of parents, various types of sexual irregularity, and witchcraft; but certain other sexual offences were dealt with less rigorously.

1-5. The brief reference to Molech worship (Lv. 18:21) is now expanded both with respect to the punishment that will overtake the offender and the fate that will also come upon those who fail to carry out the sentence of death. The love which the Israelites are to show to strangers carries with it a reciprocal responsibility in that the sojourner has to abide by covenant law. This stipulation was designed to halt the spread of pagan worship in which resident aliens might wish to indulge whilst in Israelite company. The supremacy of God Himself is threatened by the worship of false deities; hence He will intervene directly by cutting off the offender, presumably by sudden death. The phrase *people of the land* (2, Heb. *'am hā'āreṣ*), may perhaps be a technical term describing a legislative council appointed to act on behalf of the nation. This body would then carry out the sentence of death by stoning, an ancient Hebrew form of execution. The expression 'people of the land' seems to have referred originally to the indigenous inhabitants of the territory (*cf.* Gn. 23:7; 42:6; Nu. 13:28, *etc.*). According to some interpretations the term referred specifically to male landowners who exercised certain civic and cultic responsibilities, but this meaning would hardly apply to the Israelites in Egypt, who were referred to frequently as *'am.* In reaction to the concept of a legislative or authoritative body, other scholars considered the *'am hā'āreṣ* to be the poor and common people. A more moderate interpretation sees the expression in terms of peasant proprietors who worked the land and fought to defend it periodically. References in pre-exilic authors would suggest that the 'people of the land' comprised an influential body, and might even have been considered capable of civil leadership in the absence of a king (2 Ki. 25:19). In the post-exilic period the mixed nature of the dwellers in Palestine brought about an entirely different use of the term, especially when the Pharisees came into prominence. By the time of Christ it was employed almost contemptuously of the mass of the population that was uninterested in the minutiae of the law (*cf.* Jn. 7:49).[82] Death by stoning was also

---

[82] Out of a sizable bibliography on the subject the following may be consulted: M. Sulzberger, *Am Ha-aretz, the Ancient Hebrew Parliament* (1909); idem, *Jewish Quarterly Review*, 3, 1912-13, pp. 1-18; S. Daiches, *Journal of*

prescribed for blasphemy (Lv. 24:16), idolatry (Dt. 13:6–10), desecration of the sabbath (Nu. 15: 32–36), and occultism (Lv. 20:27). The punishment is severe because the offender has defiled the sanctuary and profaned God's holy name. Those of the *'am hā' āreṣ* who condone the atrocities of Molech worship are as guilty as the ones who commit the crime, being accessories to it. By overlooking the offence they imply a certain sympathy towards it, and such an attitude would demoralize the covenant community very quickly. Stern sanctions are therefore needed as reinforcement for the ideal of holiness.

6. The penalty for indulgence in necromancy, forbidden in Leviticus 19:31, is stated in the same personal terms as that applicable to Molech worship. The desire to communicate with departed persons reaches back into the remote past, but however natural it might be thought to be, the practice of necromancy was nevertheless forbidden to the Hebrews. While modern spiritualist mediums purport to make meaningful contact with deceased persons there is seldom anything of abiding value in the 'messages' that are transmitted, and sometimes considerable fraud as well. The Christian can be allied only with those powers that confess Christ as the incarnate Lord (1 Jn. 4:2).

7–8. The demand for personal and communal holiness is reiterated here. Individual consecration to the ideals of the covenant will establish a standard of holy living which will be specifically moral as well as ceremonial in character. Unswerving obedience to God's commands is one indication of a sanctified life in both the Old and New Testaments.

9. Capital punishment, presumably by stoning, is prescribed for those who curse father or mother. Since the parents symbolize God's authority, being His surrogates from the standpoint of the children in the family, cursing them would

---

Theological Studies, 30, 1929, pp. 245–249; L. Rost in *Festschrift Otto Procksch* (1934), pp. 125–148; L. Finkelstein, *The Pharisees* (1938), pp. 25–42; S. Baron, *A Social and Religious History of the Jews*, I, (1952), pp. 278–280; G. von Rad, *Studies in Deuteronomy* (1953), pp. 63–66; M. H. Pope, *IDB*, 1, pp. 106–107; W. T. Dayton, *ZPEB*, I, pp. 128–129.

be comparable to blasphemy. Elaborate curses, many of which appear to have the nature of magical spells, were current in the ancient Near East, and amongst superstitious people often worked with devastating effect since in the eastern mind the curse carried within itself its own power of execution. The curses here would no doubt involve the pronouncing of some such formula in which the name of God would most probably occur. Christians are commanded by Christ to bless rather than curse (Lk. 6:28), *i.e.*, to quicken life rather than to destroy it.

10–16. Much of this material is paralleled by Leviticus 18:6–23, except that here the penalties are stated. In verse 10 there is some difficulty in the text, the Hebrew reading, 'If a man commits adultery with the wife of, if a man commits adultery with the wife of his neighbour . . .' Such 'double readings' arise from a wide variety of causes, but in this instance the conflation is very ancient, being repeated also in the versions. It is at least possible that in this instance the repetition was deliberate, comprising a stylistic device which was meant to draw attention to an important item of legislation. In this section the capital crimes include adultery (10; *cf.* Lv. 18:20; Dt. 22:22), coition with primary kin (11–14; *cf.* Lv. 18:7–8, 15, 17), homosexuality (13; *cf.* Lv. 18:22), and bestiality (15–16; *cf.* Ex. 22:19; Lv. 18:23). The method of execution was not specified except in the instance of a man who married a woman and her mother, all of whom had to be *burned with fire* (14). In cases of bestiality, the animal was killed along with the human participants. These abhorrent crimes, familiar as they were to ancient Near Eastern peoples, were inimical to the concept of covenantal holiness, and were therefore forbidden to the Israelites.

17–21. This section contains a list of sexual offences against covenant morality which would be punished by divine intervention. Since Hebrew marriages were generally contracted with persons close to the immediate family circle, it was important for the limits of acceptable consanguinity to be understood clearly. God will cut off the one who cohabits with his sister (17; *cf.* Lv. 18:9, 11) or has sexual relations with a menstruating woman (18; *cf.* Lv. 18:19). An individual who cohabited with an aunt by marriage (20) or a sister-in-law (21;

cf. Lv. 18:16) would along with the offending partner bear the penalty of childlessness. This would be a serious matter only if the parties concerned were actually married. If a man indulged in coition with a blood aunt (19; *cf.* Lv. 18:12–13), both would *bear their iniquity*, a penalty that seems less severe than being 'cut off'. Under normal conditions the punishment for the various crimes would be sufficient to deter all but the most persistent deviants, unless other factors such as intoxication were involved.

22–26. The rationale of this legislation is explained against a background of Israel as God's elect people. Before they even enter the promised land, the nation is warned of the grave moral dangers ahead. Only by keeping all God's statutes and ordinances can they expect to survive as a holy people. If they succumb to the temptations of Canaanite life the land will expel them violently, just as it was shortly to expel the Canaanites and others at the hands of the invading Israelites. The covenant people are to live lives of distinct moral and spiritual purity in the thriving land that God has given them, because He has separated them specifically from all other nations that they might reflect His intrinsic holiness. The laws given in Leviticus will serve as guides to the proper worship of God, as well as furnishing detailed rules for holy living. God's elect people must be recognizably distinct from those who are not dedicated to the ideals of holiness, an emphasis that is equally valid for the people of the new covenant. Christians are urged to be obedient children, and holy in their manner of living (1 Pet. 1:14–15), and to avoid all the works of the flesh (Rom. 13:13; Gal. 5:19–21; Col. 3:8, *etc.*).

27. The penalties for those indulging in necromancy having been stated already (6), the legislation now deals with those individuals who act as a *medium* or a *wizard*. Whatever their psychic abilities their activities do not enhance God's holiness, but instead lead people into superstition and bring them into bondage to demonic powers. Such practitioners are to be stoned to death, lest God's holiness be profaned. To be God's elect implies serious responsibilities as well as great privileges. The way of holiness is clearly defined, but like the path that leads to eternal life in Christ (Mt. 7:14) it is narrow and sometimes hard to follow. The regulations of the covenant are meant to enable the chosen people to glorify God by their way of life, and if followed would certainly make the Israelites unique in the Near East. Quite apart from morals and ethics, the enactments would also frequently confer a positive physical benefit in terms of individual health and well-being, which would have its own effect upon community life. The pattern of existence which the elect were to follow was therefore not one of unremitting hardship, but of joy and peace in fellowship with a loving and provident Father. Difficulties would arise only when the believer disobeyed the ordinances of God, thereby bringing upon himself a disruption of the fellowship as well as some personal punishment. In Leviticus the Israelites are urged constantly to live a holy life in this world, thereby glorifying the God who has chosen them as His own. But because there is always the possibility that the flesh will overcome the spirit (*cf.* Gal. 5:17), the enactments serve as guidelines for conduct and warnings to potential offenders. By this means the way in which holy living can be attained is made abundantly clear.

c. Rules for priestly holiness (21:1 – 22:33)

Leviticus emphasizes repeatedly the concept of divine holiness as the ideal at which individual and community life must be aimed. Whereas earlier chapters have dealt with the circumstances of the average Israelite, the present section is concerned with the standards of holiness expected of the priests. Because much has been given to them as representatives of God in the community, much more will be required of them as a result (*cf.* Lk. 121:48) than of the ordinary Israelites. The material can be divided readily into six sections by noting the closing formula which speaks of the Lord as the sanctifier (21:8, 15, 23; 22:9, 16, 32). The regulations for priestly holiness in this section were paralleled to some extent in the exilic period by the ordinances which formed part of Ezekiel's vision of a restored temple in Jerusalem (Ezk. 44:1–31). There are certain differences in the two accounts, however, which are worthy of note. In the first instance, the Mosaic legislation was primary, having been revealed directly by God to Moses, whereas the material in Ezekiel was in the nature of a vision, and was therefore subjective rather than objective. Instead of prescribing ordinances and statutes, the prophet Ezekiel is merely describing the behaviour of priests who are already living according to those enactments. Secondly, the visionary experience recapitulates an aspect of the Torah in true prophetic fashion, and does not introduce anything of an innovative or distinctive nature into the priestly duties. Furthermore, whereas the material in Leviticus describes the priestly role in considerable detail, the vision of Ezekiel merely summarizes it as part of the description of activity in the temple that he saw. There seems little doubt as to the prolonged antecedent existence of the levitical prescriptions, of which the material in Ezekiel constitutes a rather general reflection. Both sections, however, emphasize the fundamental requirement of holiness in the service of the Lord.

1–9. Being one of the Lord's priests was a highly responsible position, since the person who exercised it was in effect a substitute for God among the people. Like other living offerings presented to the Lord, the priest had to be free from physical and ceremonial blemishes, so that he would be acceptable to God (*cf.* Rom. 12:1). His way of life was hedged in by restrictions which were designed to maintain his special state of holiness to the Lord. A priest must therefore avoid all contact with the dead, since this would make him unclean (Nu. 19:11–13). The only exception to this rule involved very close relatives (2–3), for whom the priest would have personal responsibility. His young unmarried sister was included in this select category, since she would not have a husband to attend to the funeral rites, and perhaps not even parents. There is no mention of the priest's own wife, but defilement for her sake would be expected since they were one in marriage. The instructions given to the exiled priest Ezekiel were most unusual (Ezk. 24:15–18), but if his wife's death occurred about the time that Jerusalem fell in 587 BC, his bereavement would be representative of the grief that the exiles would experience. He was not to mourn for a dead past, but was to live for the future by the power of God.

Verse 4 is better translated, 'He shall not defile himself, being a leader among the people, thus profaning himself.' The pollutions seem connected with mourning rites, as in the following verse, and not with a priest contracting an improper marriage. Shaving the head (*cf.* Lv. 19:27–28) was forbidden, along with other pagan mourning practices, partly to prevent the introduction of heathen customs into Israel, but also because defacing the body in any way impaired its perfection and violated the idea of holiness. Priests, above all others, had to lead holy lives, having been set apart to offer *the bread of their God* (6), the word 'bread' being an ancient sacrificial term for 'flesh' (*cf.* Lv. 3:11, 16; 21:21). Those who minister the things of the Lord must be circumspect in behaviour, and must not be unequally yoked in marriage (*cf.* 2 Cor. 6:14) with a *defiled* or *divorced* (7) woman. The mention of a *harlot* is intended to remind the Israelites that cultic prostitution of the Canaanite variety had no place whatever in the life of the covenant community, since such behaviour would profane God's holy name. Because the priests present the holy offerings on behalf of the congregation, they are to be given the respect appropriate to such an exalted position. The holiness of the priests extends to the members of their families also, so that if a daughter indulges in immorality she profanes her father as well as herself. The punishment for so grave an offence was death by burning.

10–15. The high priest also is bound by special regulations relating to mourning and marriage. At a time of bereavement he must not display any of the usual signs of sadness (10), nor must he have any contact with dead persons, even very close relatives, lest he be defiled. Having been vested and anointed with the special consecration oil, he was required to maintain his state of ceremonial holiness. Restrictions of this kind constituted a severe imposition upon persons who by nature and inclination behaved in a demonstrative fashion in the presence of death. The wife of the high priest was to be chaste at the time of marriage (13), since anyone less pure would defile his own sanctity, and perhaps already have or produce a child of non-priestly stock. In the matter of mourning and marriage, therefore, his behaviour must be exemplary, since he is the supreme representative of God to the congregation. Paul endeavoured to commend his own ministry by means of purity, kindness, love and the Holy Spirit, coupled with an attempt to avoid offence, lest his own priesthood came under censure (2 Cor. 6:3–6) along with that of others. In a corrupt, adulterous generation, holiness and purity of life can be attributed only to the sanctifying work of the Spirit in the believer's life.

17–24. The person who approaches the sanctuary as God's priest must be as free from physical imperfections as the sacrificial animal that he offers. A priest who is blemished physically is prohibited from presenting sacrificial offerings, but can still partake of sacrifical meat (*cf.* Lv. 2:3, 10; 6:17–18, 29). The imperfections listed included blindness, facial mutilations, limbs of uneven length such as could result from poliomyelitis, hunchback, whether a congenital deformity or the product of some ailment such as spinal tuberculosis, achondroplasia or dwarfism,[83] and itching diseases of various kinds. A castrate, or a man suffering from orchiotrophy (20), was also blemished and therefore unfit for sanctuary duties. Genetic mutations such as polydactyly would also exclude a person from the priesthood, and although such conditions were rare they undoubtedly existed in Old Testament times (*cf.* 2 Sam. 21:20). Physical normality and ceremonial holiness are closely associated here, the inference being that the priests can be most effective in God's service only when they are in ordinary health and free from physical imperfections. These

---

[83] The Heb. term *gibbēn*, 'hunchback', has also been interpreted to mean 'brow', 'forehead'; hence the NEB rendering 'mis-shapen brows.' The word occurs nowhere else in the Hebrew Bible, and must therefore be regarded at best as a technical term of uncertain meaning. If 'hunchback' is a correct translation, it would describe a person suffering from spinal tuberculosis (Pott's disease), marked among other things by spondylitis and curvature of the vertebrae. A model of an Egyptian suffering from this disease was recovered from the Old Kingdom period (*c.* 2700–2200 BC) tomb of Mitri at Saqqara. The replica was made of plaster, but had been painted brown to simulate wood. If the NEB rendering is the correct one, it would suggest the possibility of a genetic defect. The term *daq* which follows immediately has been rendered by 'dwarf' in most translations, perhaps by association with 'hunchback'. The connection may not be entirely accidental if the basic meaning of the word ('thin', 'sparse', 'fine') is taken as an indication of tuberculosis. The word appears in Leviticus only, and is used to indicate a person with some sort of condition that made him unacceptable for the priesthood. The NEB associated the infirmity with ophthalmic disease. While some dwarfs exhibit tubercular lesions, the ordinary physiological dwarf is merely an undersized individual rather than a deformed person. Phocomelic and micromelic dwarfs, however, have abnormal limbs.

prerequisites are very important, if only because of the emotional and sometimes physical strain that the conscientious servant of God experiences in ministering the things of eternal life. In all things God must be glorified, and His holiness is profaned by anything that is obviously less than perfect, whether it be sacrificial animal or a sacrificing priest.

22:1–9. The Aaronites are reminded in this section that they, too, can become defiled ceremonially, just like any other member of the congregation. Purity is mandatory for those officiating at the sacrifices, so if they become defiled in any way they must *keep away from* (2) the sacrificial offerings of the people, lest the name of God be made unholy. Any priest who undertakes sanctuary duties while unclean in any way has polluted the sacred area, and will be *cut off* (3) as a punishment. Uncleanness can result from a number of situations, ranging from discharges to contact with unclean creeping species. Where such a condition exists, it lasts until the evening, and the priest has to wash his body completely before he can regain his ritual purity. He must be scrupulous in observing food laws (8), lest by transgressing in such matters he dies or profanes God's sacred name. The holiness of the priest must be marked by a high degree of ceremonial and moral rectitude, as an example to the congregation.

10–16. Because a priest's holiness was shared by the members of his family, they too could participate in the food reserved for the use of the priests. This privilege, however, was denied to those who were not priests (RSV 'outsider'; NEB 'stranger'), or who were the priest's visitors or hired servants. A non-Israelite slave who was part of a priest's family was permitted to eat consecrated food, being a regular member of the household. A priest's daughter who married a lay person was no longer considered a member of the immediate family, and so was disqualified from eating the priestly portions. If she returned to her father's household under the conditions outlined (13), she could once again participate as a full family member. If a lay person accidentally ate priestly food, he had to give to the priests an amount equal to the original offering plus a fine of an additional fifth (14), as with the guilt offering. These enactments remind the priests that they have to be scrupulous in their dealings with the sacred offerings of the people in every respect, lest they be punished for profaning the name of the God who has sanctified the offerings.

17–33. The priests are instructed to ensure that all offerings are unblemished, and the catalogue of physical disabilities which disqualified the descendants of Aaron from sanctuary service is applied to sacrificial animals (22, 24). The only exception is that of animals which apparently exhibit genetic damage (23), and even these can be sacrificed only as freewill offerings. Castrated or similarly mutilated animals, whether of native or imported stock, were prohibited for sacrifice, since they were less than perfect physically and thus would not reflect divine holiness adequately (25). No animals younger than eight days are to be offered in sacrifice (*cf.* Ex. 22:30), nor is a cow or a ewe to be killed with her young on the same day, whether for sacrificial purposes, as in some pagan cults, or for ordinary food consumption. This is in harmony with laws prohibiting such wasteful practices as taking a bird as well as its eggs (Dt. 22:6–7), or the indiscriminate destruction of trees (Dt. 20:19–20). In all these matters the main purpose is that God's name shall be hallowed (*cf.* Mt. 6:9; Lk. 11:2) by His elect people. The regulations carry the personal imprimatur of God ('I am the Lord'), and as they are obeyed they will show the degree to which the Israelites are truly living in fellowship with God.

In the New Testament Christ constitutes the perfect, unblemished sacrifice (Heb. 9:14; 1 Pet. 1:19), where the Greek word *amōmos* is the equivalent of the Hebrew *tāmîm*, 'unblemished'. Here as in Ephesians 5:27 the significance of the term transcends the purely cultic usage, and refers to the moral and spiritual implications of Christ's self-offering. His death was intended to free the sinner from his iniquities; to make the body of Christian believers holy; and to remove blemishes of any kind from it. It is against this background that the members of the Christian church are exhorted to be without blemish themselves (Phil. 2:15; 2 Pet. 3:14). The term *amōmētos* occurs only in 2 Peter 3:14, and describes the lack of moral blemish that must typify the character of Christians who believe in divine judgment. In the same epistle, false teachers are spoken of as blemishing the body of Christ (2 Pet. 2:13).

The feasts of Leviticus 23 and other Old Testament calendars

MONTH				OCCASION	REFERENCE
Early Designation	Later Name	Modern Name	Date		
'Abîb First month	Nîsān	April	14	Passover	Lv. 23:5 Dt. 16:2
			15	Unleavened bread	Ex. 23:14–17
	Sîwān	June	6	Pentecost	Dt. 16:9–12
				First fruits and harvest	Ex. 23:16 Lv. 25:8–9
Seventh month	Tišrî	October	1–2	Trumpets	Lv. 23:24
			10	Day of atonement	Lv. 23:27
			15–21	Tabernacles	Lv. 23:34 Dt. 16:13

d. Consecration of seasons (23:1–44)

This section comprises a list of the holy seasons in the Israelite religious calendar, including the three great celebrations of passover, pentecost and tabernacles. The list was probably compiled in the first instance for the guidance of the priests, but no doubt formed part of the instruction which they passed on to the congregation. Beginning with sabbath observance, the list concluded with the joyous feast of tabernacles, with its emphasis upon God's deliverance of captive Israel from Egypt.

1–2. The celebrations are described as *appointed feasts* (Heb. *môʿēd̲*), the term used in the expression 'tent of meeting' (*ʾōhel môʿēd̲*). They are thus assemblies of the people taking place at set times, and as *holy convocations* they are celebrated at the tabernacle. The description of these events as feasts (*ḥag̲*) indicates their joyful character, and shows that not all the gatherings within the sanctuary precincts were necessarily solemn or filled with foreboding.

3. The weekly sabbath was the first set occasion to be observed, and followed the pattern of God's rest from creative activity (Gn. 2:3). The seventh day was sacred (Ex. 20:11) because it was hallowed by God, and this sanctity was reinforced by the giving of manna in the wilderness (*cf.* Ex. 16:5, 23–29). The sabbath ('day of rest') was a time when all work ceased and the period of time recognized as the Lord's own day. While the idea of the sabbath was familiar to the Mesopotamians, the days that were observed as such were far less regular than those of the Hebrews, and had a strictly superstitious basis. For fear of offending various deities in the pantheon, the Babylonians observed a *šabattū* on the seventh, fourteenth, nineteenth, twenty-first and twenty-eighth days of the month. Special sacrifices were offered to the gods on these occasions in order to avert their wrath or to propitiate them. Apparently only certain classes of Babylonian society were affected by 'sabbath' restrictions upon their normal activities, but these groups included the ruler and some priests. In Israel the sabbath was an occasion for regular worship of God as the author of covenantal mercies and the sustainer of national life. The sabbath was sometimes mentioned in connection with the new moon (2 Ki. 4:23; Am. 8:5; Is. 1:13), and was always venerated by the prophets who condemned the Israelites for their casual attitude towards sabbath observances (Is. 56:2, 4; Je. 17:21–27; Ezk. 20:12–24). The distinctive character of the sabbath was emphasized in the Mosaic period by the fact that two lambs were sacrificed at that time, whereas one sufficed on other days of the week (Nu. 28:9, 19). On that day a dozen loaves of shewbread were also presented to God (Lv. 24:5–9; 1 Ch. 9:32). Desecration of the sabbath was accompanied by serious consequences (Nu. 15:32–36), because the rest imposed on this basic holy day was more comprehensive ('in all your dwellings') than was required for other prescribed festivals, when only servile work was prohibited. During the Persian period Nehemiah took punitive action against those who violated the observance of the sabbath by conducting business affairs at that time (Ne. 10:31; 13:15–22). As the Judean theocracy developed, the sabbath not merely became the opportunity for weekly synagogue worship, but also a time when the law was read and studied. In conjunction with this there emerged the many details of sabbath observance that were formulated by the scribes.

In the New Testament the 'first day of the week' (Mt. 28:1; Mk. 16:2), commemorating Christ's resurrection, replaced the Jewish sabbath as a regular period for Christian worship. Sunday worship is a weekly reminder of the fact that Christ has risen from the dead, as well as being a time of instruction and fellowship. A rest interval of one day in seven seems admirably suited to the needs of the human body. Intervals of greater or lesser extent have been tried from time to time, but they have not proved as successful as the biblical sabbath.

4–8. The most important of the annual festivals was the passover, the rites and meaning of which are described in Exodus 12:1–28. The ceremony was unique to the Israelites, and any suggestion that the festival had pagan origins is entirely unsupported by fact. The passover was celebrated on the fourteenth evening of the first month (Nisan, in later terminology) in the spring (March-April), when the barley harvest was about to begin. It commemorated the deliverance of the enslaved Israelites from Egypt by a mighty act of divine redemption, and marked the establishing of the offspring of Jacob as a nation. The day following the passover celebration saw the beginning of the feast of unleavened bread, the rituals of which are described in Numbers 28:16–25. This festival lasted for seven days and, along with the feasts of pentecost (weeks) and tabernacles, had the character of pilgrimage celebrations. All adult males in Israel were enjoined to observe these three great feasts (Ex. 23:17; Dt. 16:16). The festival of unleavened bread was a *holy convocation* (7), and no laborious work was to be undertaken while it was being celebrated. This regulation is less stringent than that required for the sabbath (3), partly because a longer period of time was involved, and it applied also to the other major festivals (verses 21, 25, 35–36). The passover and the festival of unleavened bread served as a valuable annual period of instruction, reminding the Israelites of the theological issues involved in the exodus from Egypt, and also of the implications of covenant relationship. The observance of the great Christian feasts serves exactly the same didactic purpose, bringing to the attention of the worshipper that what is being commemorated happened in historical time to real people. Like the Hebrew passover, the Lord's supper focuses on a sacrificial Lamb who brings redemption and spiritual security through the shedding of blood.

9–14. The beginning of the barley harvest, the first grain to be reaped, was also the occasion on which the Israelites were commanded to bring an offering of first fruits to God. The enactment looks forward to the sedentary occupation of Canaan, and is one of four laws (*cf.* Ex. 13:5; 34:18; Nu. 29:12) that were to be observed then by the nation. The *sheaf* (10), Hebrew *'ōmer*, had to be 'waved' by the priest before the Lord, a process which may have involved the officiant making the sign of the cross. This token offering was accompanied by a sacrificial lamb, a cereal gift of *two tenths of an ephah of fine flour mixed with oil* (13), perhaps about 7 litres, and one-quarter of a *hîn* of wine, possibly as much as 1.7 litres. The ceremony acknowledged God as the real author of all the land's produce by making a representative presentation of the crops to Him, thereby consecrating them. The drink offering of wine (Ex. 29:38–42) always accompanied the cereal gift, but is mentioned here for the first time in Leviticus, apparently to draw attention to the fact that, with bread and meat, it typified the staple elements of diet. The concept of first fruits was popular

217

among New Testament writers, being employed of the earliest converts as the first fruits of the Spirit (Rom. 8:23); of the Jews as precursors of the Christian church (Rom. 11:16); of individual believers (Rom. 16:5); of Christ as the first fruits of resurrection (1 Cor. 15:20); of believers born again by the word of truth (Jas. 1:18); and of the group which had been redeemed as first fruits (Rev. 14:4).

15-22. The festival of pentecost (weeks) occurred at the termination of the harvest season, and was regarded by later Jewish authorities as the complement or conclusion of the passover celebrations, since it followed the latter by seven weeks. This interval gave rise to the name 'pentecost' or 'fiftieth'. The celebration lasted for one day only (Dt. 16:9-12), and was a joyous occasion in which the entire nation gave thanks to a provident heavenly Father for His abundant gifts of food. This latter was symbolized by two loaves which were *baked with leaven* (17) and presented to the Lord, along with sacrificial animals, cereal gifts and drink offerings. No hard work was to be done during this period of *holy convocation* (21), and the needs of the *poor* and *the stranger* were remembered at this time (22). The feast reminded the Israelites that God's care and control reached into every area of life, making no false distinction between material and spiritual blessings. Christ taught that not merely does our heavenly Father give us the things of which we have need, but that He will give the Holy Spirit to those who ask Him (Lk. 11:13). It was on the feast of pentecost that the Holy Spirit was first poured out upon the apostles (Acts 2:1-4).

23-32. The seventh month of the year, subsequently known as Tishri, was also holy just as the sabbath or seventh day of the week was. This is yet another indication of the great degree of sanctity attached to the number seven. The period was marked by three distinctive festivals, the first being the feast of trumpets. Held on the first day of the month, it was *a day of solemn rest* (24) on which trumpets were blown in order to assemble the congregation (Nu. 10:10). In the post-exilic period the Torah was generally read in public, and the atmosphere was one of celebration and rejoicing. At that time the seventh month also marked the beginning of the Jewish civil year, so that after the exile the festival of trumpets was in effect a new year's festival also. The people were reminded of God's mercies to them through the covenant, which if obeyed would sustain them through another year.

The second great celebration was that of the day of atonement (26–32), held on the tenth day of the seventh month. In Leviticus 16:1–34 it had been considered from the priestly standpoint, but here the duties and responsibilities of the lay Israelites are examined. The people had to prepare for this most solemn day by 'afflicting' themselves, perhaps by fasting or other forms of self-discipline, neglect of which carried with it a severe penalty (29). An offering by fire had to be made, and anyone who performed any kind of work would be destroyed by God. Quite clearly this celebration was much more of a fast than a festival, for on it the high priest made atonement for the sins of accident and omission committed during the previous year by the Israelites. It has become *a statute for ever* (31), being celebrated annually by Jews through-out the world. The sacrificial blood presented to God in the most holy place of the tabernacle by the high priest was a token of the people's penitence, and enabled them to be reconciled to God. The one atoning act of Christ for human sin has made such ceremonies obsolete, and in addition has provided for sins committed in defiance of God's known regulations, a situation for which nothing could avail under the old covenant (Nu. 15:30).

33–44. From the solemnity of the day of atonement, the Israelites emerged each year into the joyous celebration of the feast of tabernacles, the third great commemorative occasion in the Hebrew festive calendar. Known also as the feast of booths or ingathering, it had an historical occasion, as the passover did. At the feast of tabernacles, held on the fifteenth day of the seventh month, the Israelites gathered in *solemn assembly* (36) at the end of the harvest season for an eight-day celebration. During this period they lived in booths made from the branches of palms, willows and other native trees,[84] as a

---

[84] The *goodly trees* (40) were interpreted by the NEB as citrus trees, and in a marginal note the 'willows from the riverside' were rendered as 'poplars'. The latter most probably comprised the Euphrates poplar (*Populus euphratica*), a tree which reaches twelve or more metres in height. The stiff-textured leaves grow on weak petioles, and the tree is found throughout Syria and Palestine,

reminder of the way in which the Israelites wandered about in the wilderness after the exodus, living in tents and temporary shelters. The festive period was marked by numerous regular daily offerings, details of which are recorded in Numbers 29:12-38. The feast of ingathering was an opportunity for joyous celebration, which in the later post-exilic period took on something of a carnival atmosphere. Nevertheless, the occasion was a reminder of God's goodness, rooting His mercies in history, and asserting His sovereignty over His material creation and His covenant people. Gratitude for the gifts of nature and divine grace revealed in Jesus Christ should always form a prominent part of Christian praise and prayer.

e. Sacred objects: sin of blasphemy (24:1-23)

This chapter deals with two principal topics, namely regulations governing the holy place, and an instance of blasphemy. The latter probably occurred shortly after God had given Moses instructions about the holy oil and the bread of the presence (2-9), since it is usual for narrative to be intermingled with legislation in the book of Leviticus. The insistence upon ritual propriety found in earlier chapters is very much in evidence here also.

1-4. The golden lampstand (Ex. 25:31-40) with its seven lamps was to be kept burning continually in the tabernacle, and was to be replenished with fuel consisting of *pure oil from beaten olives* (2), as prescribed in Exodus 27:20-21. The lampstand was put in the holy place, which otherwise would have been completely dark. It was the high priest's daily responsibility to attend to the filling and trimming of the lamps (4), since he was the first person to light it (Nu. 8:3). In Exodus 27:21, however, it is made clear that the duties were to be shared with other members of the priesthood, since the ritual was to extend over many generations. Some interpreters, following the vision of Zechariah 4, have seen the lampstand as typical of Israel, which in God's purpose was meant to be a

---

growing vigorously in the Jordan valley. *Cf.* H. N. and A. L. Moldenke, *Plants of the Bible* (1952), p. 183. The species *Populus alba*, the white poplar, which grows in the hills of Palestine, has been suggested as preferable by W. Walker, *All the Plants of the Bible* (1958), p. 168.

light to the ancient Near Eastern nations. But the true light for revelation to the Gentiles, and for glory to His people Israel, was Jesus Christ (Lk. 2:32). The Christian is bidden to let the light of Christ's salvation shine in daily life, to the glory of God the Father (Mt. 5:16; Eph. 5:8; Phil. 2:15).

5–9. Little is said about the shewbread, or bread of the presence, in Exodus 25:23–30, the details of which are supplied here by way of integrating the two books. Twelve cakes, comprising one-fifth of an ephah of fine flour each, were to be baked and placed in two rows or heaps or six cakes each. Frankincense was put with the bread as a *memorial portion* (7), which would be burned on the altar of burnt offering (*cf.* Lv. 2:2) when the cakes were replaced every sabbath day. The old cakes formed part of the priests' perquisites (9), but could not be eaten by members of their families (*cf.* Mt. 12:4). Some expositors have seen in the frankincense a symbol of prayer, particularly that God would grant His people their daily bread (*cf.* Mt. 6:11; Lk. 11:3). Others interpret the cakes as typifying the twelve tribes, who are reminded continually that all the blessings they experience are a gift from a bountiful God.

10–12. An instance in which God's name was desecrated occurred at Sinai, when an unnamed man, the son of an Israelite mother and an Egyptian father, blasphemed during a quarrel in the camp. His curses brought contempt upon God's sacred name, and since at that period there was no specific penalty for blasphemy, the offender was placed under arrest until God's will on the matter was known. The mention of the mother's name and pedigree would identify her for future generations, and remind the mothers of Israel to bring up their children in the fear of God.

13–14. The sentence ultimately made known was death by stoning outside the camp, so that the ritual purity of the tabernacle and congregation would not be violated. Those who had actually heard the blasphemy had to make a token gesture signifying their involvement in the crime, after which the man was executed. The precise method is not mentioned, but perhaps the offender was made to lie down, after which his head was crushed with large stones and the remainder of his body covered with smaller ones to form a cairn. This procedure would prevent anyone incurring accidental ceremonial defilement, and as long as the congregation remained in the area the heap of stones would serve as a reminder of the crime that had been committed.

15–23. The sentence does not differentiate between native Israelite and foreigner, for whoever among the populace is guilty of blasphemy bears his own punishment (16). Those who enjoy covenant blessings must be careful not to repudiate the author of the covenant in any way. The occasion furnishes an opportunity for God to remind the Israelites of various offences, for which retaliation in kind is deemed proper. In the Hebrew text this list is arranged in a concentric pattern, indicating that its occurrence at this point is neither haphazard nor an afterthought of some supposedly late compiler or editor. The one who kills a man shall be executed, while the person causing the death of an animal is under obligation to replace it (18, 21). Personal disfigurement is to be recompensed in terms of the *lex talionis*, an important principle which states the maximum amount of retaliation allowed under specific conditions. Beyond those limits a person was forbidden to exact revenge, thereby ensuring that the retribution was proportionate to the offence. These regulations applied uniformly to all members of the nation, whatever their racial origin, and like other enactments carried the assurance of God's imprimatur (22).

The holiness of God is reinforced by the drastic penalty prescribed for blasphemy. In the Near East the name of a person was bound up intimately with his character, so that in the case of God, blasphemy was in effect an act of repudiation. This would also seem to be true of modern times, in which blasphemy is incredibly widespread. So far from blaspheming, the Christian is counselled not to swear any kind of oath (Mt. 5:34–37), but to let a simple 'yes' or 'no' suffice. Ancient legal codes contained many more capital offences than in modern western jurisprudence. In general, the Hebrew scriptures followed a policy of retribution, but premeditated murder and blasphemy were considered capital crimes. Even in the New Testament times both Jesus and Stephen were regarded as blasphemers by the authorities, and condemned to death on these grounds (Mt. 26:65–66; Acts 6:11). The expressions *fracture for fracture, eye for eye* (20) are perhaps part of ancient

Semitic legal phraseology which expressed the *lex talionis* principle, and need have been applied literally. It is important to notice that public justice was being exacted by this legal concept, thereby removing the sentence from the area of blood-feuds or other forms of private revenge. In His teachings Christ modified this concept dramatically (Mt. 5:38–41) by requiring His followers to give additional amounts instead of demanding restitution or offering active resistance. Only a truly strong person can respond voluntarily along these lines. The weak have no option but to do as they are told.

f. Sabbatical and jubilee years (25:1–55)

This chapter continues the cycle of consecrated seasons dealt with in Leviticus 23:1–44, but extends the principle of sabbath rest to the seventh year and to that which follows the completion of seven seven-year cycles, namely the fiftieth or jubilee year. The conservation of natural and other resources which is prescribed by this legislation forms the basis of good agricultural and ecological practice.

The jubilee legislation had as its basic theme the liberation of that which was bound. As a result it reminded the Israelites every fifty years of the fact that once the people of God had been bound in Egypt, victims of an oppressive native regime, but that they had been liberated at the time of the exodus by a miraculous display of divine power. They were now free citizens, living in their own land, which itself was a gift of God, but being bound to Him by a covenant relationship they were only free to serve Him to the exclusion of all other gods. As a holy nation, their hearts and minds were to be set upon God and His holiness, and they were not to think in terms of accumulating vast holdings of property over periods of time lest they succumbed to the materialism of the surrounding nations. The prescribed interruption in the normal course of national life once each half-century would furnish an opportunity for reflection upon covenant values, and remind the nation that man does not live by bread alone.

The legislation itself provided first of all for those Israelites who were in servitude to any of their fellows by restoring to them their liberty. It established an equitable correlation between the price of a slave and proximity of the jubilee year

(25:50). Secondly, those who had had to dispose of their ancestral holdings because of the force of economic circumstances were permitted to repossess them under the jubilee legislation. This meant that it was impossible for the Israelites to dispose of land permanently, or purchase property in large amounts with a view to accumulating a vast estate. Finally it was made mandatory for the ground itself to remain fallow, even though it had just passed through a sabbatical year.

In the period of jubilee the people were required to live simple lives, and this was another reminder of the discipline of body and spirit needed to survive the rigours of a wilderness milieu which had been the lot of their ancestors who finally entered the promised land. During the jubilee year the food that had been stored in preparation for the event could be consumed, along with anything that grew spontaneously from the land, but nothing was to be grown for food. By this means God is clearly reasserting His ownership of the land, and emphasizing the importance of keeping it holy. In turn, the legislation reminds the Israelites that they are to trust the God who delivered the nation from Egypt in earlier days and provided His chosen with a land in which to live, a trust that extends to His provision for the non-productive years of the sabbatical and jubilee. The legislation is thus a demand that the Israelites shall be obedient to the Lord their God, and serve Him as a holy nation all the more consciously during the period in which many of their normal duties would be suspended. In so far as the jubilee year enactments were observed, the event would occur only once in a normal lifetime.

1–7. This legislation, given on Mount Sinai, looks forward to the time when the Israelites would be in sedentary occupation of Palestine. The principle of sabbath rest is now applied to a seven-year period in which the final year is to be observed as *a sabbath to the Lord* (2). At that time the land will lie fallow, while orchards and vineyards will remain untended. During the sabbatical year there must be no systematic harvesting of self-seeding crops, or such fruits as figs or grapes. Anything of this nature that the land produces without human aid is the property of all, and people are to obtain their food wherever they can find it, just as the Israelites did in their wilderness wanderings. This provision would be of particular importance for the poor and those who did not own land (*cf.* Ex. 23:11). The sabbatical year demonstrated that God was the supreme provider, and that while man could assist the process by his co-operation it was from God that all things came. Man's chief duty, therefore, was to glorify God by observing regular sabbaths of worship and spiritual fellowship, and not to concentrate upon the accumulation of material possessions to the exclusion of all else. This same principle underlies Christ's instructions to His followers to seek God's kingdom first and foremost (Mt. 6:33).

8-12. After seven sabbatical years, the fiftieth year was to be proclaimed on the day of atonement by means of trumpet blasts throughout the land. It was a sacred year in which the slave population was emancipated, and people returned to their family holdings. This *jubilee* (11) year probably took its name from the blowing of the ram's horn (*yôbēl*) which proclaimed its beginning. The term was of ancient origin, whatever its meaning, since in Joshua 6:6, 8 it needed the additional word *šôp̄ār* ('ram's horn') to explain its meaning. Like the sabbatical year, the jubilee was to be holy to the Lord, and the land had to remain idle.

13-17. Under jubilee year regulations, land had to be returned to its original owners, thus restoring the traditional division of the land among the tribes (*cf.* Nu. 36:9). The property laws in this section are based on the concept that God retains the title to all land (*cf.* Ex. 6:4; Dt. 5:16), an idea that was to be found also in other Near Eastern cultures. For this reason the land of Canaan was assigned to the Israelites by tribes, and those who settled on it regarded themselves at best as tenants rather than outright owners. Land could therefore not be sold in the conventional sense, and any payment for property amounted to the purchaser taking a lease on it until the next jubilee year. Under these conditions the cost of property bought would be proportionate to the balance of time remaining in the forty-nine year cycle.

18-24. Since only the produce of the land could thus be properly bought or sold, the question of food supplies was very important, particularly since a sabbatical year always preceded a jubilee year.[85] Hence large harvests were promised, which would suffice until the jubilee period had ended and crops could be reaped once more. The jubilee year was clearly a time for faith in God's ability to provide food, and an opportunity for the poor and debtors to make a new beginning in life. Because of its enforced rest, the land's resources would be conserved and its continued fertility ensured. Such provisions represent an early example of land planning and the application of ecological principles in general. The social effects of the jubileee redistribution of territory were of a significantly egalitarian nature. Ideally there would be no well-marked division of society into classes, and no exploitation of the poor by rich landowners. That this did not occur, despite the intent of the legislation, is indicated by the pronouncements of such eighth-century BC prophets as Isaiah (5:8) and Amos (2:6).

25–34. Although in theory the land belongs to God, situations will arise in which the tenant-owner has to dispose of his property. Only extreme hardship would prompt such a course, since family inheritances were greatly treasured (1 Ki. 21:3). Under such conditions a close family member was expected to buy it, so that it would not pass into alien hands (25). Where a man is able to repurchase his property, the cost of redemption is governed by the length of time the holdings have been under different control. The *overpayment* (27) represented the excess of the sale price over the total value of the crops obtained from the land. If a person could not afford to redeem his property, he had to wait until the jubilee year, when it would revert to him by law (28).

The rule of jubilee release did not apply to property *in a walled city* (29–30), which if not redeemed within a year of sale belonged permanently to the purchaser. Perhaps this arrangement was devised because farm land as such would not be involved in the purchase. Houses in unwalled villages, however, came under the regulation governing the disposal of general property, since such houses would most probably be

---

[85] For the view that, by inclusive reckoning, the fiftieth year was actually the forty-ninth, see R. North, *The Sociology of the Biblical Jubilee* (1954), pp. 109–112.

sold with some accompanying land. Another exception was made in the case of the Levites, who in the disposition of territory in the settlement period were allotted forty-eight cities and their accompanying land (Nu. 35:1-8; Jos. 21:1-42). Any Levite who sold his property under such conditions had permanent right of redemption, since his home was his perpetual possession. The RSV rendering, *and if one of the Levites does not exercise*, inserts a negative, as in the Vulgate, but this addition is unnecessary since otherwise the continuity with the previous verse is not preserved. The meaning is that if one Levite disposes of his property to another Levite, the rule of reversion to the original owner in the jubilee year still applies.

35-38. The practical application of loving a neighbour as oneself is stressed here. Whatever the cause of a brother's poverty, he is to be given the hospitality accorded to a stranger or alien, and not be allowed to die of starvation. The concept of the covenant community as comprising brothers and sisters in the Lord applies to financial as well as to moral and spiritual matters. It is not enough to wish the needy every success in their search for sustenance, for in addition to this, practical help adequate to meet the person's needs must be forthcoming (Jas. 2:15-16). A needy Israelite must not be exploited by his fellows, and the Torah is distinctive here in its insistence that loans to the poor must be free of interest.[86] God uses His own generosity to the Israelites in liberating them from bondage as an example for the spiritual community to follow (*cf.* 1 Jn. 4:11).

39-45. If a man became so poor that he sold himself as a servant to a wealthier Israelite, he must still be accorded the dignity of a brother. While he obviously has to work, he must be treated as a *hired servant* (40), not as a slave. Normally such persons went free in the seventh year (Ex. 21:2; Dt. 15:12), but if the jubilee year intervened his period of service would be shortened correspondingly. The person who hired him was also responsible for the care of any immediate family members that the man might have (41). This regulation was intended to preserve the humanity and dignity of the poor or the debtor

---

[86] R. P. Maloney, *Catholic Biblical Quarterly*, 36, 1974, pp. 1-20.

without allowing such persons to evade their social and financial responsibilities. Like the Torah, the New Testament discourages parasitic behaviour (*cf.* 2 Thes. 3:10–11). Having once been redeemed from slavery, the Hebrews can never again be sold as slaves (42). Such is not the case with non-Israelites, however, who can be both bought and sold in that way, and even bequeathed to one's successors (46). A situation could arise whereby an Israelite became the slave of a wealthy alien family (47), in which case he should be redeemed by a near relative, since his service would not terminate after six years. The redemption price is to be calculated in terms of the number of years until the jubilee, as though the individual had hired himself out on an annual basis for that whole period (52). Whether ransomed or not, the Hebrew servant is to be dealt with in a humane manner, because all Israelites are truly the property of the God who redeemed them formerly from bondage in Egypt. In His atoning work on Calvary, Christ paid the supreme price for redeeming those who were in bondage to sin, and has made possible the highest degree of freedom for those who serve Him.

Just how widely the concept of the jubilee year was observed through the history of the Israelites is difficult to state for lack of direct evidence. That the legislation is early rather than late seems indicated by the appropriateness of such idealistic enactments occurring at the beginning of Hebrew community life in Canaan rather than towards the end of it, when the covenant people were somewhat less than masters in their own household. Furthermore, the Hebrews do not seem to have been entirely alone in the general concept of the jubilee, since certain Mesopotamian rulers between the nineteenth and seventeenth centuries BC enacted somewhat comparable legislation.[87] The fact that the jubilee year is not mentioned outside the Pentateuch does not necessarily indicate that it

---

[87] *Cf.* J. J. Finkelstein, *Studies in Honor of Benno Landsberger* (1965), pp. 233–246; D. J. Wiseman, 'Law and Order in Old Testament Times', *Vox Evangelica*, 8, 1973, pp. 5–21 (esp. p. 12) has shown that the periodical regulation of the economy by royal decree freeing certain fiscal and personal debts, as practised throughout the ancient Near East, is a major motive behind so-called 'reforms' such as those enacted by Hezekiah and Josiah.

was not observed to any extent beyond the time of Moses. Indeed, one authority has claimed that the only 'late' feature in the legislation is the requirement that the cycle of releases shall occur regularly every fifty years.[88] North has argued persuasively that the jubilee concept was much more likely to have been embraced by the followers of Moses than the spiritually debilitated inhabitants of Judea in the time of Haggai, Zechariah or Malachi.[89] The view that the jubilee was celebrated periodically in pre-exilic days has been supported by van Selms, on the ground that it occurs in parts of the Pentateuch (Lv. 27:18, 21; Nu. 36:4) in contexts which deal with other matters. Furthermore, he argued that no convincing etymology of *yôbēl* as the designation of the jubilee year was known in post-exilic times, thereby indicating the antiquity of the institution.[90] There are very few references in fact to other major festivals of the Hebrew religious year, the most probable explanation for which is that the occasions were so normal a part of national life as to be taken for granted, and therefore were not singled out for particular mention. In 1 Maccabees 6:49, the land is spoken of as having a sabbath during the Maccabean period, a circumstance which made it very difficult for the beleaguered defenders of Bethsura to hold out because of a shortage of food. The narrative here does not indicate whether a sabbatical or jubilee year was in progress, but if the former was being observed it is more probable that the latter would be also.

An emphasis upon humanitarianism and social justice is a pronounced feature of the legislation in this chapter, and it should be noted that the tenor of the laws pursued a middle course between the extremes of unrestricted capitalism and rampant communism. The absolute rights of the individual to his personal freedom and his ancestral holdings are written into law so that they are guaranteed, a situation which is underlined by the injunction to the Israelites that they should love their neighbours as themselves. Brotherly love could be

---

[88] R. Westbrook, *Israel Law Review* (1971 ed.) pp. 209–226.

[89] R. North, *Sociology of the Biblical Jubilee*, pp. 204–206.

[90] A. van Selms, *IDB Supplementary Volume*, pp. 496–498. See also N. Sarna in H. Hoffner (ed.), *Orient and Occident*, pp. 143–149.; R. North, *Sociology of the Biblical Jubilee*, pp. 96–101.

expressed most directly in the concern for the impoverished, a tradition which was maintained by the members of the primitive Christian church (*cf.* Acts 4:34–35; 2 Cor. 9:1–2; Phil. 4:15, *etc.*), who supported the needy and indigent as an expression of Christ's law of love (Gal. 6:2).

These enactments demonstrate that an equitable society has to be based upon moral and spiritual principles. Indeed, the spirituality of the jubilee is grounded in the concept of the sabbath and the sabbatical year, of which it is the logical extension. The legislation confirms and enhances the acknowledged sovereignty of God over His people, who themselves were hopelessly enmeshed in bondage at a certain period of their history, and continued in this condition until God liberated them by a dramatic act of redemption. Release from captivity and oppression were promised by Isaiah (61:1), and were fulfilled in the work of Christ, the Messiah of God, who cited that very prophecy at the beginning of His ministry (Lk. 4:18–19). Freedom from bondage to sin, true humanity and the realization of the dignity attached to being a child of God are all the outcome of Christ's atonement for human sin.

VI. CONCLUDING BLESSINGS AND PUNISHMENTS (26:1–46)

In the ancient Near East it was customary for legal treaties to conclude with passages containing blessings upon those who observed the enactments, and curses upon those who did not. The international treaties of the second millennium BC regularly included such sections as part of the text, with the list of curses greatly outnumbering the promises of blessing. In the Old Testament this general pattern occurs in Exodus 23:25–33, Deuteronomy 28:1–68, and Joshua 24:20. The maledictions of Mesopotamian legal texts or the curses in the treaties of the Arameans, Hittites and Assyrians were threats uttered in the names of the gods which had acted as witnesses to the covenants. That these threats could be implemented was part of the supersitious belief of people in the ancient Near East, and could have had some coincidental basis in fact. For the Israelites, however, there was no doubt that the God who wrought the mighty act of deliverance at the Red Sea will indeed carry out all that He has promised, whether for good or ill. Obedience to His commands is the certain way to obtain a consistent outpouring of blessing, whereas continued disobedience is a guarantee of future punishment. The phrase 'I am the Lord your God' divides this chapter into convenient sections. The double mention of God's name in verses 1–2 and 44–45 matches that in Leviticus 19:2–3, 36–37.

a. Blessings (1–13)

1–2. Certain prohibitions precede the blessings proper (3–13). The kind of idolatry current in Canaan is strictly prohibited. The *idols* (Hebrew *ᵉlîlîm*) are the non-existent things referred to in Leviticus 19:4, while the *graven image*, legislated against in the Decalogue (Ex. 20:4) was a cultic representation of deity such as has been found at several sites in Canaan. The *pillar* (Hebrew *maṣṣēbâ*) was apparently made of stone and was probably intended to comprise a tangible indication of the presence of El or Baal, the two principal deities of Canaanite religion. The *figured stone* (Hebrew *maśkît*) would no doubt have contained some carved picture of a Canaanite deity, such as one depicting Baal hurling thunderbolts, dated about 1800 BC and unearthed at Ras Shamra (Ugarit). Observance of the sabbath and punctilious attendance to worship at the sanctuary will be the best means of forestalling the corruptions of Canaanite religion.

3–13. Because the Sinai agreement between God and Israel is just as much a covenant as the familiar second-millennium BC international treaties were, it is both natural and proper for a section of blessings to be included here. They fall into three divisions (verses 4, 6, 11), each of which is prefaced by the phrase 'I will give'. Obedience to the covenant stipulations will be recompensed by material prosperity (3–5), victory over the nation's enemies (6–9), the assurance of God's presence in the land (11–12), and the dignity of personal freedom (13). The mention of God's deliverance of Israel from Egypt is a guarantee that the Great King who has initiated the covenant with the people is able to perform all that He has promised. He will be no absentee deity, but will be with the Israelites, directing their lives and providing for all their needs. These blessings are unique in character, assuring the Israelites of

231

personal security, continued national prosperity, and above all the presence of a loving, all-powerful deity. The assurance of God's presence has been a source of strength and blessing for countless generations of believers (*cf.* Is. 11:1–16; Ezk. 36:28; 37:24–27, *etc.*). Before His ascension Christ gave the assurance of His continual presence with His disciples as a means of strengthening and encouraging them in their ministry (Mt. 28:20). Because Jesus Christ is the same yesterday, today and for ever (Heb. 13:8), this promise is still valid for every believer.

b. Punishments (14–39)

14–33. The sections of ancient Near Eastern treaties containing the curses were much longer than those describing the blessings that would accrue to the vassal consequent upon obedience to the Great King, and this pattern is seen here also. Although the possibility that the chosen people would come to abhor God's ordinances (15) might have seemed rather remote at Sinai, the prospect was faced squarely nevertheless. The punishments included *sudden terror* (16), resulting from calamities of a medical nature such as *consumption* and *fever*. The former (Heb. *šaḥepeṯ*) was a general designation of any wasting disease, and this could include such contagious and infectious conditions as dysentery, cholera, typhoid fever, typhus fever, malaria, tuberculosis and various types of cancer. The condition described as fever was explained more fully as a condition that wastes the eyes and causes life to wane. The reference may be to a form of gonorrhoeal blindness, which has been known occasionally to assume epidemic proportions. The ailment is marked by a disabling form of ophthalmia known as acute purulent conjunctivitis, which spreads rapidly from eye to eye and from person to person. It results in permanent blindness and the consequent social hardships. Rejection of covenant spirituality will also produce drought and accompanying famine. The seasonal rains will be replaced by a sky that is as merciless and unyielding as iron, and land that has a surface as hard as bronze (19). God is reminding potential transgressors that He will still be with them, but in punishment instead of blessing.

Continued disobedience will bring plagues of wild beasts

(22) such as the Asiatic lions that were found in the Jericho region in the time of David (*cf.* 1 Sa. 17:34–36), or around Samaria after the northern kingdom had gone into captivity (2 Ki. 17:25–26). This punishment will be followed by war (22), which will search out its victims and destroy them. In the Old Testament, those nations that fought against Israel were frequently being used by God as agents for punishing the covenant people (*cf.* Jdg. 2:11–15; 2 Ki. 17:18–20; Is. 10:5–11, *etc.*). The famine that will result when the supply of food is cut off ('When I break your staff of bread') will involve the rationing of what is left. This amount will be so small that one oven will be all that is needed to bake bread for ten families (26). The mention of *high places* (30) seems to point to a time when the Israelites would occupy the pagan Canaanite *bāmôt* and use them for idolatrous worship. The *incense altars* (AV 'images') were most probably of the kind found in Canaan after 1100 BC. They were made of limestone, and had projections or 'horns' on each corner. One such altar was unearthed at Megiddo in an early tenth-century BC Israelite shrine.

Further rejection of covenant responsibilities will bring even worse punishments from God. These assurances of divine retribution are based upon a concept of strict justice, since the God of Sinai is one who maintains His rights (Ex. 20:5; RSV, NEB, 'jealous god'). Cannibalism (*cf.* 2 Ki. 6:28–29; La. 2:20), the desolation of the cities, and the exile of the people (*cf.* Je. 9:16; Ezk. 5:10, 12, 14, *etc.*) will be elements of the stern punishment which God will mete out to those who have not kept the promises made to Him on Mount Sinai by the Israelites.

34–39. The period of exile will allow the land to recover from neglect of sabbatical year observances (34). The RSV 'enjoy' (mg., 'pay for') attempts to convey the idea of compensation owed to the land by Israelites who had failed to conserve its resources properly according to the law. The few who survive exile (36) will be insecure and terrified by the slightest threat,[91] while their fellows in captivity will *pine away*

---

[91] The *driven leaf* (36) has been generally identified with the aspen, because of its flattened leaf petioles that cause the leaves to move and quiver in the slightest breeze. *Cf.* H. N. and A. L. Moldenke, *Plants of the Bible*, p. 184.

(39) because of former sin. This dramatic picture of exile was to be an unhappy part of the nation's future, consequent upon the continued repudiation of covenantal responsibilities and obligations.

c. The rewards of contrition (40–46)

40–42. God does not wish the sinner to die, but rather to repent and live. If His iniquitous people confess their apostasy and treachery, showing genuine repentance and an earnest desire to *make amends* (41), God will remember that He is still bound by His everlasting covenant made with the descendants of Abraham (*cf.* Gn. 17:7). Christ taught how greatly God esteemed repentance by speaking of the joy in heaven over one penitent sinner (Lk. 15:7, 10).

43–45. The land, which was an important part of the covenant promises to Israel, will need time to recover its productivity. It will therefore be able to *enjoy its sabbaths* (43) while its former inhabitants are in exile. Though God has afflicted His people with such a drastic punishment, they themselves must bear responsibility for it. The covenant concept carries with it the implication that the cursing was in effect self-cursing. By disobeying the provisions of the covenant agreement, the vassal brings upon himself the maledictions which it contains. The responsibilities of the individual and the nation as a whole thus assume much more significant dimensions, since for the Israelites a large proportion of the responsibility for the success of the relationship devolved upon them. Having reversed the values of the Sinaitic covenant by making profane that which is fundamentally pure and holy, they can hardly complain if, after repeated warnings over a lengthy period of time, a just God reverses their own situation by taking away what had been given, and handing over to slavery once more the people that had only recently been liberated from bondage to the Egyptians. Although the fate of exile which is being envisaged prophetically here could well become a reality in the experience of the Israelites, God will not forget the covenant people in that event, for He is the sole reason for their existence (44). Because He loves His chosen nation, He places them under discipline (Am. 3:2; Heb. 12:6) instead of rejecting them completely out of hand.

46. A concluding formula in the style of a colophon repeats the general title of the section from verse 3 (*statutes . . . commandments*), mentions the scribe who wrote down the material (*Moses*), and provides a date (*on Mount Sinai*) for the occasion.

VII. REGULATIONS CONCERNING VOWS AND OFFERINGS (27:1–34)

The final chapter of Leviticus deals in detail with vows and tithes, which had been mentioned only in a rather general manner elsewhere (Lv. 7:16; 22:18–23; 23:38). A vow to God placed a person or property in a special consecrated relationship which stood outside the formal demands of the law. The daughter of Jephthah (Jdg. 11:30–31) and Samuel, the son of Hannah (1 Sa. 1:11), are instances of persons who were made votive offerings by others. Leviticus began with regulations concerning sanctuary offerings, and it is appropriate that it should conclude on the same theme.

a. Persons (1–8)

1–5. This section deals with the valuation of a male person who is offered under a vow to the Lord. The standard of valuation is that of the sanctuary shekel (see note on Lv. 5:15), and a male in his majority was considered to be worth *fifty shekels of silver* (3). This money would be paid to the priests, and in later periods was used for the general maintenance of the sanctuary. Females who were vowed to divine service were appraised at thirty shekels, probably because they were physically less strong than healthy males. A similar scale applied to persons of both sexes whose ages ranged from five to twenty years. The women would doubtless assist the priests in non-ceremonial duties connected with the sanctuary, and in addition would probably care for the more junior votaries.

6–8. The young male child dedicated in this manner to the Lord's service was valued at five shekels and his female counterpart at three shekels. Such children would be taught how to assist the priests in various duties as long as the period of their vows lasted. Persons above the age of sixty were valued at fifteen shekels for a male and ten for a female. If the individual making the vow, whether for himself or for someone else, was too poor to pay anything, then the person being vowed was valued by the officiating priest at a lower and more realistic level in the expectation that the person involved would keep his or her vow. In Old Testament times vows were regarded as extremely serious acts (*cf.* Dt. 23:21–23), and the precautions listed here were meant to dissuade overenthusiastic and unrealistic vows. Since the Torah did not contain legislation which prescribed vows, it was expected that someone who entered into that kind of voluntary relationship with God would complete whatever had been undertaken. Only those vows that conformed to the covenantal ethos would be acceptable to God. A wife's vow was invalid unless it was approved by her husband.

b. Animals (9–13)

9–10. Since all clean animal offerings to the Lord were holy, they had to meet the standard prescribed in earlier sections of the legislation. Once an animal had been vowed, it could not be replaced with one of inferior quality or one of a different species (10). If an equal exchange was made, both the original animal and its substitute were to be considered holy, and neither could be used for secular purposes.

11–13. Animals regarded as unclean by virtue of a blemish could also be vowed to the Lord, and these were accorded monetary value by the priest (12). If a situation arose whereby a man wished to discharge his vow and redeem his animal, he was required to pay a penalty amounting to one-fifth of the valued price. These regulations protected the sanctity of the vow by insisting upon proper ritual procedures, and discouraged the indiscriminate consecration of such disposable commodities as blemished animals by imposing a fine where redemption occurred.

c. Property (14–29)

14–15. Houses and land could be vowed to the Lord as well as people and animals. In the case of houses, the priest was required to make a realistic valuation of the property before accepting it. A penalty of one-fifth of the valuation price had to be paid in the event that the original owner decided to redeem what had been vowed. Once the house passed into the control of the sanctuary priests they could presumably use it as they saw fit, since it would be in a walled city and thus not associated with any land (*cf.* Lv. 25:29–30).

16–29. When land was dedicated to the Lord's service the situation was rather more complex, since under jubilee year legislation such property reverted to the original owner at that time. The land being vowed was valued by the priest in terms of the amount of seed required for sowing it annually, each *homer of barley* representing a price of fifty shekels for the forty-nine year period.[92] This is comparable to Mesopotamian practices, where a homer of barley cost a shekel. As with other measures, the exact amount comprising a homer is unknown (*cf.* Lv. 19:36), but it probably amounted to a couple of hectolitres. For a shorter length of time a pro rata reduction was made (*cf.* Lv. 25:50–51). Even though the price of a homer of barley might fluctuate, depending upon local conditions, the underlying principle of the legislation was to relate the value of the property to that of the crops it could be expected to produce. A 20% premium was payable to the priests if the field was redeemed subsequently by the owner. In the event that the land was also sold for some reason after having been dedicated to the Lord, it became the perpetual property of the priests at the next jubilee year. A temporary gift of land to the priests (22) was also valued according to the proximity of the jubilee year, and the donor was required to make a comparable payment as a *holy thing to the Lord* (23). The sanctuary shekel, which was the approved standard of valuation, consisted of twenty gerahs (*cf.* Ex. 30:13; Nu. 3:47; 18:16).

Firstlings of clean animals belonged to God in any event (Ex. 13:2), and therefore could not be vowed to the sanctuary. Unclean, *i.e.*, blemished, animals could be redeemed by paying the usual 20% premium. To discourage irresponsible acts of piety, dedicated things (Heb. *ḥērem*) were regarded as the exclusive property of the Lord, and therefore could not be disposed of or redeemed. The process by which persons were devoted to this kind of 'ban' was to be seen in Israel's

---

[92] For the sense of 'seed' meaning 'crops', see R. de Vaux, *Ancient Israel* (1961), p. 168.

237

subsequent history (*cf*. Jos. 6:17; 7:1), along with the consequences of disobeying the legislation governing this type of
dedication. Such a procedure of 'devoting' or 'placing under
the ban' is the result of God's direct instructions in given
circumstances, and is therefore quite different from acts of
individual dedication to the Lord's service.

d. Redemption of tithes (30–34)

30–31. The tithe, comprising one-tenth of all the produce,
is regarded as the offering due from the people to the true
owner of the land (Lv. 25:23). In instances where it was
necessary or desirable for the tithe to be redeemed, the normal
20% premium was payable to the priests. This provision did
not apply to animals, however, since every tenth one that was
born belonged automatically to God.

32–34. The *herdsman's staff* (32) was used to guide the sheep
and help the shepherd to walk in difficult terrain. The Hebrew
word used here, however (*šēbeṭ*), is more properly a 'rod', a
defensive weapon for warding off predators (*cf*. 2 Sa. 23:21).
When the shepherd was 'rodding' his sheep, he used it to hold
the animals back at the door of the sheepfold while he
inspected each one of them for injury or damage. The newly
born ones would be examined similarly for imperfections. This
section prohibits the owners of flocks and herds from engaging
in an arbitrary or haphazard selection of animals to be offered
to God (33); and if any attempt at exchange was to be made,
both animals were regarded as consecrated to God. A concluding pronouncement authenticates the contents of the chapter
in a manner encountered elsewhere in Leviticus.

The intent of this legislation is to outline the conditions
under which persons and property could be devoted to divine
service. Because God's holiness was at the heart of every votive
offering, stringent regulations were necessary to prevent acts of
profanation. Individual motivation is therefore of prime
concern in this chapter, so that irrational, frivolous, or overenthusiastic acts will be minimized, if not excluded altogether.
The experience of those who have made vows seems to
indicate in general that the passing of time alters the original
motivation or the circumstances under which the vows were
made. The levitical law takes cognisance of this matter, and is

sufficiently humane and flexible to allow, under certain conditions, for the redemption of what was vowed.

The seriousness of making a vow to God ought to be understood as clearly by the modern Christian as it was by the ancient Hebrew. The New Testament does not make any kind of vow mandatory, but implies clearly that any undertakings or promises to God are solemn affairs which must be honoured, whether they are baptismal vows, marriage pledges, or other similar commitments. Breaking a vow is analagous to putting one's hand to the plough and looking back (Lk. 9:62). To keep the vow of a life dedicated to the service of Christ is the most acceptable means of worshipping a holy and perfect God.

APPENDIX A: LEVITICUS 13

The following is an experimental translation of Leviticus 13 into semi-technical English. Because of the obscure nature of some of the Hebrew expressions, this rendering will exhibit faults common to all such versions. The terms 'leprous' and 'leprosy' are used in the same general sense as 'cancerous' and 'cancer', without prejudice to either clinical condition.

1. Now the LORD spoke to Moses and Aaron saying,

2. When a man exhibits a swelling, an eruption, or an inflamed spot upon the surface of his body, and a leprous condition of the epidermis is suspected, he shall be brought to Aaron the priest, or to one of his sons.

3. The priest shall then examine the lesion on the epidermis, and if the hair in the affected area has turned white and the diseased spot appears to have penetrated the epidermis, it is a symptom of leprous disease. Having examined him, the priest shall then pronounce the man unclean.

4. If the glossy area of the epidermis is white, and there appears to have been no penetration of the skin, and the local hair has not become depigmented, the priest shall then quarantine the patient for seven days.

5. On the seventh day the priest shall re-examine him, and if in his opinion the disease has been checked and there is no further cutaneous involvement, the priest shall then quarantine him for an additional seven days.

6. The priest shall re-examine him on the seventh day, and if the affected area is resuming a normal appearance and the disease is not disseminated in the skin, the priest shall pronounce him clean; it is only a macular or papular eruption. He shall wash his clothes and be religiously and socially clean.

7. But if the lesion becomes widely distributed over the epidermis after the patient has presented himself to the priest for discharge, he shall return to the priest for a further examination.

8. If the priest then sees that the lesion has achieved a serious degree of cutaneous penetration, he shall then pronounce him unclean; it is a leprous condition.

9. When a person is afflicted with leprosy, he shall be brought to the priest.

10. The priest shall then examine him, and if there is a distinct white vesicle in the skin which has turned the hair white, and if the lesion is characterized by ulcerating tissue,

11. it is chronic leprosy in the cutaneous tissues, and the priest shall pronounce him unclean forthwith and shall not quarantine him, for he is unclean already.

12. Now if a suspected leprous condition becomes widespread in the epidermis to the point where the affliction involves the entire skin of the diseased person from head to foot, wherever the priest looks,

13. then the priest shall examine him, and if the affliction has covered his body completely he shall pronounce the patient free from the disease. The skin has turned white, and he is clean for religious and communal purposes.

14. When ulcerated tissue appears in the patient, however, he shall be regarded as unclean.

15. The priest shall then examine the ulcerated tissue and pronounce him unclean. Ulcerated tissue is to be regarded as unclean; it is leprous.

16. But if the ulcerated tissue changes in appearance and becomes white, the patient shall visit the priest,

17. and the priest shall examine him. If the afflicted area has turned pinkish-white, the priest shall pronounce the sufferer free from the disease; he is ceremonially clean.

18. When there is present on a person's body a boil that has healed,

19. and on the site of the boil there arises a white swelling or an inflamed white spot, it shall be shown to the priest.

20. Now if, when the priest examines it, an obvious cutaneous penetration has occurred and the local hair has become white, the priest shall pronounce the man unclean; it is a leprous condition which has broken out in the boil.

21. But if, on examination by the priest, there are no obvious white hairs at the site of the inflammation, and it has not infiltrated the epidermis but is fading away, the priest shall then impose a seven-day quarantine.

22. If the affliction subsequently becomes disseminated throughout the skin area, the priest shall then pronounce the person unclean; he has a malignant ailment.

23. But if the swollen spot remains localized and does not spread, it is merely an inflamed boil; and the priest shall pronounce him clean.

24. Now if the body has sustained a burn upon the skin, and the raw tissue of the burn erupts into an inflamed reddish-white or white area,

25. the priest shall examine it, and if the local hair has become depigmented and the lesion appears to have penetrated the epidermis, it is a leprous condition that has broken out in the burn. The priest shall pronounce him unclean at that stage; he has a leprous disease.

26. But if, when the priest examines it, the hair in the lesion is not white, and the affliction has not actually penetrated

the epidermis but is fading away, the priest shall impose a seven-day quarantine.

27. On the seventh day the priest shall re-examine him, and if the affected area is spreading over the epidermis, the priest shall then pronounce him unclean; it is a leprous disease.

28. If the lesion is localized and does not spread in the skin but fades away, it is a swelling of the original burn, and the priest shall pronounce him clean, for it is merely an inflammation of the burn.

29. When a man or woman exhibits a diseased condition of the scalp or facial hair,

30. the priest shall examine the lesion, and if there is evidence of cutaneous penetration and the local hair is coppery-red and scanty in appearance, the priest shall then pronounce him unclean. It is an irritating lesion, a malignant condition of the head and facial hair.

31. Now if the priest examines the irritant disease, but fails to discover either frank cutaneous penetration or the presence of black[93] hairs at the site, the priest shall quarantine the person with the itching disease for seven days.

32. On the seventh day the priest shall re-examine the lesion, and if the irritation has not spread, if there is no coppery hair, and if the diseased area has not infiltrated the epidermis,

33. then the patient shall shave himself, leaving the lesion unshaven. The priest shall impose a further seven-day quarantine upon the person with the irritant disease.

34. On the seventh day the priest shall re-examine the lesion,

---

93 The LXX has 'yellow'.

and if the irritation is not disseminated across the epidermis and there is no cutaneous penetration, the priest shall then pronounce him clean. He shall wash his clothes and be religiously and socially clean.

35. But if the irritating lesion becomes widely distributed over the epidermis subsequent to his cleansing,

36. the priest shall re-examine him, and if the disease has obviously spread in the skin the priest need not look for coppery hairs; the person is unclean.

37. But if in his judgment the irritating disease has been inhibited, and black hair has grown at the site, the lesion is healed. The patient is clean, and the priest shall pronounce him such.

38. When a man or woman exhibits glossy patches or prominent white vesicles on the skin of the body,

39. the priest shall examine them, and if the vesicles on the epidermis are dullish-white in appearance, it is a mottling that has arisen in the skin; the person is ceremonially clean.

40. If a man's hair has fallen from his head he is clean, despite his alopecia.

41. If a man's hair has receded from his forehead and temples, he is still clean despite his baldness.

42. But if there is a reddish-white lesion on the bald head or the bald forehead, it constitutes a leprous condition breaking out on his bald head or forehead.

43. The the priest shall examine it, and if the swollen lesion appears reddish-white on his bald head or bald forehead similar to the appearance of leprosy on the skin of the body.

44. he is a leprous person; he is unclean, and the priest must pronounce him completely unclean. He has a malignant scalp infestation.

45. The leprous person who has the affliction shall wear torn clothing and allow the hair of his head to become unkept. He shall cover his upper lip and cry, 'Unclean, unclean'.

46. He shall remain unclean as long as he exhibits the symptoms of the disease. He is unclean, and must dwell apart in a place remote from the encampment.

47. When cloth assumes a degenerative appearance, whether it is a woollen or linen garment,

48. either in the warp or woof of linen or wool, or in a leather garment or anything made from leather,

49. if the affected area of the fabric appears greenish or reddish, whether in the warp or woof, or in a leather garment or in anything made from leather, it is a degenerative condition and must be shown to the priest.

50. The priest shall then examine the affected part, and isolate for a seven-day period the material which exhibits the deterioration.

51. He shall re-examine the area on the seventh day. If the condition has spread in the fabric, in the warp or woof, or in the leather, whatever its use, the degenerative state is of a malignant nature; it is unclean.

52. The priest shall burn the clothing, whether affected in warp or woof, whether woollen or linen, or anything made from leather, for it is a deteriorating condition and must be burned in the fire.

53. If, however, when the priest examines it, the affected area has not spread in the fabric, in the warp or woof, or in anything made from leather,

54. then the priest shall order the owners to wash the article containing the deteriorating portion, and he shall put it in quarantine for an additional seven days.

55. After it has been washed the priest shall examine the affected article again. If the deteriorating area has not altered in colour even though the infestation has not spread, it is still unclean. You must burn it in the fire, whether the threadbare portion appears on the right or the reverse side.

56. If, when the priest examines it, the affected area has faded in colour after being washed, he shall tear it out of the garment or the leather, the warp or the woof.

57. Then if it reappears in the fabric, whether in the warp or the woof, or in anything made of leather, it is spreading. You must burn the affected article in the fire.

58. But from whatever article, warp, woof or anything made from leather, the degenerative area disappears after washing, it shall be washed a second time and be clean for normal usage.

59. This is the regulation governing conditions in articles made of wool or linen, either in the warp or the woof, or in anything made from leather, to determine whether it is clean or unclean.

APPENDIX B: SEX AND ITS THEOLOGY

Much of what is taught in Scripture about sex occurs in the Old Testament, from which it emerges in a manner that is sometimes explicit and sometimes cloaked in euphemisms. Sexual differentiation is described by such terms as 'male' and 'female', 'man' and 'woman', 'husband' and 'wife'. It is continued at the level of physical structure by such general words as *bāśār* ('flesh', 'whole body', whether human or animal) being employed in a special euphemistic sense to denote the male organ of generation (*cf.* Gn. 17:11; Ex. 28:42; Lv. 15:2–18; Ezk. 16:26, *etc.*). The Hebrew term *yārēk* ('thigh', 'loin') is also used periodically for the male sex organ (*cf.* Gn. 24:2, 9; 46:26, *etc.*). Sometimes the word 'feet' was employed as a surrogate for the male genitals (Ex. 4:25; Ru. 3:7; Is. 6:2, *etc.*), and occasionally for female sex organs as well. An additional term, generally rendered 'nakedness' in the versions, has been used to denote the shameful exposure of the female genitals (Lv. 18:6–19; 20:17–21; La. 1–8, *etc.*). While euphemisms were generally employed to describe sex organs and sexual activities, such secondary sexual characteristics as the female mammary glands were mentioned by name quite openly. Both male and female genitalia were frequently described in terms of their relationship to the entire body.

Sex organs were regarded as sacred, and sometimes oaths were sworn upon them (*cf.* Gn. 24:2, 3, 9). Among the Hebrews, circumcision does not seem to have had the significance of a puberty rite, as it is supposed to have done among some other ancient peoples, but instead was the sign of introduction into the body of the chosen people. Under normal conditions the sex organs were not displayed, since Hebrew mores regarded such an activity as shameful (Gn. 9:21–23; Lv. 18:6–19, *etc.*).

Among the Israelites, sexual behaviour was regulated by law. Adultery was prohibited (Ex 20:14; Lv. 18:20, *etc.*), and various statutes dealt with such matters as the seduction of a virgin (Ex. 22:16), bestiality (Lv. 18:23), incest (Lv. 18:6–18; 20:11, 12, 14; Dt. 27:20, 22), homosexuality (Lv. 18:22; 20:13) and the utilization of its avails (Dt. 23:18). Physiological functions of a sexual orientation such as menorrhagia (Lv. 15:25–30) and normal menstruation (Lv. 15:24; 18:19; 20:18) were also covered by legislation.

Males and females had their distinctive roles in antiquity. In a patriarchal society the male was the head of the household, and was responsible for all its members over whom he had complete power. The males of a household farmed the land, cared for animals, occupied themselves with trades or commercial activities and fought the nation's battles when the need arose. The primary function of the females was that of producing children and being helpmeets to their mates. Secondary tasks came into prominence for women as Hebrew sedentary culture developed after the time of Joshua, and by the period in which the proverbs of Israel were being compiled a 'virtuous woman' led a varied and responsible life (Pr. 31:10–13).

While there was thus an obvious differentiation of sexes in terms of social roles, there seems to have been no segregation of females in the biblical period apart from such interludes as the *harim* of Solomon with its contingent of foreign women. Even there, however, the evidence for direct segregation of the females is lacking. In the book of Esther, the females of the royal household seem to have been housed in a separate area of the palace at Susa (Est. 1:9; 2:3, *etc.*). Other biblical references indicate that at least some women had their own living quarters (*cf.* Gn. 16:2; 31:3; Dt. 22:13, *etc.*). What does amount to discrimination against women occurs in those passages that deal with violations of covenant legislation. Thus a woman was punished more severely for infidelity than was the case for a man (Dt. 22:13–21).

In the ancient Near East, sexual intercourse between married people had as its primary purpose the procreation of children. The male or female prostitutes employed their sexuality with a view to strict monetary gain, while perhaps according an incidental recreational pursuit to the persons who took advantage of their services. The Old Testament is surprisingly sensitive to the emotional aspect of sexual relationships, as is indicated in the collection of love lyrics known as the Song of Solomon or Canticles.[94] Along with other

[94] For an analysis of this material see *HIOT*, pp. 1049–1056.

sources, these compositions indicate the way in which sexual desire as such can be transcended and enriched by a deep and lasting companionship between a male and a female. Sexual relationships were never described explicitly in the Old Testament, a situation that tends to emphasize the delicate and intimate nature of the activity. Instead, expressions such as 'becoming one flesh' (Gn. 2:24), 'knowing a wife' (Gn. 4:1) or 'lying' with someone (Gn. 34:7) were employed as euphemisms.

The general tenor of covenant law makes it clear that the God of Sinai is the creator and sustainer of all life. Because He exemplified lofty moral and ethical standards as a holy deity, those who are in covenant relationship with Him are expected to live in a way which will also exhibit these spiritual qualities. Bounteous harvests and large herds are His gift to a nation that has holiness and obedience to His laws at the forefront of their activities. Whatever the pagan nations may have believed about the ability of their orgiastic cultic rites to influence agricultural productivity, the law makes it abundantly clear that such beliefs and activities have no place whatever in the life of the chosen people. For them it was of fundamental importance to remain in a state of ritual holiness, lest by indulging in the sexual excesses of the Canaanites and others they polluted the land. Sexual activity was indeed a legitimate part of the life of a holy people, but only in so far as it was consistent with the regulations that governed such contacts. If the Israelites utilized their sexuality outside those guidelines they could only expect divine punishment to come upon them. The sanctity of the marriage relationship was emphasized when God used it in the days of Hosea to demonstrate the seriousness of the covenant undertakings made in the time of Moses, and contrasted that situation with the state of the covenant in the eighth century BC by depicting the nation as a faithless wife. Because of the continued apostasy of Israel, the people were warned that unless they repented and returned to God in obedience and faith they would be punished severely. God the Father loved His children with a love far transcending that of human parents for their children. In return, He demands that they reciprocate with a depth of emotion and commitment, the measure of which is expressed by the

Hebrew term 'know', itself a euphemism for sexual love (*cf.* Is. 11:2; Ho. 4:1, 6). It would thus appear from the foregoing that the affection experienced within a sexual context can point the participants to a love far greater and purer than can be conceived of by mortals.

New Testament teaching on the subject of sex is less evident than that which occurs in the Old Testament, but it stands nevertheless in the general Hebrew tradition. Sexual intercourse was regarded as a legitimate and normal function of males and females within the marriage bond, of which monogamy had long been representative. As in Old Testament times, the principal objective of sexual activity was the procreation of children, who were loved and cherished as God's precious gifts. Jesus Christ condemned adultery and sexual lust (Mt. 5:27–32; 15:19–20, *etc.*), emphasizing the importance of a pure motive in sexuality, as indeed in all other relationships. Under rather special circumstances His love extended on one occasion to the forgiveness of a woman taken in adultery, who was nevertheless warned not to pursue such immoral behaviour (Jn. 8:11 AV; RSV mg.)

Christ's teachings laid the basis for the subsequent high moral and ethical standards for sexual activity as contained in other portions of the New Testament. The ideal of a lifelong union between a man and a woman in matrimony (*cf.* Gn. 2:24) is enhanced by the injunction that it shall be 'in the Lord' (*cf.* 1 Cor. 7:39). Any form of sexual indulgence outside marriage was condemned, no matter how infrequent or casual the liaisons might be. Sexual deviations and perversions, a common feature of life in the ancient world, were also regarded as alien to the Christian concept of sexual morality. Thus homosexuality was prohibited specifically in Romans 1:27 and 1 Corinthians 6:9.

Modern psychological and medical studies have explored the complexity of homosexual behaviour, but with inconclusive results for the most part. The pluralistic nature of late twentieth-century society has encouraged the belief that one opinion is just as valid as another in a given area, and not least as far as morality is concerned, since the idea of the existence and authority of absolute spiritual principles for living has been so widely denied. Some opinion regarding homosexuality sees the practice as a violation of the biblical teachings on the topic, and therefore as a perversion of legitimate functions in the area of sexual activity. Some researchers have come to the conclusion that homosexuality is a form of psychopathology, and have recommended various types of treatment in an attempt to combat the condition in so far as such an approach was thought necessary or desirable. Other investigators have set aside concurrent values or disvalues, and have merely regarded homosexuality as a variation from the statistical norm.

This commentary is obviously not the place in which this matter can be explored in any depth. Suffice it to say, however, that in the opinion of the writer, the New Testament makes it clear that any form of homosexual practice is incompatible with a moral and holy Christian life. For a person to think of himself or herself as a 'Christian homosexual' or a 'Christian lesbian' is a complete contradiction in terms, and cannot be sustained in any manner from the Scriptures. Equally specious is the logic that would endeavour to make homosexuality appear valid as an 'alternative life-style' for the Christian.